God, Adam, and You

God, Adam, and You

How Original Sin, the Flesh, and Holiness Integrate in the Christian Life

MICHAEL M. CHRISTENSEN

WIPF & STOCK · Eugene, Oregon

GOD, ADAM, AND YOU
How Original Sin, the Flesh, and Holiness Integrate in the Christian Life

Copyright © 2015 Michael M. Christensen. All rights reserved. Except for brief quotations in critical publications or reviews, no part of this book may be reproduced in any manner without prior written permission from the publisher. Write: Permissions, Wipf and Stock Publishers, 199 W. 8th Ave., Suite 3, Eugene, OR 97401.

Wipf & Stock
An Imprint of Wipf and Stock Publishers
199 W. 8th Ave., Suite 3
Eugene, OR 97401

www.wipfandstock.com

ISBN 13: 978-1-4982-3066-7

Manufactured in the U.S.A.   11/16/2015

All Scripture quotations, unless otherwise indicated, are taken from the Holy Bible, New International Version®, NIV®. Copyright ©1973, 1978, 1984, 2011 by Biblica, Inc.™ Used by permission of Zondervan. All rights reserved worldwide. www.zondervan.com The "NIV" and "New International Version" are trademarks registered in the United States Patent and Trademark Office by Biblica, Inc.™

Contents

Introduction: Background and Starting Points | 1
   Definitions | 1
   Statement of the Problem and Questions | 3
   Plan of the Book | 4
   Presuppositions | 4
   Sources, Methods, and Principles | 5

1 Ingredients in the Theological Stew: Opinions from Jewish and Christian History | 18
   Definitions | 18
   Judaism | 19
   The Early Church Fathers and Eastern Orthodoxy | 24
   Excursus: The Pelagian and Semi-Pelagian Controversies | 25
   Roman Catholicism | 32
   Early Protestantism | 39
   Arminianism-Wesleyanism | 52
   Stone-Campbell Movement | 57
   Neo-Orthodox, Liberation, and Contemporary Catholic Theologies | 59
   Summary | 60

Section I: What do the Scriptures Say about Sin, Its Source, and Its Consequences?

2 What Is Sin? | 65
   Word Study | 66
   Knowledge and Sin | 76
   The Nature of Sin | 78
   A Definition | 80
   The Source of Sin | 81
   Summary | 83
   Interaction with Historical Definitions of Sin | 84

3 What Are the Consequences of Adam's Sin? | 85
   Universality and Persistence of Sin | 87
   Passages Relating to Original Sin | 89
   Direct and Indirect Consequences of Adam's Sin | 133
   Conclusion | 141
   Historical Interaction with the Concept of Original Sin | 144
   Old Testament Uses and Word Study | 145
   New Testament Uses and Word Study | 146

4 What are Fleshly Desires and How Do They Relate to Sin and Original Sin? | 145
   Old Testament Uses and Word Study | 145
   New Testament Uses and Word Study | 146
   What is the Flesh? | 147
   How Powerful Are Evil Desires and the Flesh? Romans 6–8 | 150
   Excursus: Compatibilism, Incompatibilism, and Human Freedom | 159
   Theologizing on the Flesh | 165
   What can we Conclude about the Nature of Evil Desires and the Flesh? | 168
   Summary and Plausible Models for Section I | 169
   Evaluation of Models According to IBE Criteria | 170
   IBE and a Cumulative Case | 181

Section II: What Do the Scriptures Say about the Definition and Nature of Holiness, God's Expectations of Us, and Our Ability to Be Holy?

5 Holiness Defined | 185
   Word Study | 185
   Types of Righteousness | 197
   The Nature of Holiness, Righteousness, and Spiritual Maturity | 200
   Conclusion | 212

6 God's Expectations of His People: What Are They and Can They be Fulfilled? | 214
   Does God Command and therefore Expect His People to be Holy? | 214
   Can We Be Holy? | 227
   Table 1: Americans Define Holiness | 228
   Table 2: American Responses to Barna Holiness Survey | 229
   Conclusion | 247
   Interaction with Historical Concepts of Holiness, Expectations, and Achievability | 247
   Summary and Plausible Models for Section II | 248
   Evaluation of Models According to IBE Criteria | 250

     IBE and a Cumulative Case | 256
7 Conclusions and Implications for Individuals and the Church | 257
     Models 1 and 3's Implications for the Individual | 257
     Models 1 and 3's Implications for the Church | 263

Epilogue | 265

Appendix: Informal Fallacies of Logic | 269

Bibliography | 277

Introduction
Background and Starting Points

DEFINITIONS

Reason: Reason is the ability to think critically. It is the ability to weigh statements using the laws of logic and the various argument forms (deductive, inductive, and abductive) to come to justified conclusions or inferences. It is sometimes referred to as the "third act of the mind."

Laws of Logic:
The law of identity states that a declarative statement/proposition (in philosophy this is represented for brevity by the letter "P") is identical to itself and therefore different from any other.

The law of non-contradiction says that P cannot be both true and false in the same way and at the same time.

The law of excluded middle states that P is either true *or* false and hence there is no third or "middle" option.

Experience: Experience refers to the complex of relationships, events, and circumstances (in our context, especially religious) that shape our life and resulting worldview.

Tradition: Christian tradition references what the various Christian movements (Eastern Orthodoxy, Roman Catholicism, and Protestantism) and their scholars have concluded are the beliefs and practices that best represent what is true about God, his kingdom, and human beings.

THIS BOOK IS BORN out of my personal struggle with what I thought God expected of me as a Christian. These expectations included my motives, my inner thoughts and attitudes, my words, and actions. Further, these expectations affected my private life, family life, life within my Christian community, and life in the world at large. For example, in all of these life venues, does God expect me to be a sinlessly perfect believer? Does he expect me to sin every day in thought, word, and deed? Does he want something in the middle of those two extremes? Through discussions with other Christians, I found that I was not alone in my confusion. Other Christians were also perplexed when trying to figure out what God expected of them. As I struggled with these questions, several related issues emerged. To illustrate, some Christians told me that I was a sinner by nature and that I couldn't help but sin and this was a remnant of the original sin that I, and every other human, had inherited from Adam. As a result, the Christian life was a struggle between two natures that warred within—the old self and the new self—and this struggle would only cease when we entered heaven. Others suggested that as a Christian I needed to have this sin nature removed by a crisis experience called "entire sanctification" (a term that will be discussed in chapter 2 under Wesleyanism). This meant I loved God with my whole heart and that I need not sin at all.

These questions and issues became more muddled due to the various Christian denominations I was affiliated with as I grew up. I was raised in the Lutheran tradition, transitioned to a more charismatic fellowship in college (to include the Assemblies of God), participated in a Wesleyan Holiness tradition in my twenties to fifties, graduated from a Reformed-oriented seminary, and have recently worshipped in Evangelical Covenant and Southern Baptist churches. Each group gave somewhat different answers to the above questions and had different "holiness" expectations of me as a believer. These differences were found within a narrow subgroup of Christianity called "Protestant evangelicalism." As I learned in seminary, there are further differences as one considers other Christian groups, such as Protestantism generally, Roman Catholicism, and Eastern Orthodoxy, with each one claiming to have the best perspective on the subject.

Not only were there differences among Christian denominations in their interpretations, but there seemed to be differing expectations depending on which biblical passages were referenced. Paul, in Romans 5–8, presents information about how Adam affected his posterity and seemingly conflicting expectations regarding Christian holiness. In the Sermon on the Mount, Jesus told his disciples that they needed to be perfect as their heavenly Father is perfect when relating to their enemies (Matt 5:48). However, later in the New Testament (NT) Paul tells the Philippians that he is not perfect in his conduct, but is pressing on toward it (Phil 3:12–14).

There obviously needs to be a thorough study of the context and likely meaning of all related texts in order to come to a plausible conclusion on how Adam and Eve's sin affects us and how well we can meet God's expectations for our motives, thoughts, and conduct. Looking more broadly, right thinking on original sin and holiness has a significant impact on our whole view of God, the message of the gospel, and how we represent God to those who are not Christians. Is God someone who has allowed us to be saddled with an irresistible urge to sin and then asked us to be holy like him? What is the eternal destiny of the unborn, infants, or the mentally challenged? How do our answers to these questions make us feel when we think of God as our "Lord" and "Father"? When we preach the gospel, how does Jesus's death on the cross relate to original sin? Does his sacrifice undo any of its alleged negative effects? Did Jesus die for our "sin state" as well as our "sins"? Does the Holy Spirit provide much help in overcoming sin? How do we respond to Christians who complain about the strength of their fleshly desires and their "inability" to overcome sin? Can we honor God's character coherently when non-Christians challenge the justice of original sin? Can we justify the goodness of Christianity when skeptics wonder if becoming a Christian makes any difference at all, considering the unholy behavior of some Christians?

STATEMENT OF THE PROBLEM AND QUESTIONS

Several questions succinctly encompass our problem. What kind of spiritual baggage do we have from Adam and our "flesh"? How does God define sin? What are God's spiritual expectations and goals for us on this earthly pilgrimage? All of this has led me to do some serious study, using the resources God has given. One resource is the help of Judeo-Christian history—what has Jewish theology and the Christian church from the first century to the present concluded? A second resource is the experience of both Israelites and Christians throughout history—what sinful and holy experiences have they both had? The third and most important resource is the Bible itself—what does a careful study of the Scriptures reveal about the effect of Adam's sin, the effect of the flesh, the definition of sin, the power of present salvation, the Holy Spirit dwelling inside, and the resultant level of holiness God expects from his people?

PLAN OF THE BOOK

The plan of this book is to arrive at the best conclusions that can be drawn from the above resources and that adequately answer our questions. This introduction will review significant issues in theological method and philosophy that impinge on this study. Topics include the proper source of theological knowledge (the Scriptures) and the appropriate use of reason, tradition, and experience (elements of the Wesleyan quadrilateral) in answering theological questions. Chapter 1 is an historical sketch of what theologians in Judaism, the early church, Roman Catholicism, Eastern Orthodoxy, the Reformation, and modern Protestantism believed about the effects of original sin, what sin and holiness are, and God's expectations regarding holiness. Chapter 2 seeks to define sin and investigate its source and nature. Chapter 3 will uncover the cost of Adam's sin. As we analyze the Scriptures and look at original sin's effects in our world, what direct and indirect consequences can we see? Furthermore, what are the effects of our personal sins and the sins of others? Chapter 4 discusses the "flesh," that concept Paul uses repeatedly to describe sinful desires. How does it relate to original sin? What is a good definition for it? Who is responsible for it and its increase? The goal of chapter 5 is to define holiness, righteousness and other similar words. What kinds of righteousness are there? What is the source of holiness and how does a holy person act? Chapter 6 follows the holiness theme by examining God's holiness expectations. How clear are they in Scripture? Can we actually fulfill them? Are the examples of past Christ-followers and the benefits of the new covenant adequate to the task? Finally, chapter 7 looks back over all we've covered, forms conclusions, and discusses implications for both individual believers and the whole church.

PRESUPPOSITIONS

The presuppositions and methods one uses to interpret biblical passages have a large effect on the conclusions reached. Presuppositions are our conscious or unconscious starting points; things we assume to be true. For the purposes of this book I will assume certain ideas, some of which certainly have evidence to support them, but providing that evidence now is beyond the scope of this book; other books adequately defend those ideas. I list my presuppositions (at least the ones that I am aware of) to clarify this book's starting points and to avoid confusion:

- The Bible is the authoritative source for spiritual truth on the subject of God and human spiritual life. The Bible is consistent in the truths

INTRODUCTION

it presents; its truths are a unity and not contradictory. There may be areas it does not address completely, which sometimes limits the conclusions we can make when formulating doctrines and theologies.

- The meaning of a biblical text is what the author intended and what the audience understood. Further, this meaning is largely knowable and is relevant to life today.
- Reason, Christian experience, and Judeo-Christian tradition are helpful and necessary adjuncts to interpreting the Bible and in arriving at spiritual truth.
- Adam, Eve, Jesus, Paul, and other Old and New Testament characters were historical persons.
- Humans have significant freedom, sometimes called libertarian freedom, (philosophers might call it incompatibilist freedom) such that they can make choices among alternatives, especially in the moral realm.
- The laws of logic apply to every field of study, to include theology.
- A reliance on paradox or antinomy[1] weakens any argument, especially when there is another plausible explanation that avoids them. It is better to investigate apparent paradoxes more deeply or more impartially to determine whether one, several, or all of various beliefs are false rather than accept a paradox. If all efforts fail, a paradox is acceptable as the best explanation.
- There are things about God, ourselves, and our relationship to God that will remain mysterious due to a lack of complete knowledge. We are finite beings with finite knowledge and abilities. However, this is categorically different from using mystery or paradox as an explanation for ideas that are incoherent or contradictory.

SOURCES, METHODS, AND PRINCIPLES

The sources, methods, and principles one uses to interpret Scripture also have a profound effect on one's conclusions. The source used in this book will be the Bible with reason, Judeo-Christian tradition, and Christian experience as adjuncts to help us understand the meaning of various passages. The Scriptures and the three adjuncts are sometimes called the Wesleyan

---

1. An antinomy is "the bringing together of two principles, statements or laws that, even though appearing to be contradictory to or in tension with one another, are both believed to be true." Grenz, et al., *Pocket Dictionary*, "antinomy."

quadrilateral, and their use is necessary to understand any biblical passage, especially ones in which the meaning is less clear or must be inferred.

Scriptural Adjunct—Reason

Reason is an essential component to finding the meaning of human communication, whether it is oral, visual, or written (the Bible is included in those types of communication.) David Clark agrees and makes the further assertion that rationality transcends worldviews. He admits that certain rational principles are situation-specific, but in general, rational principles (coherence, scope or comprehensiveness, explanatory adequacy, and livability) must be followed to make any sense of the world.[2] He defines reason as "part of our belief-forming capacities by which we draw inferences and check for consistency. The God-given inferential equipment with which each person is endowed enables us to grasp God's revelation, distinguish it from other claimed revelations, and apply it appropriately to life."[3]

When reason operates, it applies rational principles when evaluating statements making truth claims, claims that occur frequently in theology. At the base of these principles are the laws of logic: identity, non-contradiction, and excluded middle. If these laws are broken most human communication becomes unintelligible. Kenneth Kantzer affirms that these laws of logic are an expression of God's nature:

> To trust the laws of logic is not to put law or logic above God. Rather, it is to recognize that the laws of logic are an expression of the rational nature of the God of Truth. He created humans in his own image so that we, like him, can think rationally. He also created an objective world that conforms to the reason of God and to our own reason so that we can trust our senses and arrive at the truth. And it is only by the use of reason in dependence on the basic laws of thought that we are able to know the truth and rest in our knowledge of it. This is true of our Christian faith and of all else as well. If we deny the basic laws of thought and particularly the law of noncontradiction, all so-called knowledge becomes mere nonsense. Our dependence on them is a necessary guide to warn us of error and to lead us to the truth. Consequently, the Scriptures call us to make judgments on the basis of the laws of thought—as, for example, in the tests of a

---

2. Clark, *To Know and Love God*, 313.

3. Ibid., 300. In addition to Clark's definition, reason in this book will be defined by the definition given at the beginning of this chapter.

prophet (Deut 13:18), in the necessity of rejecting a false gospel (Gal 1:3), and in the application of scriptural truth (Isa 1:18).[4]

Reason is helpful to those of us who have faith in God because biblical faith involves three components, all of which rely on reason—*notitia* (understanding the Christian faith's content), *assensus* (the intellect's acceptance of the truth of some proposition), and *fiducia* (trust in God). Trust is based on what we understand and accept as true. Trust is not a leap into the dark, but a step toward what, or who, we have good reason to believe in.[5]

Reason is also a key component of philosophy, which can be used as a servant of theology. Philosophy helps clarify theological concepts and is essential to the task of integration, which involves blending our scripturally based theological beliefs with knowledge from other disciplines (e.g., history, psychology, sociology, the physical and biological sciences, and politics) into a coherent Christian worldview.[6] Further, philosophy can provide "external conceptual problems" for a theology as part of a rational evaluation of theories within it (e.g., when Galileo's astronomical evidence for a sun-centered solar system came in conflict with the then current theological idea of an earth-centered system).[7] Clark agrees that philosophy helps serve theology by demanding clear definitions and distinctions, requiring logical form, identifying underlying assumptions, exploring latent presuppositions within a viewpoint, critically evaluating the evidential status of truth claims, and qualifying conclusions.[8] In short, philosophy inspects and evaluates theological foundations much like a building inspector would a physical structure.

Types of Reasoning

Reasoning is frequently divided into two major types—deductive and inductive—and both are used in theology. *Deduction* starts with two premises or declarative statements (the first is usually a broad general statement and the second is more specific), followed by a conclusion based on those statements. If the conclusion follows the formal rules of logic and avoids informal fallacies (see Appendix), the argument proposed is called *valid*; if it doesn't, the argument is *invalid*. However, to be a *sound* argument, the

---

4. Kantzer, "A Systematic Biblical Dogmatics," 474–75.
5. Moreland and Craig, *Philosophical Foundations*, 18.
6. Ibid., 15, 17.
7. Ibid., 25.
8. Clark, *To Know and Love God*, 298, 317.

form must be valid *and* the premises must be true. If these two conditions aren't met, the argument is *unsound*.[9] For example, consider:

Premise 1: I am a person.

Premise 2: Paul declares that all persons have sinned (Rom 3:23).

Premise 3: Paul asserts that Christ died for us while we were still sinners (Rom 5:8).

Conclusion: I am a sinner for whom Christ died. This is a sound argument (true premises and valid form).

Induction usually starts with observations or particular statements and is followed by a general conclusion. Because the statements are individual bits of information and the conclusion is usually general in nature, the conclusion can never be totally certain, but can only possess varying degrees of probability, depending on the apparent truthfulness of the premises (and sometimes the number of them—the more the better).[10] For example, if we observe many times in the Scriptures and see statements declaring that God is impartial, and see a few instances where he appears to be partial, this still leads to the conclusion that God is impartial. Osborne concludes that both deduction and induction are important forms to use in theological interpretation. They are interdependent and must be kept in dynamic balance.[11]

A third type of reasoning is called *inference to the best explanation* (IBE), or sometimes *abduction* or *adduction*. This technique involves evaluating plausible yet competing explanations for data we are concerned with. In our case, it would be evaluating which theory of human anthropology and holiness best fits the scriptural data as interpreted by tradition, reason, and experience. Although there is debate over which criteria produce the best explanation, Moreland and Craig suggest there is general agreement that the following are helpful:

1. Explanatory scope: Which theory explains the widest range of data?
2. Explanatory power: Which theory makes the data the most epistemically probable?
3. Plausibility: Which theory is implied by the greatest variety of accepted truths?
4. Less *ad hoc*: Which theory produces the fewest new suppositions?

---

9. Moreland and Craig, *Philosophical Foundations*, 28–29.
10. Ibid., 59, 310.
11. Osborne, *Hermeneutical Spiral*, 385.

5. Accord with accepted beliefs: Which theory, when combined with accepted truths, implies the fewest falsehoods?
6. Comparative superiority: Which theory bests its rivals in items 1–5?[12]

Osborne proposes a similar list of criteria for judging the veracity of our theological theories. He holds that these criteria function in a *critical realism* approach to theology, which seems the most appropriate approach for the way God has revealed truth to us (e.g., in history, through inspired persons, who use language and leave writings). It is *realistic* in that it asserts theological ideas are valid representations of the way things are. Further, theological assertions can be subject to various criteria of verification like other knowledge in the sciences or history. The approach is *critical* since it realizes that assertions approximate truth and do not define it for all time. The process is one of continual improvement in methods and conclusions. Hence, there is a "hermeneutical spiral" that spirals closer and closer to the truth. As we humbly allow our interpretations to be evaluated by the text of Scripture and this then refines our interpretations, we spiral inward toward the truth. Practically, there is also a contextual spiral in which our contextualizations more properly apply the text's meaning to Christian life today.[13]

Several authors have produced similar groups of criteria that aid in verifying theological claims. Earlier, Clark listed several principles helpful in verifying truth claims—coherence, scope or comprehensiveness, explanatory adequacy, and livability. Harold Netland's list includes internal consistency among beliefs, freedom from *ad hoc* hypotheses, congruence with other fields of study (such as history and the sciences), and the ability to explain basic aspects of human experience (explanatory power).[14] Vanhoozer advances five necessary rules of reflective discourse that overlap somewhat with these: clarity, logical consistency, conceptual coherence, comprehensiveness, and criticizability.[15] William Wainwright suggests the criteria used to evaluate metaphysical systems (e.g., naturalism, religious truth statements [from Christianity or other world religions], and religious pluralism) can also be used to evaluate doctrinal schemes and reduce interreligious disputes. Germane to the present discussion, we suggest Wainwright's criteria, which overlap significantly with the foregoing criteria, can help resolve intra-religious disputes within Christianity. Wainwright describes three formal criteria: 1) internal consistency and freedom from logical error. This

---

12. Moreland and Craig, *Philosophical Foundations*, 61–62.
13. Osborne, *Hermeneutical Spiral*, 22, 32, 398–99.
14. Netland, *Encountering Religious Pluralism*, 291.
15. Vanhoozer, "Christ and Concept," 132.

includes freedom from *ad hoc* hypotheses, which are only used to enable the system to cope with counterevidence. 2) Coherence—the ability of a set of ideas to hang together and be mutually reinforcing, 3) simplicity, as preferred over complexity. Two further criteria relate to a theory's explanatory power: 4) scope, which describes a theory's ability to account for a wide range of human experience (the physical universe, general human experience, religious experience), and 5) explanatory adequacy, which describes a system's ability to integrate data and concepts from other domains—science, art, psychology, sociology, ethics, etc. The last criteria, 6) existential effects, asks: Does the theory help an individual cope successfully with his or her total environment and the challenges of life?[16]

Kenneth Samples lists nine criteria by which to evaluate philosophical or religious worldviews. He uses several ingredients represented by many of the above schemes. What some put under the umbrella of scope or plausibility he calls correspondence—does a worldview correspond with well-established facts and general human experience? His "pragmatic" and "existential" tests are what others call existential livability. He includes "verification" and relates this more to empirical and scientific data. His "cumulative" and "competitive competence" tests really summarize the whole IBE process.[17]

Nancy Pearcey uses cues from Romans 1 to affirm that all worldviews must deal with the facts of general revelation (the physical creation and human nature) and can be tested to the extent they either explain or fail to explain it. She uses five strategies to critique worldviews, 1) identify the idol, 2) identify the idol's reductionism, 3) test the idol: does it contradict what we know about the world? 4) test the idol: does it contradict itself? and 5) replace the idol: make the case for Christianity.[18] Though these criteria apply to worldviews outside Christianity, they mimic the strategies that can evaluate any truth claim, whether outside or inside Christianity.

Hermeneutics

Under the umbrella of reason is the science and art of biblical interpretation or hermeneutics. *Hermeneutics is a science in that it provides helpful laws and principles of effective interpretation. It is an art because it demands skill and insight to apply the laws and principles without breaking them. It is also spiritual, because biblical interpretation is a task for those who know God and*

---

16. Wainwright, "Doctrinal Schemes," 79–81.
17. Samples, *World of Difference*, 33–37.
18. Pearcey, *Finding Truth*, 24, 42–50.

who humbly seek the Holy Spirit's guidance in their efforts.[19] The Holy Spirit directs our minds to the spiritual truths we need to hear, especially those truths necessary for our salvation and holiness. He doesn't seem to work by directly imparting every Scripture's meaning to our minds, but seems to push us to skillfully use the tools of interpretation. Christians have wrestled with some biblical passages and doctrines for millennia without knowing exactly what they mean (consider the millennium, for example). These are things that are not critical for our salvation or holiness and we must be content to know some things without total certainty.

To find the meaning of a text, hermeneutics addresses several aspects. There is the meaning the biblical author intended, the meaning the words and grammar of a text convey, and the meaning the reader understands. These should all be in agreement. The original readers wanted to know what the author meant by the words and sentences used. We twenty-first century readers of Scripture want the same thing; we want to know what the biblical author, and the God that inspired that author, meant for them and us. Because each biblical text came from a certain author with a set of pre-understandings, at a certain time in history, in a specific culture, and with a specific purpose for the intended audience, we must incorporate these ingredients if we want the fullest understanding.[20] This authorial intent can only be known, however, through the written text with its words and grammar.

Further, to arrive at the intended meaning certain contexts must be taken into account. *Historical-cultural context* deals with the identity of the author and audience, the date the text was written, the purpose and themes of the text, and the customs and norms of the surrounding society. The *literary context* examines the sentences and paragraphs immediately around a text and expands to consider the whole biblical book, books by the same author, the testament, biblical genres, and the Bible as a whole.[21] These expanding contexts give useful insight into the meaning of the words, phrases, or sentences the author uses.

Examining the text itself is the task of *exegesis*. Word studies in the Bible's original languages (Hebrew and Greek), grammar studies, the structure of sentences (syntax), and the literary genre of a text (e.g., narrative, letter, parable, poetry, wisdom literature, apocalyptic) make up this task. The main task of hermeneutics, then, is to discover the author-centered textual meaning. The best approach to finding that meaning is to use the four

19. Osborne, *Hermeneutical Spiral*, 22.
20. Klein, et al., *Introduction to Biblical*, 169–71.
21. Ibid., 37–39.

ingredients of literary context, historical-cultural background, word meanings, and grammatical structure. Klein, Blomberg, and Hubbard concur, proposing that regardless of the genre, "an interpretation that is not faithful to all four of these aspects of the text is unlikely to be the meaning the writer intended."[22]

The above exegetical contexts are used to interpret biblical *passages*. On the shoulders of this process we use hermeneutical procedures to crystallize a *whole biblical doctrine*. Grant Osborne lists several helpful steps when forming a biblical doctrine: 1) Discover and acknowledge our presuppositions and let the biblical text influence them. 2) Inductively collect all passages that apply to the doctrine studied. 3) Exegete all passages in their context. 4) Organize the texts into a biblical theology. 5) Trace the doctrine through church history. 6) Study competing models of the doctrine. 7) Recontextualize the doctrine for the current culture, showing the interdependence of this doctrine with other doctrines. 8) Rework your existing systematic theology if necessary. 9) Work out the implications of any reformulations for the individual Christian and the church as a whole.[23] Osborne, in a different section of his book, lists another important guideline, the "analogy of Scripture," which assumes the clarity and unity of the main points of the Bible. The guideline asserts that when formulating doctrines that clearer, more numerous, and more intentionally didactic (teaching) passages should carry more weight than single, obscure, or descriptive passages. This implies that doctrines should summarize what *all* of Scripture has to say (*tota scriptura*). By further implication, if there are no clear passages, then a dogma (an established teaching on a subject) should not be made from them.[24]

Gordon Lewis and Bruce Demarest propose a comparable paradigm for doing theology in their work, *Integrative Theology*. Their theological method involves six successive steps: 1) Identify the theological problem or question under consideration. 2) Identify the various solutions to the problem in the history of Christian thought. 3) Using the primary source of theological knowledge, the Bible, apply responsible hermeneutical procedures to interpret the relevant passages. 4) Order the various passages into a coherent doctrine, verifying one's conclusions via the threefold test for truth—logical consistency, agreement with Scripture, and existential viability. 5) Defend

---

22. Ibid., 214.

23. Osborne, *Hermeneutical Spiral*, 407–9.

24. Ibid., 28, 361–62, 30–31. Similar points are made by Klein, et al., *Introduction to Biblical*, 462–63.

your doctrinal conclusions against competing theologies, philosophies, or religions. 6) Apply the theology to specific life situations.[25]

In conclusion, it appears hermeneutics has a goal beyond understanding a certain passage of Scripture. This goal is to construct a systematic theology—a theology that is true, coherent, and comprehensive,[26] which reminds us of the list of criteria for developing an IBE and the hermeneutical spiral. We will incorporate all of these elements in arriving at a procedure that will spiral us toward the truth regarding original sin, sin, the flesh, and holiness.

Scriptural Adjunct—Experience

Osborne helpfully defines experience as the complex of events and circumstances (especially religious) that shape our life and resulting worldview. More specifically to our discussion, our subjective experiences and the beliefs that are affected by them influence the way we interpret biblical evidence.[27] This experience is best seen as the experience of the church as a whole and not just that of the professional theologian, pastor, or believer. Further, experience's influence could be either positive or negative. Experience could be a positive when it is a "seasoned wisdom." As a seasoned wisdom it then acts as a dialogical partner, along with tradition and reason, revering Scripture as the source of Christian truth. It acts as a negative when it is used as an autonomous authority, asking reason, previous tradition, and the Scriptures to submit to it.[28]

Scriptural Adjunct—Tradition

The concept of tradition involves referencing what the various Christian movements (Eastern Orthodoxy, Roman Catholicism, and Protestantism) and their scholars have concluded are the beliefs and practices that best represent what is true about God, his kingdom, and human beings. In other words, using the Bible, reason, their own tradition, and Christian experience, what have Christian groups in the past determined to be good theology? There is value in mining the centuries of Christian wisdom and

---

25. Lewis and Demarest, *Integrative Theology*, vol. 1, 7–8.
26. Osborne, *Hermeneutical Spiral*, 374, 398–99.
27. Ibid., 383.
28. Maddox, "The Enriching Role," 127. Thomas Noble makes the same point. See Noble, "Scripture and Experience," 292.

writings that relate to a theological subject. Theological treatises, apologies, and creeds are all helpful and have been developed by careful thought and consensus. No single person possesses every insight and we learn when we understand the thinking patterns, methods, and conclusions of those who have diligently studied before us.[29] Further, tradition shields us from being blown away with "every wind of doctrine." It gives us a place to start until we develop a firm grasp of what the Bible teaches on a subject. If our tradition is confirmed we can feel confident about our beliefs.

Tradition is helpful but it is not primary when searching for what the Scriptures teach. Lewis and Demarest call tradition a "provisional authority." It is provisional until we verify its faithfulness to the total revelation of the Bible and check that it provides the most coherent account of the biblical text. If it does, it should be kept; if not, it should be modified or discarded.[30] No belief should be validated by a theological tradition alone since a tradition was itself established by human beings who studied and came to certain conclusions in a certain historical context. Tradition should be evaluated by its agreement with Scripture and its relevance to the current context.[31]

Sometimes it is difficult to determine *which* Christian tradition to prefer. Should the early church fathers take precedence? Should my particular Christian division have sway (Eastern Orthodoxy, Roman Catholicism, or Protestantism)? Should my denominational affiliation have the greatest weight? Maybe a well-respected theologian should be given preeminence.

If a tradition is maintained for its own sake, it can become *traditionalism*. Clark describes it:

> Traditionalism . . . is a degenerating conservatism that expends too many resources staking out territory and defending boundaries. At times this growing conservatism identifies itself with a particular form of theology from the past. It begins to position itself primarily as the guardian of this tradition, and it digs in its heels against innovations that threaten change. When it takes up this role, traditionalism can lose capacity for honest self-criticism. It can forget that any model has limits and requires ongoing correction. . . . It can even hide political agendas or power interests, as various postmodern analyses make clear.[32]

By nature, traditionalism abhors change. Osborne suggests such changes can be dangerous for those rocking the theological boat. Nontraditional

---

29. Supporting this view is McGrath, "Engaging the Great Tradition," 139–58.
30. Lewis and Demarest, *Integrative Theology*, vol. 1, 34.
31. Osborne, *Hermeneutical Spiral*, 380–81.
32. Clark, *To Know and Love God*, 226.

ideas challenge the theological community and can result in the loss of one's job or ministry—professors lose posts, candidates are disqualified for job openings, students have papers rejected, or alternative ideas are neglected or rejected by those in power.[33] There is deliberate pressure to conform and the questioning of beliefs is repressed. Further, traditionalism can stifle any meaningful interaction with those who have different traditions. It feels threatened by conflicting ideas and doesn't want to confuse persons within its ranks with those ideas.

It appears, then, that tradition can have both positive and negative effects on our doctrinal formulations. Positively, it provides a rich background from which we can see how previous generations have wrestled with finding the truth and we can learn from their efforts. Negatively, it can limit our thinking, prejudice our judgment, and prevent us from entertaining ideas that are closer to the truth than ones we now possess.

The relationship among Scripture and the three adjuncts is depicted well by the following figure. Our theology is created and is most valid as the three adjuncts work on the foundation of the Scriptures.

Figure 1: A Modified Wesleyan Quadrilateral.

Conclusion

Based on the above discussion, how should we proceed? It seems that reason and logic (which include hermeneutical principles) are very helpful in interpreting Scripture and are aided by the positive aspects of experience and tradition. Consequently, we will use a combination of Osborne's and

---

33. Osborne, *Hermeneutical Spiral*, 399.

Lewis and Demarest's steps for developing a doctrine/theology. These steps seem to mark the most appropriate course for our task:

1. Acknowledge presuppositions (see mine above).
2. Identify the problem or question under consideration and identify parameters (see above).
3. Identify the solutions to the problem (competing models) in Judeo-Christian history (tradition and experience, chapter 1).
4. Inductively collect all relevant passages from both testaments and exegete them in their context (chapters 2–6).
   a. Use clear definitions of terms.
   b. Follow the laws of logic and avoid informal fallacies.
   c. Use deduction and induction dialogically.
   d. Adhere to an author-centered hermeneutic, using the four contexts: literary, historical-cultural, word meaning, and grammatical structure.
   e. Use the "analogy of Scripture" principle.
5. Interact with secondary sources (commentaries, etc.) and develop a final interpretation (chapters 2–6).
6. Organize interpretations into a biblical and systematic theology and compare with competing models (end of both chapters 4 and 6). Revise if necessary.
   a. Apply IBE criteria and select the model that provides the best overall explanation for the data. Which provides the best cumulative case?
      i. Explanatory power and scope: Which theory best explains the biblical revelation, human religious and general experience, and the physical universe? Which theory can best account for or explain what it attempts to explain? Relatedly, which one can explain the widest range of data?
      ii. Logical consistency: Which theory follows the laws and principles of logic, which God has built into the human mind? Which theory is most free of logical error?
      iii. Coherence: Which theory has the best internal consistency among beliefs? In which theory are the beliefs the most mutually reinforcing?

iv. Less *ad hoc*: Which explanation needs the fewest extraneous or makeshift hypotheses (e.g., assumptions, explanations, definitions, exceptions), which are used to prevent a theory from being falsified?

v. Integration: Which explanation best integrates biblical revelation with accepted truths in other fields of knowledge (from psychology, sociology, history, biological sciences, physical sciences)?

vi. Existential livability: Which explanation can best be lived out? Does it enable the Christian to cope with his or her total environment and deal with life's challenges? Which theory best enables a Christian to live the life God has directed?

7. Lay out your conclusion's implications for individuals and the church (chapter 7).

Steps six and seven are necessary final steps, because in the end, theology's goal for using proper sources, methods, and principles is practical. J. I. Packer says it well: "The systematic theologian's goal must accordingly be to use his mind to grasp and state in order as much as possible of all the things that God teaches in Scripture, so as to be able then to go to God knowledgeably in the exercise of faith and prayer and to discern his will in each situation for the practice of faithful obedience."[34]

---

34. Packer, "Is Systematic Theology," 25.

1

Ingredients in the Theological Stew
Opinions from Jewish and Christian History

DEFINITIONS

The fall: The first sins of Adam and Eve when they ate the forbidden fruit in the Garden of Eden against God's command not to do so.

Original sin: 1. The same as the fall. 2. The *negative effects* of the fall on subsequent humanity. An author's context determines which meaning is intended. The negative effects commonly associated with original sin are listed at the beginning of chapter 3.

Cause: When referring to forces outside of human thoughts, attitudes, and actions, a cause is an irresistible force, a coercion. Within the human person the individual is the absolute originator or cause of actions.[1]

---

1. Moreland and Craig further define the nature of humans causing their own actions: "... when it comes to the free acts of persons, the person himself as a substance and as an agent occupies the first term in the causal relation (the cause) and the act is the second term (the effect). Persons are agents and, as such, in free acts they either cause their acts for the sake of reasons (called agent causation) or their acts are simply uncaused events they spontaneously do by exercising their powers for the sake of reasons (called a noncausal theory of agency). Either way, persons are seen as first causes or unmoved movers who simply have the power, as free agents, to exercise the ability to act as the ultimate originators of their actions. It is the I, the self that acts; not a state in the self that causes a moving of some kind." Moreland and Craig, *Philosophical Foundations*, 278.

Influence: When referring to human thoughts, attitudes, and actions, an influence is a persuasion; an influence is resistible.

IT IS A WISE person who learns from the past, and as the saying goes, if we don't learn from it, we are doomed to repeat the negative parts of it. Heeding this warning, we now turn to what theological history has to tell us about human nature, sin, holiness, and God's holiness expectations for his people. Israel and the church were blessed with great thinkers who contributed significantly to our understanding on these topics and who help us when setting a foundation for the building of a Christian theology.

JUDAISM

Although Christian history sometimes begins with Jesus and the twelve disciples, by the first century there already existed a foundation of Jewish thought on the nature of humanity and holiness. Besides the Torah and the rest of the Hebrew Bible,[2] oral laws developed over the long history of Israel, which were eventually written down near the year 200 AD in a document called the *Mishnah*. Later, further contributions, the *Tosefta*, and commentaries on both of them, *Gemara*, were added. Altogether, these documents were called the *Talmud*. Another source of information about Jewish beliefs comes from Jewish rabbis. After the overthrow of Jerusalem and the destruction of the temple in 70 AD, rabbinic schools of thought developed, in which the rabbis wrote in-depth commentaries (*midrashim*) on many of the books of the Hebrew Bible. The oldest copies available today date from the second century through the seventh century AD.[3] Other documents of that era, called the *apocrypha* and *pseudepigrapha*, discuss human nature, but were never generally accepted as canonical by either Jewish or Christian scholars,[4] and because of this they are not considered in this book.

Craig Blomberg believes that if we have evidence that a Jewish belief or tradition was discussed by the rabbis during the first three centuries AD, such tradition could very well have existed during the time of Christ and been an influence on the writers of the NT. Even if these traditions developed later, they still helped shape the rabbinic and general Jewish view of human nature and holiness that has come to exist today.[5] Solomon Schechter sees general agreement among the rabbis, even when looking at

---

2. The thirty-nine books from Genesis to Malachi comprise what Christians call the Old Testament.
3. Blomberg, *Jesus and the Gospels*, 42–44.
4. Ibid., 9. Also see Schechter, *Some Aspects*, 5.
5. Blomberg, *Jesus and the Gospels*, n. 45, 41–42.

the large time frame of the second through tenth centuries and considering the scarcity of documents. The doctrinal teachings of the second century Palestinian rabbis are largely in agreement with Babylonian rabbis, R. Ashi of the fifth century and R. Sherira of the tenth.[6] Schechter remarks that even though the rabbis were in general agreement, they unfortunately had no compunction to apply theological or logical principles to their conclusions or to seek logical consistency. Therefore it is difficult to compile a systematic rabbinic theology. Schechter therefore cautions the reader to not press rabbinical writings too much in order to "fill them with meaning" that the author never intended them to have.[7] Schechter's distillation of the Jewish view of sin is in close agreement with the ideas expressed by the well-known writer on Judaism, G. F. Moore, whose research we discuss next.

Moore narrowed his focus on Judaism to the age of the Tannaim (the first three centuries of the Christian era), and pertinent to this book, discussed Jewish views on sin and holiness. He notes the fact that all humanity had sinned was the testimony of Scripture and experience. According to the rabbis, universal sin was due to every person having a conflict with an evil impulse. Moreover, when this impulse is repeatedly yielded to it becomes a habit and exerts a growing power over the sinner. Small sins can lead to larger ones for those who are reckless, just as a spider's silk may grow as thick as a cart rope.[8] The rabbis acknowledge that sin began with Adam and that his sin led to the deaths of all the generations of his descendants. The idea of the solidarity of families, clans, and nations was familiar to the Jews and they saw no injustice in God's death punishment. Although this is true, individual responsibility for sin is also a hallmark of Judaism. In an ancient Midrash the righteous dead reproach Adam for causing their deaths, but he responds that he was guilty of only one sin, but they of many. Every person deserves death and they do not die because of the guilt of Adam's sin.[9] Judaism affirms the tempter Satan draws or influences people toward sin. Satan, as the serpent, appealed to Adam and Eve's desires and ambitions that were already inherent in them before they sinned. Therefore, Adam and Eve's sins were like those of any other person who follows the leadings of their human nature. In fact, Adam was mentally and morally alike to his posterity.[10] Moore remarks that in Judaism "there is no notion that the original constitution of Adam underwent any change in consequence of the

---

6. Schechter, *Some Aspects*, xi–xii.
7. Ibid., 13, 15–17.
8. Moore, *Judaism in the First Centuries*, 467–70.
9. Ibid., 475–76.
10. Ibid., 478–79.

fall, so that he transmitted to his descendants a vitiated nature in which the appetites and passions necessarily prevail over reason and virtue, while the will to good is enfeebled or wholly impotent."[11] N. P. Williams agrees, affirming that the theory of the fall and original sin does not rest on anything found in Genesis 3:

> It's true foundations are psychological, based on the bed-rock facts of ethical and spiritual experience—the consciousness of the moral struggle, and the feeling of a ceaseless strain and tension between duty and the clamorous appetites, which ever and anon burst victoriously forth into crude external expression, whilst reason looks on in helpless dismay and shame.[12]

Williams also quotes Romans 7:19 to the same effect, "the evil that I do not want to do—this I keep on doing." In other words, the theory of the fall and original sin were developed to explain the general human experience of giving in to temptation. But, if Adam and Eve are not the source of a sinful tendency, then what or who is? Williams sees the rabbinical literature as pointing to God himself—he implants it in each individual.[13]

The "evil impulse" is named the *yetzer hara* (*yetzer* is sometimes spelled *yeser*, *yetser*, or *yezer*) and is based on the phrases found in Genesis 8:21 and 6:5. This impulse is not intrinsically evil or sinful, but is only evil if the impulse is yielded to so that conscious sin follows.[14] Moore summarizes how the rabbis pictured it acting:

> The opportunity or the invitation to sin may come from without, but it is the response of the evil impulse in man to it that converts it into temptation. It pictures in imagination the pleasures of sin, conceives the plan, seduces the will, incites to the act. It is thusly primarily as the subjective origin of temptation, or more correctly as the tempter within, that the *yeser ha-ra* is represented in Jewish literature. Since it compasses man's undoing by leading him into sin, it is thought of as maliciously seeking his ruin—a kind of malevolent secondary personality. Throughout his life, from infancy to old age, it pursues its deadly purpose, patiently biding its time.... It is man's implacable enemy. Only in the world to come will it be extirpated by God.[15]

---

11. Ibid., 479.
12. Williams, *Ideas of the Fall*, 31.
13. Ibid., 69.
14. Moore, *Judaism in the First Centuries*, 480–81.
15. Ibid., 481–82. Williams agrees, referencing Rabbi Simon ben Eleazer, and depicts it like iron, which can be cast into the blacksmith's fire and made into vessels for

The evil impulse is sometimes given a "personality," and when this is done, it is frequently personified as a tempter, as Satan, or as the angel of death.[16]

Summary

A good summary of the rabbi's views follows in the form of answers to questions:

Since God created everything good, how could he create something that brings about evil?

The rabbis assert that God *did* create the *yetzer hara* impulse, but it is more of an appetite or passion, in the sense of spurring someone to have the ambition to build a house, marry, beget children, or be a diligent worker. These impulses are necessary for society to function and therefore are not to be destroyed, but channeled and controlled. However, if the impulse leads someone toward sin, the proper response is to resist and subdue it.[17]

How is one to resist or subdue what is evil?

Traditional teaching affirms that we also possess a good impulse that resists evil, called the *yetzer hatov*.[18] Some rabbis use the word "heart," which encompasses our mind and will, to describe the source of our good and evil actions. It is the heart that devises evil thoughts and purposes. The good impulse should be stirred up to overcome the evil, and is associated with the right use of our rational faculty. If extra help is needed, the good is aided greatly by dwelling on and studying the Torah, which acts like a medicine to preserve life.[19] Other methods to help overcome evil involve dwelling on the bad consequences of sin (to include final judgment), dwelling on sin's folly,

---

good or evil use. The *yetzer hara* wells up from the intrinsically good heart God has given us and should be directed toward social and moral goods and in following the Law. But it can bend toward evil when the person allows it overcome sexual restraint or to defy the rights of God and our fellow humans. Williams, *Ideas of the Fall*, 67.

16. Moore, *Judaism in the First Centuries*, 492.

17. Ibid., 482–83.

18. Early Judaism did not see a dualism between the evil *body* and the good *soul*, as is seen in some Hellenistic thought. Both impulses are part of our total being. If we do good or evil, all parts participate, not just one.

19. Moore, *Judaism in the First Centuries*, 484–86, 490.

taking an oath to do good, confessing one's faith in God, and reminding oneself of the duty to love and obey God supremely.[20]

But what if one gives in to evil and commits sin?

The rabbis always lead the sinner to the remedy of repentance, which can overcome any sin.[21]

How is one to know what evil or sin really are?

Judaism insists that sin is anything against God's revealed rules for life, whether in moral issues or religious observance. These rules are in the Torah and what the prophets reveal in the rest of the Hebrew Scriptures. Furthermore, because sin involves the heart (will and mind), it is the person's *intentions* that count the most. Although an Israelite could sin unintentionally, the use of the word "sinner" is generally used for someone who willfully sins or neglects a known duty in a persistent manner.[22] The Hebrew words used for sin also suggest different severities of sin. *Het* occurs almost six hundred times in the Hebrew Bible and means, "to miss the mark." It refers to both intentional and unintentional sin and is the only word used to describe the least serious type of sin—an inadvertent breaking of a ritual law. The next most frequent word is *awon,* which is frequently translated as "iniquity." This suggests a more deliberate and serious offense, and is usually used to define breaking of social or ethical law. A third word is *pasha,* which means to "transgress" or "rebel," and signifies the most serious form of sin. The rebellion is deliberate and directed against God and his laws.[23]

Can a person be righteous, and if so, what does that mean?

Yes, a Jew could be righteous and his or her life would be distinguished by a life of repentance (consider the moral evil done by a venerated leader, such as David, and his subsequent repentance) and not by sinless perfection. God knows our finiteness and frailty and has given us ways to deal with sin. God is reasonable and does not demand from us a perfection we cannot

---

20. Ibid., 489, 491.
21. Ibid., 492.
22. Ibid., 493.
23. Wigoder, *New Encyclopedia,* s. v. "sin."

achieve.[24] God has granted humans the ability to choose between right and wrong, informed them of the consequences for obedience and disobedience, and given them the power to perform what he asks. The rabbis did not pursue whether there was any conflict with this human freedom and God's providence. They saw both as existing together. In the end, humans are responsible before God for their thoughts and conduct.[25]

What can we conclude about Judaism's views on sin and righteousness? It seems reasonable to conclude that Judaism saw little direct effect of Adam and Eve's sin on their progeny. Mainstream Judaism rejects the notion of an inherited sinful nature derived from our first parents' "original sin." There are influences to sin and temptations (*yetzer hara*), but these are not coercive. Humanity is blessed with the ability to freely choose good or evil and is responsible to God for the choices they make. Should they sin, they can respond to God in repentance, a door that is always open.[26] They may also choose to obey God's commands, commands that are not burdensome, and by such obedience God will declare them righteous.

THE EARLY CHURCH FATHERS AND EASTERN ORTHODOXY

The Eastern Orthodox tradition is considered alongside the early church fathers since it relies so heavily on their teachings. The early fathers are generally considered ones from the first century through the eighth century, but Eastern Orthodoxy recognizes luminary theologians from medieval times and up to the present. Although Augustine lived in this time period, his ideas will be discussed with the Reformation because his thoughts match more closely those of that era.

Early Church Fathers

The views of the early church fathers[27] are not uniform regarding our topics, but there is enough of a consensus that a general conclusion can be made

---

24. Moore, *Judaism in the First Centuries*, 494–95.
25. Ibid., 453–54.
26. Wigoder, *New Encyclopedia*, s. v. "sin."
27. The church fathers that significantly address the topic of sin, original sin, and holiness are Justin Martyr, Tatian, Theophilus of Antioch, Athenagoras, Irenaeus, Clement of Alexandria, Origen, Methodius, Athanasius, Cyril of Jerusalem, Basil, Gregory of Nazianzus, Gregory of Nyssa, John Chrysostom, Theodore of Mopsuestia, Tertullian, Cyprian, Ambrose, and Augustine.

about their beliefs. A survey reveals that they were almost unanimous in concluding that physical death was a result of the fall (initial sin of Adam and Eve). Some suggested that humanity was represented by Adam or that somehow all persons were involved in Adam's sin, but the nature of this relationship was not clearly expressed. Of those that discussed the issue, many believed that we inherit spiritual death from Adam and Eve and some believed that the image we received from God is retained, but it is marred or damaged by the fall. This frequently meant that we are now more prone to sin than to holiness, or that we now have a moral corruption or "concupiscence" that predisposes us toward sin. Only a few fathers suggested that we are personally guilty for Adam's sin. Many affirmed that Satan and his demons push humans toward sin, but that we still retain our freedom to sin or not. The early fathers do not seek to resolve the nature of the interplay of the fall's effects on Adam's posterity and human free will. They assert that Adam had a negative effect on all humanity's choice to sin or not, but fall short of saying this effect was a direct cause or coercion. Humans are still able to choose between good and evil, are able to obey the commands God has given, and are held responsible for whatever choices they make.[28]

EXCURSUS: THE PELAGIAN AND SEMI-PELAGIAN CONTROVERSIES

Two controversies relate directly to the topic of sin and holiness and to our ability to respond positively to God's commands; these are the Pelagian and Semi-Pelagian disputes. The Pelagian controversy involved a British ascetic, Pelagius (354 AD–?), and Augustine in the early fifth century. Pelagius was dismayed at the corruption he found in both Rome's parishioners and clergy. He reinforced the importance of human freedom and its relation to virtue. His interpretation of Romans 5 was that Adam's original sin was harmful to the whole race, not by transmission, but by example. Along with Adam's sin, the sins of those around us and the temptations of the devil sway us toward sin. Pelagius believed the original sin did not taint humanity directly, but each person retained the ability to do good, since that was part of God's creating grace. To Pelagius sin is not a substance, but a chosen thought or deed. Humans retain the ability to not sin and can keep God's commandments. This does not mean that anyone is or ever was sinless, but that when converted, someone can be without sin by the synergy of their own efforts

---

28. Christensen, M. "Original Sin," 11–12. Tennant, *The Sources*, 273–345 summarizes the views of many of the church fathers on this topic. See also Smith, *With Willful Intent*, ch. 1; and Toews, *Story of Original Sin*, ch. 2–6.

and God's grace.[29] Augustine greatly opposed Pelagius's views. Augustine believed that all Adam's posterity participated in and are responsible for his fall, and with Adam, are held guilty for it. The result of this sin was both physical and spiritual death. Spiritual death includes the total loss of the image of God and an irresistible inclination to do what is sinful and evil (concupiscence), especially sexual sin. Humanity is only able to sin and can do nothing good unless God sovereignly enables them. In response to the controversy, the church's leaders held the council of Carthage (418 AD), in which it was decided that: 1) death was a penalty imposed on humans due to Adam's sin (and not an evil that attached itself to human nature), 2) original sin inherited from Adam is present in everyone and therefore infants must be baptized to remove it, 3) grace is not given so we can *more easily* obey God's commands, but is absolutely *necessary* to obey his commands.[30]

Later, the Semi-Pelagian controversy developed and was part of a string of Western controversies over the relationship between God's grace and human freedom. Along with the aforementioned Pelagian dispute, this string included the Gottschalk (ninth century), DeAuxiliis (sixteenth century), Jansenist (seventeenth century), and Calvinist-Arminian debates (seventeenth century to present), which battled over similar issues. The Semi-Pelagian dispute was over the relative contributions of God's added grace and the God-given freedom of humanity to respond to God and obey his commands. In the early fifth century, certain monks in the monastery at Hadrumetum, North Africa, were upset with Augustine's writings that seemed to destroy the effect of human free will. Augustine maintained that salvation and the power to respond positively toward God was all of God's grace. The monks perceived this as a denial of the connection between human striving, assisted by God's grace, and their rewards in heaven. (For the monks, the combination of God's grace and their own efforts was the basis of their spiritual life).[31] The monks of southern Gaul in France also read Augustine's writings. One of their leaders, John Cassian, wrote a number of *Conferences,* which were dialogues between himself, his companion Germanus, and the ascetic desert fathers of Egypt. In these writings on the Christian life, *Conference 4* describes the struggle between the flesh and the spirit. Cassian contended that fleshly desires are not necessarily evil, but distract us from what is spiritual. Every descendant of Adam has this struggle and it must therefore be a part of the human nature given us by our Creator. This struggle is over obedience to God and is given to us so

29. Christensen, M. "A Description," 2.
30. Kelly, *Early Christian*, 361–66, 369–70.
31. Weaver, *Divine Grace*, 1.

that we would not do only what our flesh desires.[32] Several other of the twenty-four *Conferences* relate to grace, free will, and our human nature, but *Conference 13* has a very concentrated discussion. In it, Cassian sees a synergistic relationship between God's grace and human freedom. God inspires good thoughts, actions, and good will, and gives us opportunities to carry these out.[33] Therefore, his grace is necessary for every aspect of salvation since human weakness can accomplish none of it.[34] This grace works on our will, and fans and fosters any small spark of good will that we express. God enlightens us, strengthens the sparks he sees in us, and urges us on toward salvation since he desires no one to perish.[35] Cassian asserted that God made humanity with the capability to do what is good as well as evil. If humans could only do one or the other, God would not have granted them a free will. He relates this situation as applying first to Adam:

> And, in this case how will that first statement of the Lord made about men after the fall stand: "Behold, Adam is become as one of us, knowing good and evil?" For we cannot think that before, he was such as to be altogether ignorant of good. Otherwise we should have to admit that he was formed like some irrational and insensate beast: which is sufficiently absurd and altogether alien from our Catholic faith. Moreover as the wisest Solomon says: "God made man upright," i.e., always to enjoy the knowledge of good only, "But they have sought out many imaginations," for they came, as has been said, to know good and evil. Adam therefore after the fall conceived a knowledge of evil which he had not previously, but did not lose the knowledge of good which he had before. . . . And with the same meaning the Lord rebukes by the prophet the unnatural but freely chosen blindness of the Jews, which they by their obstinacy brought upon themselves, . . . and that no one might ascribe this blindness of theirs to nature instead of to their own will, elsewhere He says: . . . "having eyes, but ye see not; and ears, but ye hear not."[36]

Rebecca Harden Weaver interprets Cassian's view of the fall by saying that he saw human nature as severely injured and unable to heal itself. Humans are lost and cannot find their way to God although they may desire and seek to find that way. We need God's additional grace, but God's original

32. Cassian, *The Conferences*, 4.7. The *Conferences* are accessible online at http://www.osb.org/lectio/cassian/conf.
33. Ibid., 13.3.
34. Ibid., 13.6.
35. Ibid., 13.7, 13.8.
36. Ibid., 13.12.

grace in creation has not been totally lost such that we have lost all freedom to will what is good.[37]

Debate over these issues continued for over a century until Caesarius, bishop of Arles, France, called a synod in Orange (529 AD), at which the bishops in attendance produced twenty-five canons, some of which related to the Semi-Pelagian controversy. They concluded that Adam's sin had so impaired humanity, body and soul, that no one could respond to God, love God, or do good until divine grace had enabled him or her. This grace is not found in the free will of humans, for grace is needed to even begin to will what is good or to will salvation.[38]

According to John McGuckin, many of the eastern Greek fathers, as opposed to the western Latin fathers, see that humanity's created image from God has not been lost but severely tarnished, so that humanity's original "silver mirror" does not reflect the glory of its Maker.[39] McGuckin references the fathers, especially Athanasius, in saying that they invariably mean that:

> The believer ought to correspond with the prevenient grace of God in an active (if unequal) synergy with the divine grace of redemption and mercy that has been given in Christ. Almost all the ascetical fathers argue that the gift of God's grace is given in measure, appropriate to the degree of seriousness with which the believer responds to the initial grace, and with which he or she continues on the Christian path of responsiveness. God calls his people to himself, but expects them to respond, and does not generally force the presence on the unwilling or the unresponsive . . .[40]

Interestingly, McGuckin's summary sounds very much like John Cassian and others who supported the Semi-Pelagian doctrine during that controversy.

Eastern Orthodoxy

The Orthodox Church relies heavily on the views of the early fathers when formulating their theology.[41] Kallistos Ware, a present-day Orthodox

---

37. Weaver, *Divine Grace*, 123.
38. The Canons of the Council of Orange.
39. McGuckin, *Orthodox Church*, 189.
40. Ibid., note 27, 263.
41. Ibid., 100.

thinker, summarizes the views of the fathers by saying that they frequently asserted the free choice of humans as part of their endowment in the image of God. Ware refers to Irenaeus, who believed that Adam and Eve were created immature and in need of growing into God's perfection. Humans were created innocent, and in cooperation with God's grace, were called to gradually develop into God's likeness; they were given the opportunity to grow into a full fellowship with him.[42] Ware summarizes Orthodox thought by stating that evil entered the world by a double fall—the fall of both the angels and humans. Each used the gift of free will incorrectly; therefore evil is in itself not a thing, being, or substance, but a wrong attitude toward what is good. Adam and Eve's "original sin" was a conscious act of disobedience, a freely chosen and deliberate act of turning away from God to self.[43]

What were the effects of the original sin? Ware maintains the effects were physical and moral. Physically, humans became subject to physical pain, disease, toil, great pain in childbirth, disability, physical decline, and eventually physical death.[44] Morally, humans began to experience toilsome work, frustration, weakness of will, and a divided self in which desires and actions don't always match. To the Orthodox, the word "flesh," as St. Paul uses it, is not the same as the body, but describes whatever is sinful and opposed to God in us (both body and soul are fallen). Asceticism is Orthodoxy's answer to the flesh, and is the struggle against it. This struggle is for all Christians and not just for those who take monastic vows. The struggle can be successful, since the Orthodox tradition does not hold to some of the tenets of "total depravity" (part of which affirms the idea that the image of God was lost and the will is unable to do what is good). However, the total effect of Adam's and every succeeding generation's sin, which includes every individual's sin, has set an unbridgeable gulf between God and humanity that only God's grace can traverse. How that bridge is crossed will be discussed under the topic of deification/theosis/union with God. Further, the moral consequence of the fall does not extend in a juridical sense to personal guilt. Adam's posterity are not held guilty for his sin, but only for their own sins. However, Adam's sin had wide-ranging consequences. We live in an environment where it is easier to do evil and harder to do good. We, as fellow humans made in the image of God, are interdependent; we are

42. Ware, *Orthodox Way*, 51–52.

43. Ibid., 57–58.

44. Ibid., 60. On a side note, Orthodox scholars see physical death as a blessing and not primarily as a punishment. God did not want humans to go on living perpetually in a fallen, sinful state. Death was the merciful way of escape in that it opened the door to the renewal that will occur when body and soul are reunited at the resurrection of the dead.

not islands. The actions of others, including Adam and Eve, have affected us. We are not guilty of the sins of others, but we are always involved.[45]

Another current Orthodox theologian, Michael Pomazansky, adds further details. He stresses that God gave humans three great gifts at the outset: freedom, reason, and love. With freedom there was the possibility of wavering and therefore being tempted. Reason's temptation was to grow proud, not acknowledging God's supreme wisdom (consider Adam and Eve not trusting God with the knowledge he gave them—they allowed the serpent to persuade them there was a better way than God's). Love's temptation is to replace love for God and our fellow humans with a supreme love of our own desires—to replace the higher and eternal with the lower and temporary. A moral consequence of the fall, which the Orthodox prefer to call the *ancestral sin*, was that, as St. Paul says, a "law of sin" entered. Our inclinations now do not lean toward the good; sinful inclinations, such as lust and pride, reign. We have inherited a spiritual disease. Furthermore, when Adam sinned, his posterity became corrupted by sin and lost the indwelling grace with which they were created. This led to spiritual death and later to physical death. The greatest consequence of the fall was the loss of Paradise, or the Kingdom of God. Death, hell, darkness, and God's rejection now loomed. God, however, did not reject humankind—we retain our image, freedom, and reason.[46] Pomazansky concludes that the early fathers do not express the "how" of the effects of the ancestral sin, merely that Adam's sin negatively reached unto all those who followed after him.[47]

John Romanides, who has devoted a whole book to the questions of the ancestral sin in the minds of the early church from the NT writers through the second century, has considerable agreement with the above authors. Adam's sin, influenced by the efforts of the devil, resulted in physical and spiritual death for himself and all his descendants. Our sins spring from the fact that we are dead and have thus inherited a corrupt nature, a nature that strongly inclines us toward sin.[48]

Sin Defined

Sin for the Orthodox is the turning of the human will away from the will of God, his commandments, and the moral law written in our consciences.[49]

45. Ibid., 60–62.
46. Pomazansky, *Orthodox Dogmatic*, 155, 157–61.
47. Ibid., 169.
48. Romanides, *Ancestral Sin*, 162–63.
49. Pomazansky, *Orthodox Dogmatic*, 152.

Since God's goal for us is union with him, when we sin we miss the mark—we fail to strive for communion with God and fail to base our life on the life and actions of Jesus Christ. Further, sin can be conscious or unconscious, active or failing to act, but in either case the sinner is personally accountable to God.[50]

The Orthodox and Holiness

How does this Orthodox view of the fall affect their views on holiness? As hinted above, the Orthodox see humanity as created innocent and immature. Neither Adam and Eve nor anyone today is born in complete union with God, but we do have the ability to communicate with God, a free will, and a lifetime to grow in fellowship with him. This is akin to the "image" that God created humanity with; it is an endowed potentiality to become godly. We then acquire the "likeness" of God as we use our freedom to cooperate with God's grace and journey toward union with God and moral perfection (this process is sometimes called *theosis* or deification). This struggle is a life-long pilgrimage and is the calling of every Christian.[51]

Theosis for the Orthodox is more understandable in the West by the terms transformation, sanctification, becoming Christlike or godly, communion with God, or sharing in God's life. It is not becoming like God in his essence, but in his character.[52] The Christian participates not in God's essence but in his "energies," which are his divine life outside of his essence. Examples of his energies are the fruit of the Spirit in Galatians 5:22–24.[53] As we advance toward God, he shares these energies with us, especially the virtue of love. This is the first aspect of *theosis*.

The second aspect is our union with God. This is intimately tied to the first aspect, becoming godly, because godliness flows from union with God. God calls his followers to take part in his very life, the fellowship shared within the Trinity itself.[54] McGuckin describes *theosis* as the process of "ascent," of always becoming more and more like God. However, this is preceded by God's descending and reaching toward us. His divine grace reaches out to his children and allows them to experience his presence. His presence is like holy light, and as it radiates onto us we become cleansed and

---

50. Orthodox Church in America, "What is Sin?"
51. Fairbairn, *Eastern*, 66–68.
52. Ibid., 68, 71.
53. Another list of energies are mentioned in 2 Pet 1:3–7 and are the result of our participation in God's nature.
54. Ibid., 72.

transformed.[55] As God draws us and we ascend, we are drawn to our true destiny, which is to love God and others as ourselves. Our union with God overflows in love towards our brothers and sisters in Christ and in drawing non-Christians toward that love. Thus, we develop the "mind of Christ."[56]

The third aspect is our participation in God's immortality. Because of our union with God, we share his eternalness and incorruptibility so that this union will be never-ending. In the West it might be called experiencing God's "eternal life."[57] God is eternal and incorruptible by nature, but we can share in it by grace.[58]

In reviewing the Orthodox views, there are similarities with Judaism. Humans are created with and retain their moral freedom. Adam's sin has harmed humanity and there is a definite inclination toward sin that resides within us. However, God in his grace calls all people to participate in his divine life. Unlike Judaism, this life is experienced in a relationship with the divine Trinity—Father, Son, and Holy Spirit. This life of godliness flows from union with God and grows until it is perfected in the new heavens and earth.

ROMAN CATHOLICISM

Through the ages, the Roman Catholic Church's teaching on sin and original sin has been influenced by several well-known theologians, such as Augustine, Anselm, and Thomas Aquinas. It was Augustine who seems to have had the greatest influence. His views on original sin influenced the conclusions of the provincial (not ecumenical) Second Council of Orange (529 AD), which was later approved by Pope Boniface II. The later Council of Trent (1546 AD) made several decrees on original sin that included the content of Orange with a more systematic presentation.[59] The decrees of the Council of Trent still stand as the official view of the Roman Catholic Church. The five canons of the fifth session of the council summarize their views: When Adam transgressed God's commandment, he lost humanity's original holiness and justice, incurred death, came under the power of the devil, and was changed for the worse in body and soul. Adam transferred both the death of the body and of the soul to the whole human race by natural propagation (having offspring). The sin of Adam is taken away by the

---

55. McGuckin, *Orthodox Church*, 198–99.
56. Romanides, *Ancestral Sin*, 112–13.
57. Fairbairn, *Eastern Orthodox*, 71–72.
58. Romanides, *Ancestral Sin*, 128.
59. Schoonenberg, *Man and Sin*, 161, 163.

merits of Jesus Christ, whose benefits are administered to both infants and adults by the sacrament of baptism. Baptism confers the remission of sins, expiates the sin of Adam, regenerates through its cleansing, and remits the guilt of original sin. However, the baptized still keep concupiscence, which the Christian must resist through the grace of Christ. Concupiscence came from Adam's sin, it is not sin, but does incline one toward sin.[60]

These canons also form the basis for the teachings in the Catechism of the Catholic Church. The Catechism teaches that when Adam and Eve sinned they lost their original state of "holiness and justice," with the original holiness given so they could participate in his divine life. Original justice consisted of: freedom from suffering and death, inner personal harmony, accord between man and woman, and harmony between humanity and the physical creation. Adam and Eve had mastery of their own selves and were free of the three concupiscences—subjugation to the pleasures of the senses, covetousness, and self-assertion, all of which are contrary to reason. The consequences of their sin not only affected them, but brought death to all—thus sin became universal.[61] The Catechism gives further detail beyond the Council of Trent; it states that all humanity is somehow implicated in Adam's sin. The whole human race was in Adam's action; but the "how" of this transmission is a mystery. All are born afflicted by Adam's sin (the death of the soul). As a result, Adam and Eve's personal sin affects the human nature of all who follow—their nature is fallen since it is deprived of original holiness and justice. However, the "original sin" of Adam and Eve is only called "sin" by analogy—it is contracted, not committed, a state and not an act.[62] Contrary to Trent, the Catechism does not mention that humanity bears guilt for Adam's fall, but seems to suggest that the fall's main effect was on human nature and therefore did not bring *personal* guilt, which would attach to *personal* sins.[63] As suggested in line 377, concupiscence is now part of human nature. Although not totally corrupted, since humans retain their freedom, human nature is now wounded in its natural powers, is liable to ignorance, suffering, and death, and is inclined toward sin. Though baptism brings life and removes the guilt of original sin, concupiscence remains,

---

60. The Council of Trent, "Fifth Session."
61. Catechism, 375–77, 399–401.
62. Ibid., 402–4.

63. Ibid., 404–5. The guilt from original sin is therefore not personal guilt, but is guilt in a broader or "analogous" sense (McDermott, "The Theology," 512). Therefore, it would still be possible for an unbaptized infant to enter heaven, considering the greatness of God's mercy and Christ's redemption (Thils, *Christian Holiness*, 239–40). It seems modern Catholic theologians have softened the traditional Catholic stance that Adam's posterity inherits the guilt of his fall.

which, along with the devil's influences, must be battled throughout this earthly life. The battle is intensified since the personal sins of all those in the world around us (past and present), to include sin perpetuated in social structures, form what Catholics call the "sin of the world."[64]

Recent Catholic scholarship, however, has reinterpreted the views of Augustine and the Council of Trent in an attempt to make the teaching relevant to the modern world. Catholic scholars still see original sin as the sinful condition of the race that traces its beginning to the fall of humans at the dawn of human existence. However, the teaching must be interpreted in light of modern knowledge that reveals more accurate dating for the age of the earth, advances in the study of human evolution, similarities between humans and other creatures, the invalidity of guilt without responsibility, and a more positive view of matter and the human body.[65] Therefore, the story of Adam and Eve is reinterpreted as a symbol that mediates a more transcendent reality. Their story is a myth rather than history, but the story is effective because it allows us to properly interpret our own selves. Further, Paul personifies sin in Romans 7 (For I do not do the good I want . . .) as a universal power in individuals and society that keeps our human freedom in bondage. Paul's intent in Romans 5:12–21 is not to say that universal sin is caused by an inheritance from Adam (a doctrine that was read back into the passage), but that from the beginning until now all are sinners and need to be saved by Christ. Genesis and Romans teach us that all humans have a propensity to sin (concupiscence), temptation is inward more than outward, God created the world good, sin is not from God (rather, it is a result of human freedom), and because of sin we all need God's salvation in Christ.[66] In this newer view, concupiscence is not an evil itself, but the finite situation in which our desires and impulses are not disposed toward trust, faith, and love toward God. We therefore experience temptation to go against what God's gift of freedom was meant to lead us to.[67] The result seems paradoxical in that the concupiscent condition lies prior to the exercise of freedom, and exercising freedom results in real sins, which are both inevitable and free. Sin is neither necessary nor caused by God's good creation, and persons are always offered God's grace by which they could trust in God. However, humans *don't* trust in God and personal sinning is universal.[68] It seems the modern scholars have come to similar conclusions

---

64. Catechism, 405–9.
65. Haight, "Sin and Grace," 85–86.
66. Ibid., 89–95. See similar conclusions in Koszarek, *The Catechesis*, 42–54.
67. Haight, "Sin and Grace," 96–97.
68. Ibid., 99. See a similar discussion in McDermott, "The Theology," 505–12.

as Trent (except on guilt for Adam's sin), but deny the historical basis for these same doctrines.

Sin Defined

Based on the above discussion, what is a Roman Catholic definition of sin? Catholic theologians make a distinction between original and actual sin. Actual sin has to do with moral evil, which is the lack of conformity to right reason and the law of God. If an act does conform, it is good; if it does not, it is evil. "God has endowed us with reason and free-will, and a sense of responsibility; He has made us subject to His law, which is known to us by the dictates of conscience, and our acts must conform with these dictates, otherwise we sin (Romans 14:23). In every sinful act two things must be considered, the substance of the act and the want of rectitude or conformity (St. Thomas, I–II:72:1)."[69] The essence of sin is in line with actual sin:

> As regards the principle from which it proceeds sin is original or actual. The will of Adam acting as head of the human race for the conservation or loss of original justice is the cause and source of original sin. Actual sin is committed by a free personal act of the individual will. It is divided into sins of commission and omission. A sin of commission is a positive act contrary to some prohibitory precept; a sin of omission is a failure to do what is commanded (St. Thomas, I–II:72:5).... As regards their malice, sins are distinguished into sins of ignorance, passion or infirmity, and malice: as regards the activity involved, into sins of thought, word, or deed (*cordis, oris, operis*); as regards their gravity, into mortal and venial.[70]

> The division of sin into original and actual, mortal and venial, is not a division of genus into species because sin has not the same signification when applied to original and personal sin, mortal and venial. Mortal sin cuts us off entirely from our true last end; venial sin only impedes us in its attainment. Actual personal sin is voluntary by a proper act of the will. Original sin is voluntary not by a personal voluntary act of ours, but by an act of the will of Adam. Original and actual sin are distinguished by the manner in which they are voluntary (*ex parte actus*); mortal and venial sin by the way in which they affect our relation to God (*ex parte deordinationis*). Since a voluntary act and its disorder are

69. Catholic Encyclopedia, "Sin, Nature of sin."
70. Ibid., "Sin, Division of sin."

of the essence of sin, it is impossible that sin should be a generic term in respect to original and actual, mortal and venial sin. The true nature of sin is found perfectly only in a personal mortal sin, in other sins imperfectly, so that sin is predicated primarily of actual sin, only secondarily of the others.[71]

Catholicism and Holiness

There is significant emphasis in Catholic teaching regarding the call to Christian holiness. The Catechism of the Catholic Church teaches that the vocation of the Christian is to fulfill the Beatitudes as expressed by Jesus in Matthew 5:3-12. The ultimate beatitude that God calls us to is to partake of his coming Kingdom such that we see God face to face ("Blessed are the pure in heart, for they shall see God," Matt 5:8). This "beatific vision" allows us to become partakers of the divine nature and eternal life once we reach the heavenly Kingdom.[72]

Although this experience is not possible in our earthly life, the Catechism affirms that Christ's followers walk the path toward it:

> The beatitude we are promised confronts us with decisive moral choices. It invites us to purify our hearts of bad instincts and to seek the love of God above all else. It teaches us that true happiness is not found in riches or well-being, in human fame or power, or in any human achievement... The Decalogue, the Sermon on the Mount, and the apostolic catechesis describe for us the paths that lead to the Kingdom of heaven. Sustained by the grace of the Holy Spirit, we tread them, step by step, by everyday acts. By the working of the Word of Christ, we slowly bear fruit in the Church to the glory of God.[73]

As Christ's followers continue to walk the path, they develop the various virtues. Virtues are defined as:

> ... firm attitudes, stable dispositions, habitual perfections of intellect and will that govern our actions, order our passions, and guide our conduct according to reason and faith. They make possible ease, self-mastery, and joy in leading a morally good life. The virtuous man is he who freely practices the good.

---

71. Ibid., "Sin, The capital sins or vices."
72. Catechism, 1716–22.
73. Ibid., 1723–24.

The moral virtues are acquired by human effort. They are the fruit and seed of morally good acts; they dispose all the powers of the human being for communion with divine love. . . . The human virtues acquired by education, by deliberate acts and by a perseverance ever-renewed in repeated efforts are purified and elevated by divine grace. With God's help, they forge character and give facility in the practice of the good. The virtuous man is happy to practice them. . . . It is not easy for man, wounded by sin, to maintain moral balance. Christ's gift of salvation offers us the grace necessary to persevere in the pursuit of virtues. Everyone should always ask for this grace of light and strength, frequent the sacraments, cooperate with the Holy Spirit, and follow his calls to love what is good and shun evil.[74] The four cardinal virtues are prudence, justice, fortitude, and temperance.[75] The theological virtues are faith, hope, and charity (love). The theological virtues form the base of the Christian's moral life and give life to all the rest of them. They are "infused by God into the souls of the faithful to make them capable of acting as his children and of meriting eternal life."[76] Love is key to the practice of all the virtues and inspires all the rest. It gives each their proper order among the others. In fact, "love is itself the fulfillment of all our works. There is the goal; that is why we run: we run toward it, and once we reach it, in it we shall find rest."[77]

Further, the Catechism lists the gifts and fruits of the Spirit. The gifts (wisdom, understanding, counsel, fortitude, knowledge, piety, and fear of the Lord) sustain the virtuous moral life. They "complete and perfect the virtues of those who receive them. They make the faithful docile in readily obeying divine inspirations."[78] The fruit of the Spirit (charity, joy, peace, patience, kindness, goodness, generosity, gentleness, faithfulness, modesty, self-control, and chastity) "are perfections that the Holy Spirit forms in us as the first fruits of eternal glory."[79] The Catechism emphasizes that the holy Christian life is the calling or vocation of every Christian. The full Christian life in which one is perfected in love is the call of Jesus to all his followers (Matt 5:48). As one makes spiritual progress toward that end there is ever more intimate union with Christ. This is a "mystical" union since it involves

74. Ibid., 1804, 1810, 1811.
75. Ibid., 1805.
76. Ibid., 1813.
77. Ibid., 1829.
78. Ibid., 1831.
79. Ibid., 1832.

partaking of the sacraments (holy mysteries), which through Christ, allows union with the whole Holy Trinity. Like Christ, this way toward perfect love is cruciform since it involves renunciation and spiritual warfare. The believer lives an ascetic life that mortifies the flesh and allows one to enjoy the peace and joy of the Beatitudes.[80] The late Pope John Paul II confirmed the attainability and need for Christian holiness:

> To ask the catechumens: "Do you wish to receive Baptism?" means at the same time to ask them: "Do you wish to be holy?" It means to set before them the radical nature of the Sermon on the Mount: "Be perfect as your heavenly Father is perfect." (Matt 5:48)
>
> ... The time has come to re-propose wholeheartedly to everyone this *high standard of ordinary Christian living*: the whole life of the Christian community and of Christian families must lead in this direction.[81]

Ralph Martin affirms that holiness involves the process of having our heart transformed into one of love. This heart will fulfill the two Great Commandments—to love God and our neighbor with all our hearts. This heart brings its will into unity and conformity to God's will. What holds us back from attaining greater spiritual growth is not external circumstances but a sluggish heart. Sometimes this manifests itself in procrastination, thinking that further purification will be taken care of in purgatory. However, Martin asserts that holiness is the whole purpose of our creation, therefore it is not optional but is necessary for us to be united with God and to spend eternity with him. The untransformed will not see God and will be separated from him forever in hell.[82]

Martin, in his overview of the stages on the spiritual journey, accentuates three generally chronological stages—the purgative, illuminative, and unitive—and uses seven Doctors of the Church to explain these stages. The purgative stage includes coming to conversion, turning from sin and toward obedience to the moral law, and the beginning of the habits of prayer, piety, and faithfulness in church life. The illuminative stage involves growth in all the previous, including growth in the virtues, love, surrender to Christ, detachment from the world, and union with God. Here one experiences greater trials, blessings, and "mystical phenomena." The unitive stage involves deep and regular union with God, resulting in deep joy and humility,

---

80. Ibid., 2013–15.
81. Martin, *Fulfillment*, 2.
82. Ibid., 2, 7–8.

freedom from fear, a great desire to serve God, and increased fruitfulness. Here, one experiences a great insight into God and his ways, and any suffering that occurs is seen as a participation in Christ's redemptive suffering. One's deep union with God is thought of as a "spiritual marriage" or a "transforming union."[83]

In summary, Roman Catholic teaching on original sin and holiness has broad agreement with the previous two traditions. Humans have inherited a tendency to sin, but not Adam's personal guilt, and they still retain the human freedom to pursue holiness. Gustaf Thils provides a good summary:

> A true concept of original sin will affect our effort at holiness. The moderate eudaemonism of Christianity will make the faithful always vigilant, but basically rooted in joy. Christian holiness will be at its basis prudent watchfulness and a triumphant hope. The effort of sanctification will always be guided by the necessity of reestablishing this balance which has been upset, but it will also always be strengthened by the certitude of the supremacy of grace and the definitive victory.[84]

EARLY PROTESTANTISM

Protestantism began as a "protest" against some of the doctrines and practices of the Roman Catholic Church in the 1500s. Martin Luther and John Calvin were preeminent early Protestant theologians, and they relied heavily on Augustine for their ideas on sin and holiness. The Anabaptists rejected infant baptism and believed one could experience significant holiness because original sin was less of a hindrance. John Wesley, an Anglican and the founder of Methodism, lived in the 1700s, and had somewhat different views on sin and greater differences on holiness when compared to Luther and Calvin.

Martin Luther

Luther believed the image of God was lost when sin entered the world, which likely included our natural endowments of memory, mental acuity, and will. These have all been severely weakened. Sin entered the world through Adam and by his disobedience all humans were made sinners, resulting in death for all and a greater susceptibility to the devil's wiles. Further, humanity

---

83. Ibid., 11–12.
84. Thils, *Christian Holiness*, 242.

inherited Adam's corrupt nature, which leads to disobedience of all sorts, especially of the Ten Commandments. The totality of these negative effects is called original sin.[85] This original sin is imputed to us; all have sinned and become guilty through Adam's sin.[86]

Luther spends much time describing the effects of our inherited corrupt nature. We have lost all uprightness in our body and soul and are prone to evil, abhorring what is good. We now turn away from knowledge and wisdom and prefer ignorance (darkness). We have a spiritual sickness that pervades the wholeness of our being. We are in a dilemma—we are sickened by what is good for us and desire those things that harm us. Original sin is then the law of the flesh, a tyrant that enfeebles our nature.[87]

The flesh is defined as anything that is opposed to spirit and reason, anything that is outside of the grace and Spirit of Christ, or anything that does not come from faith. The flesh is first and foremost self-directed or selfish; it is prideful and self-assertive. The word flesh has physical overtones, but it is more than physical—it entails the whole of our being and thus includes our heart and soul. Thus, the flesh surpasses the idea of concupiscence (sensuality overruling reason) to include the broader concept of humanity's total resistance to God in soul and spirit. This means that sin is more than just our evil thoughts, words, and deeds, but is the corrupt nature from which these spring. What we do flows from who we are; all our sins are born from this essential sin.[88]

Luther believes this flesh greatly limits what our free will can do—our wills are bound. Humans have the power to consciously obey the exterior requirements—God's commands and laws—but have no power to affect the heart and its thoughts and desires. Thus, even when we outwardly obey God's commands, there remains an inner resistance and reluctance of the heart that is controlled by the flesh. Our love is never as free as it should be because it lacks complete genuineness and freedom. Our good deeds are still corrupt and never fully fulfill the law of God since there is always a mixture of outer obedience and inner unwillingness. We sin even when we do right, sometimes more and sometimes less, depending on the strength of our flesh.[89] Though sin is inescapable, it still carries guilt with it. Since Adam's sin, God has condemned humanity; he has imprisoned their wills and removed the original freedom Adam had. We are unable to change this

---

85. Luther, *Compend of Luther's Theology*, 80, 84.
86. Luther, *Luther*, 165–66.
87. Ibid., 167–68. Note that Luther equates original sin with the flesh.
88. Althaus, *Theology*, 153–55.
89. Ibid., 151–52.

sinful will. We are also subject to Satan's slavery. As a result, we have no power to turn to what is good. There is no active ability to respond to God, but there remains a passive aptitude, which is able to be taken ahold of by God's Spirit.[90] That is humanity's only hope.

When God does work on us he changes our will by the Holy Spirit so that we desire and act willingly. When God so acts there is no force that can compel us to desire anything that is evil.[91] So the human will sits before God and Satan. "Thus the human will is, as it were, a beast between the two. If God sit thereon, it wills and goes where God will: as the Psalm saith, 'I am become as it were a beast before thee, and I am continually with thee' (Ps 73:22–23). If Satan sits thereon, it wills and goes as Satan will. Nor is it in the power of its own will to choose, to which rider it will run, nor which it will seek; but the riders themselves contend, which shall have and hold it."[92]

Luther and Holiness

Luther's view on holiness begins with the purpose of the gospel, which is to restore the lost image in humankind and even to exceed the original. Christians are born again not only unto life but unto righteousness. This life and righteousness is grasped by faith, and is a beginning of what will be perfected in heaven. On this earth our righteousness is imperfect, but the Holy Spirit helps us to resist unbelief and other temptations to sin.[93] To Luther, original sin and the effects of the flesh remain and are forces that must be struggled against during this life. "Original sin, after regeneration, is like a wound that begins to heal; though it be a wound, yet it is in course of healing, though it still runs and is sore. So original sin remains in Christians until they die, yet itself is mortified and continually dying. Its head is crushed in pieces, so that it cannot condemn us."[94] So Luther believes that Christians will continue to struggle against the flesh and make some progress toward holiness:

> You are to understand, if you are a Christian, that you must experience all kinds of opposition and wicked dispositions in the flesh. For wherever there is faith, there comes a hundred evil thoughts, a hundred strugglings more than before; only see to it that you act the man, and not suffer yourself to be taken captive;

90. Ibid., 156–57.
91. Luther, *Compend of Luther's Theology*, 88–89.
92. Ibid., 90.
93. Ibid., 83.
94. Ibid., 87.

and continue to resist, and say, I will not, I will not. For we must here confess, that the case is much like that of an ill-matched couple, who are continually complaining of one another, and what one will do the other will not.

That may yet be called a truly Christian life that is never at perfect rest, and has not so far attained as to feel no sin, provided that sin be felt, indeed, but not favored. Thus we are to fast, pray, labor, to subdue and suppress lust . . . While flesh and blood continue, so long sin remains; wherefore it is ever to be struggled against. Whoever has not learned this by his own experience, must not boast that he is a Christian.[95]

The righteousness that the Christian experiences is an imputed or "alien" righteousness, since it comes from Christ. God considers the Christian righteous for Christ's sake. We are passive in the process and can do nothing to become righteous. Righteousness happens to us; all we can do is receive it. It is imputed as we daily receive forgiveness for our sins by faith.[96] Along with imputed righteousness comes humanity's transformation to a new obedience. However, the transformation in this life is only partial. Christians live at present through this alien or imputed righteousness and remain sinners throughout their lives. Our current obedience is partial and imperfect and will only be perfected in the new heavens and earth. This leads to Luther's concept of Christians being both totally righteous and sinners at the same time. Luther sees this illustrated in Paul's words in Romans 7:14–25, which Luther interprets as the conflict within Christians, not unbelievers. There is the continual inner battle with the flesh or the old man, and it requires daily surrender, grace, and forgiveness so that the flesh's effects become weaker and weaker and the new man becomes stronger and stronger.[97]

With this understanding, how holy does Luther expect Christians to be? He believes that salvation, righteousness, and faith always lead to good works and love of God and neighbor. He contends that there is a measure of victory over sin, but it is a hard-fought struggle. He comments on Romans 6:14 ("For sin shall have no dominion over you"):

> We must understand that this refers not only to the sinful desire for temporal goods and prosperity but also to our tendency to run away from temporal evils and adversities. For a man who has Christ through true faith does not desire any worldly goods

---

95. Ibid.,114.
96. Althaus, *Theology*, 227.
97. Ibid., 240–45.

(nor life itself), however much they may intrigue him; nor does he fear any evils and even death itself, however much they may frighten him. He stands firm on solid rock; he does not seek an easy life and does not mind getting hard knocks, not that he is not tempted to flee when fear overcomes him, or to yield to sinful desire when it entices him (for he is not insensitive to either lust or fear), but in the end, he does not surrender, even though it costs him utmost exertion and pain just barely to resist and to come out on top, in accordance with the word of 1 Peter 4:18: "The righteous man is scarcely saved." In this trial and struggle, the righteous man always resembles more a loser than a victor, for the Lord lets him be tested and assailed to his utmost limits as gold is tested in a furnace.[98]

John Calvin

Calvin describes the effects of the fall of Adam and Eve in his life-long work, *Institutes of the Christian Religion*. In it he describes the result of Adam's sin, and the guilt he incurred, as a curse, which spread to all his offspring. Further, our original image has been obliterated so that all the blessings that Adam and Eve had—wisdom, holiness, truth—were replaced by things such as impurity, vanity, and injustice. These replacements make up our inherited corruption or "original sin" and are testified to by such Scriptures as Romans 5:12 and Psalm 51:5. All humans now descend from impure seed and are born with an already existing infection; we are already soiled and unclean.[99] Calvin summarizes:

> Original sin, therefore, seems to be a hereditary depravity and corruption of our nature, diffused into all parts of the soul, which first makes us liable to God's wrath, then also brings forth in us those works which Scripture calls "works of the flesh" [Gal 5:19]. And that is properly what Paul often calls sin. The works that come forth from it—such as adulteries, fornications, thefts, hatreds, murders, carousings—he accordingly calls "fruits of sin" [Gal 5:19–21], although they are also commonly called "sins" in Scripture, and even by Paul himself.[100]

Calvin especially comments on sin's effect on human freedom. He believes that a person's unaided will can perform no good works unless helped

---

98. Luther, *Luther*, 189.
99. Calvin, *Institutes*, 246–48.
100. Ibid., 251.

by the special grace that the elect receive through regeneration. Moreover, the unregenerate act wickedly by choice and not by compulsion. They are willing slaves to sin.[101] This slavery is due to the fact that when sin entered the world all our spiritual gifts were completely lost, such as the ability to have faith, the ability to love God and neighbor, and the desire to be righteous. However, our *natural* gifts were only weakened. Our ability to mentally understand and make judgments became depraved. Our will did not die but was so constrained by evil desires that it can no longer pursue what is right.[102] Calvin concludes his chapter on refutations of free will by discussing human abilities:

> Of course he [a human] has a mind capable of understanding, even if it may not penetrate to heavenly and spiritual wisdom. He has some judgment of honesty. He has some awareness of divinity, even though he may not attain a true knowledge of God. But what do these qualities amount to? Surely they cannot make out that we are to abandon Augustine's view, approved by the common consent of the schools: the free goods upon which salvation depends were taken away from man after the Fall, while the natural endowments were corrupted and defiled. Therefore let us hold this as an undoubted truth which no siege engines can shake: the mind of man has been so completely estranged from God's righteousness that it conceives, desires, and undertakes only that which is impious, perverted, foul, impure, and infamous. The heart is so steeped in the poison of sin that it can breathe out nothing but a loathsome stench. But if some men occasionally make a show of good, their minds nevertheless ever remain enveloped in hypocrisy and deceitful craft, and their hearts bound by inner perversity.[103]

Sin Defined

The resulting definitions of sin by Luther and Calvin are quite similar. They both stress that sin has both original and actual aspects. Luther sees sin as referring not only to "sins," but also to the root behind them, namely the heart and its powers. At the bottom of the sinful heart is unfaith and egocentricity. Unfaith despises God and does not fear, love, or trust him. Unfaith produces a particular attitude—ingratitude—which is self-satisfied

---

101. Ibid., 262, 264.
102. Ibid., 270–71.
103. Ibid., 340.

and trusts only in itself and its own righteousness.[104] For Luther, the source of unfaith and self-centeredness is the "flesh":

> The pride and self-assertion which prevent a man from achieving genuine love either of men or of God is not an occasional distortion; it is the nature of fallen man. This means that sin is not only individual acts of commission and omission but the impurity of one's entire being. When we speak of sin, we may not, as Luther's opponents—the scholastic theologians—did, think only of the transgressions of the law in thoughts, words, and deeds. When we do that, we fail to understand the full depths of sin, that is, its root and the real sickness. "Our weakness lies not in our works but in our nature; our person, nature, and entire being are corrupted through Adam's fall. Man's acts reveal that his entire nature is impure, that is, there is simply nothing in us except sin."[105]

Likewise, Calvin linked the concepts of original and actual sin in his definition of sin. Original sin produces "works of the flesh" in us—adulteries, thefts, hatreds, etc., that are the fruits of sin (Gal 5:19–21). Calvin believes this is Paul's concept of sin.[106] Further, humans sin by necessity, because their will is bound by sin. This bondage occurs because we have given ourselves over to this necessity, not because we lack will, but because we lack soundness of will.[107]

Modern Reformed theologians follow Luther and Calvin's trend. Lewis and Demarest differentiate between sin (singular) and sins (plural). *Sin* is the tendency of humans since the fall of Adam and Eve to disbelieve God, become disillusioned with him, and to disobey his moral laws by commission or omission. This is our rebellious nature/inclination. *Sins* are self-determined and responsible thoughts, words, deeds, or any inactions that yield to our inherently depraved natures, misuse God-given abilities, disrespect the rights of others, break moral laws, and throw off God's rule over our lives.[108] Therefore, our moral nature inherited from Adam is the cause of actual sins. This depraved nature, or the "flesh," as Paul describes it, is the harmful tendency of persons to use their *power of contrary choice* to oppose the will of God.[109] Curiously though, later Lewis and Demarest

---

104. Althaus, *Theology*, 144–45.
105. Ibid., 153.
106. Calvin, *Institutes*, 251.
107. Ibid., 294.
108. Lewis and Demarest, *Integrative Theology*, vol. 2, 220.
109. Ibid., 208–9.

assert that the flesh is *unable* to do what is good and is able only to sin.[110] Since the fall unbelievers do *not* have the power of contrary choice of loving and serving God. Their ability is limited by their fleshly nature.[111] These theologians conclude by saying, "Everyone sins because everyone has an innate disposition to sin. We are sinners by choice because we are sinners by nature, and we are sinners by nature because we are sinners by choice. We are self-determined, but the nature of the self is inclined to rebel against moral norms."[112] Self-determination is what it means to be free and not always to have the ability of contrary choice. Humanity's moral nature before regeneration is a slave to sin, and every self-determination made according to that nature (sins) are free and responsible.[113] Similarly, Millard Erickson states that "sin is not merely wrong acts and thoughts, but sinfulness as well, an inherent inner disposition inclining us to wrong acts and thoughts. We are not simply sinners because we sin; we sin because we are sinners. . . . Sin is any lack of conformity, active or passive, to the moral law of God. This may be a matter of act, of thought, or of inner disposition or state."[114] Sin's essence is the displacement of God as the supreme authority/love in one's life with anything else. It is not letting God be God in one's life. Erickson also recognizes the "flesh," and describes it as the selfish life, one that rejects God's rule. The flesh has become a part of human nature since Adam's fall. However the nature of the flesh is that we are now *less* able than Adam and Eve, not *unable*, to choose what is right.[115]

Calvin and Holiness

The only way out of this predicament is for humans to be regenerated by God's sovereign grace and to become holy as he is holy. The end object of regeneration is for God to display a harmony between God's righteousness and a believer's obedience, thus confirming their adoption as sons (Gal 4:5, 1 Pet 1:10). Calvin affirms that the law of God has within itself the newness by which his image can be restored in us. However, we humans are lethargic in our response and we need goading and a pattern to follow to keep us on the right path. The goading and the pattern are found in the Scriptures.

---

110. Ibid., 210–11. See also vol. 1, 324.

111. Ibid., 215. Apparently the power of contrary choice refers only to the power to choose contrary to God's ways. It does not refer to the power to do what is good.

112. Ibid., 221.

113. Ibid., 233.

114. Erickson, *Christian Theology*, 596.

115. Ibid., 616.

First, the Scriptures motivate us to love righteousness because our nature is biased toward the opposite. The Scripture motivates by warning us that we must be holy because God is holy (Lev 19:2). We must rely totally on God and depend on him so that his holiness can be infused into us and so we may then follow his commands. We have no union with him without this. The strongest motive to holiness comes from the love shown to us by God sending Christ as our redemption and example, whose pattern we ought to display in our lives.[116]

The second element the Scriptures provide is a pattern for ordering one's life. The law of the Lord is the best model, but the Holy Spirit adds other helps, proclaiming through the apostle Paul that our goal is to present our bodies as living, holy, and acceptable sacrifices. When we have done this we, will be transformed by the renewal of our minds (Rom 12:1–2). Because we are God's and have been bought at a price (1 Cor 6:19–20), we are to both live and die for him. Calvin summarizes these ideas by saying the goal of the Christian life is to deny ourselves. We deny ourselves by seeking and obeying God's will supremely, putting off our old nature (Titus 2), esteeming others above ourselves (Phil 2:3), seeking the benefit of our neighbor, cultivating a sincere inner love of our neighbor, devoting ourselves totally to God's will, and trusting in God's provision and blessing alone.[117] A companion metaphor that is a part of self-denial is bearing the cross as Jesus instructed (Matt 16:24).[118] By bearing our cross as Jesus did, we are conformed to his image (Rom 8:29). Specifically, our cross can lead us to develop important virtues, such as perseverance, patience, and obedience. Our patience and obedience, however, are only the ones that God has already given us. God doesn't want these graces to lie hidden within the Christian, but wants to put these excellent gifts on display as ones he has conferred.[119]

Though God motivates us and sovereignly gives us gifts of virtue, to what extent can we model Christ's holiness? Calvin responds:

> I do not insist that the moral life of a Christian man breathe nothing but the very gospel, yet this ought to be desired, and we must strive toward it. But I do not so strictly demand evangelical perfection that I would not acknowledge as a Christian one who has not yet attained it. For thus all would be excluded from

---

116. Calvin, *Institutes*, 684–86.

117. Ibid., 689–99.

118. Ibid., 702. Calvin suggests that bearing one's cross involves a toilsome and unquiet life, surrounded by all kinds of evils. By bearing our cross God tests us, but we also share the comfort of knowing that not only will we share Christ's sufferings, but his glory (Acts 14:22).

119. Ibid., 704–5.

the church, since no one is found who is not far removed from it, while many have advanced a little toward it whom it would nevertheless be unjust to cast away.

... But no one in this earthly prison of the body has sufficient strength to press on with due eagerness, and weakness so weighs down the greater number that, with wavering and limping and even creeping along the ground, they move at a feeble rate. Let each one of us, then, proceed according to the measure of his puny capacity and set out upon the journey we have begun. No one shall set out so inauspiciously as not daily to make some headway, though it be slight. Therefore, let us not cease so to act that we may make some unceasing progress in the way of the Lord. And let us not despair at the slightness of our success; for even though attainment may not correspond to desire, when today outstrips yesterday the effort is not lost. Only let us look toward our mark with sincere simplicity and aspire to our goal; not fondly flattering ourselves, nor excusing our own evil deeds, but with continuous effort striving toward this end: that we may surpass ourselves in goodness until we attain to goodness itself. It is this, indeed, which through the whole course of life we seek and follow. But we shall attain it only when we have cast off the weakness of the body, and are received into full fellowship with him.[120]

Lutheranism and Calvinism Today

The core of these theologians' ideas continued in those who followed them and in modern Lutheran and Reformed denominations and confessions. Luther's ideas on sin and holiness were formalized by such documents as the Augsburg Confession, the Formula of Concord (art. I), and the Smalkald Articles (pt. III, art. I). These documents are treated as authoritative by such denominations as the Evangelical Lutheran Church in America and the Lutheran Church, Missouri Synod.[121] Reformed confessions (Belgic, art. XV; French Confession of Faith, art. IX, XI), the Heidelberg Catechism (Lord's Day 3, Q&A 7–9), the Thirty-Nine Articles of Religion (art. IX), and the Westminster Confession (ch. 6, 9, 13) all affirm Calvin's general conclusions on sin, holiness, and the bondage of the will.[122] These Reformed statements

---

120. Ibid., 688–89.
121. Evangelical Lutheran Church in America, "Faith: ELCA Teaching."
122. Lewis and Demarest, *Integrative Theology*, vol. 2, 193.

are generally held by modern denominations, such as Christian Reformed, Presbyterian, Anglican, and some Baptist denominations.

Modern Reformed theologians propose a "compatibilist"[123] form of God-human interaction on holiness. The Christian is to be liberated from the power of sin by an active and Spirit-enabled pursuit. This objective is to be holy as God is holy. The desires of our old nature are put away and the desires of the new nature are fostered. Christians develop control over their thought and emotional life and their Spirit-renewed wills can now say "No" to sin. They can now develop holy habits because they are responsible agents who can determine their own activities. Though being agents, sanctification and holiness is a response to the Holy Spirit's initiative, just like conversion is.[124] Conversion took place because God "effectually called" the elect. The Spirit supernaturally renewed the sinner's depraved ability to know, love, and act on spiritual matters. He overcame the sinner's spiritual bondage and brought her to a place of sinful unbelief and the beginnings of spiritual life. The Spirit produced an "infallible attraction," such that the elect respond positively to the gospel.[125] This means it is not possible for a person not to believe.[126] In like manner, the Spirit's work in sanctification does not irresistibly coerce but providentially stimulates human cooperation rather than being dependent on it, as in Arminianism or the Semi-Pelagianism of Roman Catholicism.[127] God's will is larger than the human will and in the divinely initiated synergism,[128] God works for good in those who are actively yielded to him.[129] Reformed theologians Lewis and Demarest propose a God-controlled but robust sanctification here. However, some Reformed traditions (e.g., that follow the Westminster Larger Catechism) affirm that Christians daily break God's commands in thought, word, and deed:

---

123. See Excursus discussion on compatibilism and incompatibilism in chapter 5.

124. Lewis and Demarest, *Integrative Theology*, vol. 3, 206–9.

125. Ibid., 54–56.

126. Moreland and Craig, *Philosophical Foundations*, 281.

127. Lewis and Demarest, *Integrative Theology*, vol. 3, 23. Lewis and Demarest describe Arminianism's view as holding that salvation is a synergism—God's grace and the human will both are causes of salvation. God's Spirit does not work irresistibly but through human free will. God initiates the process of salvation and humans cooperate.

128. It is apparent Lewis and Demarest's definition of synergism is not the same as Arminianism's. They seem to suggest that synergism is God-dominated and that God ultimately controls the human desires that lead to actions and therefore indirectly all human actions. Unfortunately, they do not formally define it. In like manner, it is unclear what "actively yielded" means in such a view, since the human response seems passive.

129. Lewis and Demarest, *Integrative Theology*, vol. 3, 214.

> Question 149: Is any man able perfectly to keep the commandments of God?
>
> Answer: No man is able, either of himself, or by any grace received in this life, perfectly to keep the commandments of God; but doth daily break them in thought, word, and deed.[130]

In a related question a similar answer is given:

> Question 78: Whence arises the imperfection of sanctification in believers?
>
> Answer: The imperfection of sanctification in believers arises from the remnants of sin abiding in every part of them, and the perpetual lustings of the flesh against the spirit; whereby they are often foiled with temptations, and fall into many sins, are hindered in all their spiritual services, and their best works are imperfect and defiled in the sight of God.[131]

Therefore, there seems to be a spectrum of Reformed views on how Christlike we can become.

The Anabaptists

A further expression of Reformation thinking occurred in the early 1500s in Switzerland, Moravia, and the Netherlands. Refusing to baptize their infants according to Roman Catholic and political edicts, the early Swiss leaders of Anabaptism made their stand, believing scriptural baptism is only appropriate for faith-confessing youth and adults. The descendants of these early pioneers are today's Mennonite and Hutterite segments of Christianity.

Early on they also espoused doctrinal beliefs about original sin, sin, and holiness that differed in several ways from other Reformation movements. Though these early leaders wrote sparsely on original sin, what they did write differed from Luther and Calvin. They avoided the term "original sin" since it is not found in Scripture. They held that what humankind did receive from Adam was physical (temporal) death and an evil tendency or an inclination toward disobedience. However, this tendency is not sin until it has been consciously acted on by the will. This means Adam's sin does not impair those who do not freely make sin part of their own being through sinful acts. Adam's "foreign sin" brings condemnation on no one. This is made clear especially by the OT prophet Ezekiel, who reminded

---

130. Westminster Larger Catechism, "Question 149."
131. Westminster Larger Catechism, "Question 78."

the Israelites that persons are held accountable for only their own sins and not those of either their parents or children (Ezek 18). These evil urges and thoughts of the flesh are not totally removed by regeneration. The Christian must continue to fight against them during this earthly life.[132]

When asked about the fate of infants or those who have not reached the age of moral accountability (age of discernment), Anabaptists declare that these young persons are pure and innocent. They suffer no eternal consequence for Adam's sin; they belong to God. When they reach the age at which they can discern right and wrong and willfully choose evil, youth are then rightly said to sin.[133] They, along with adults, have been graced with freedom of will and are thus able to overcome evil tendencies and obey God's commands. Humans can cooperate with God's grace, enter the Kingdom of God, and once entered, can begin a life of obedient discipleship.[134]

Sin and Holiness

Anabaptists adhere to a definition of sin that emphasizes sin's willfulness and consciousness. Sin is fundamentally disobedience exhibited through transgression of God's laws, the will acquiescing to the influence of the fleshly body and sinful world in which it lives. As mentioned above, the believer still struggles with the influences of the flesh until death, but the new life in the Spirit is characterized by faithful discipleship, an Anabaptist hallmark. Christians live according to their new nature in Christ. Christ-followers are tempted and do sin, but they generally:

> Live in unconditional obedience to the Word of God; follow the example of Christ in word and deed; love the other members of the household of God, the unity of which is rooted in their love; serve the needs of the deprived and oppressed of the earth; hate "all impure carnal works and resist the world with all its

---

132. Friedmann, "The Doctrine," 208–10, 212–13. See Toews, *Story of Original Sin*, for a more detailed exposition of Mennonite views on original sin. Toews surveys historical views on the subject and concludes that the biblical and early church fathers' views on original sin are more in line with the Anabaptist views described above and are significantly different from the traditional Augustinian interpretation.

133. Weingart, "Meaning of Sin," 31.

134. Ibid., 31–33. Historic Anabaptist beliefs on original sin, sin, and holiness are congruent with the views of current Mennonites as reflected in the Confession of Faith in a Mennonite Perspective (July 1995), published by two North American Mennonite bodies, the Mennonite Church and the General Conference Mennonite Church. See especially Articles 7, 17, and 18. US Mennonite Brethren hold very similar views. See their Confession of Faith, Articles 4 and 10.

lusts"; and like Christ bear the cross of suffering because of the enmity of the perverse world. These are the lineaments of the life of discipleship voluntarily assumed by the believer obedient to Christ.[135]

ARMINIANISM-WESLEYANISM

Disagreement also arose in the early 1600s on some of the Reformation's doctrines. Dutchman James Arminius and his followers, called Remonstrants, disagreed with certain points of Calvinism by saying that human choice and faith work synergistically in salvation with God's grace and that God's grace is resistible. Believers could even resist God's grace to the extent they could lose their salvation. Arminius and his followers would disagree little with the Reformed doctrines on sin and original sin. In the 1700s Methodism's founder John Wesley accepted many of Arminius's views, but further emphasized the ability of Christians to overcome the effects of original sin and to live a life without sin. This *was* a departure from the traditional Reformed view.

Like Arminianism, Wesley and modern Wesleyanism[136] have much in agreement with the Reformed doctrine of sin and original sin. Wesley states that 1) humankind was originally righteous or holy, 2) original righteousness was lost by Adam's sin, 3) humans experienced death of every kind, since 4) Adam's sin was as a public person, whom God appointed to represent all his posterity, therefore 5) all his posterity are by birth "children of wrath," devoid of all holiness, and possess a propensity to sin.[137] This propensity to sin comes from a human nature that is entirely depraved, a depravity that has the general character of atheism, idolatry, pride, self-will, and a love of the world.[138] This depravity affected both the physical and spiritual nature of humankind and was total in that it touched all areas of humanness, not that all aspects were depraved to the greatest degree. In one sermon Wesley writes:

> Know that you are corrupted in every power, in every faculty of your soul; that you are totally corrupted in every one of these,

---

135. Weingart, "Meaning of Sin," 28.

136. Modern churches in the Wesleyan tradition include the Church of the Nazarene, Wesleyan Church, Salvation Army, Christian and Missionary Alliance, Free Methodist Church, Church of God (Anderson, IN), and the United Methodist Church.

137. Wesley, *Works of John Wesley*, vol. 9, 415.

138. Wesley, "Sermon 44, Original Sin," 183.

all the foundations being out of course. The eyes of your understanding are darkened, so that they cannot discern God, or the things of God. The clouds of ignorance and error rest upon you, and cover you with the shadow of death. You know nothing yet as you ought to know, neither God, nor the world, nor yourself. Your will is no longer the will of God, but is utterly perverse and distorted, averse from all good, from all which God loves, and prone to all evil, to every abomination which God hates. . . . All your passions, both your desires and aversion, your joys and sorrows, your hopes and fears, are out of frame, are either undue in their degree, or placed on undue objects.[139]

However, no one is left in the natural state. Wesley believed God works in all persons to do his good pleasure. Commenting on Philippians 2:12–13, he believed because God works in us, we can work out our own salvation. On our own we can do nothing since we are dead in our trespasses and sins; we cannot make the slightest movement toward God. However, God calls us to come out of our sins and quickens us. We are dead in sin by nature but there is no one who is solely in the state of nature. All persons experience God's preventing (prevenient or that which goes ahead of) grace to one degree or another. Everyone has some degree of spiritual light that enlightens them and some response of conscience when he or she rejects that light.[140] Likewise, "have not Christians, in common with other men . . . an immaterial principle, a spiritual nature, endued with understanding, and affections, and a degree of liberty; of a self-moving, yea, and self-governing power? (Otherwise, we were mere machines, stocks, and stones.)"[141]

Modern Wesleyan theologians would generally agree with Wesley's ideas. A well-known twentieth-century Nazarene theologian, H. Orton Wiley, exemplifies that agreement. He believed original sin is best seen as an inherited depravity, a result of all persons since Adam being born in a state of spiritual death. This inherited depravity, sometimes referred to as a fallen human nature, is akin to what Paul calls the "flesh." He quoted a formal definition from the articles of faith of the Church of the Nazarene:

> Original sin, or depravity, is the corruption of the nature of all the offspring of Adam, by reason of which every one is very far gone from original righteousness, or the pure state of our first parents at the time of their creation, is averse to God, is without spiritual life, and is inclined to evil, and that continually; and

---

139. Wesley, *Compend of Wesley's Theology*, 121.
140. Ibid., 149.
141. Ibid., 149–50.

that it continues to exist with the new life of the regenerate, until eradicated by the baptism with the Holy Spirit.[142]

This deprivation is of the image of God, and consequently, original righteousness. This is because the gift of the Holy Spirit has been removed. Wiley, like Wesley, believes that the result of this deprivation is guilt in the sense of a liability to punishment due to Adam's sin. This does not mean Adam's posterity is culpable for his sin; only Adam carries the weight of that. Like Wesley, modern Wesleyans believe in the total depravity of humanity (all human faculties are harmed by sin), that there is no positive good in our natural moral state, and that prevenient grace is given to all humanity so that 1) they are not condemned eternally for Adam's sin due to Christ's atonement, 2) they are culpable for their own freely chosen sins only, 3) the Holy Spirit works to awaken and convict sinners, and 4) enables sinners to respond to the gospel.[143]

Sin Defined

Wiley does not produce one definitive sin definition but rather refers to many theologians in the Wesleyan tradition when he defines sin. William Burt Pope defines sin as a voluntary separation of the soul from God. Wesley also stresses sin's voluntariness and its nature as a transgression of a known law. A. H. Strong describes sin as a lack of conformity to the moral law of God by either act, disposition, or state. James Arminius defined sin, not using act, disposition, or state, but the words thought, word, and deed. To him sin was either thoughts, words, or deeds done against the law of God or an omission of what the law required. John Miley emphasized that sin is conditional on free moral agency and the opportunity to know the law. William Newton Clark adds that sin's inner motive is to place self-will or selfishness above love and duty toward God.[144] Several recurring themes occur in these definitions—sin is voluntary, done knowingly, and is against God and his law.

Holiness and Entire Sanctification

Unique in Wesleyanism is their doctrine of holiness, to include the post-regenerational crisis experience of entire sanctification. Wesley's views are

---

142. Wiley, *Christian Theology*, 121.

143. Ibid., 123, 126, 128–29, 135–36.

144. Ibid., 86–87.

summarized in his book, *A Plain Account of Christian Perfection*. Wesley thought that a Christian could experience a total love and consecration to God such that he or she would not sin. He admitted that frequently a Christian approaching death would reach such a degree of love to God and progress in holiness that there was a "repose in the blood of Christ; a firm confidence in God, and persuasion of his favor; the highest tranquility, serenity, and peace of mind, with a deliverance from every fleshly desire, and a cessation of all, even inward sins."[145] Using many biblical allusions, Wesley described this Christian perfection as having the mind of Christ, walking as he walked, being cleansed from all filthiness of flesh and spirit, not committing sin, being sanctified, walking in the light as Christ is in the light, having the blood of Christ cleanse us from all sin, being crucified with Christ, being holy as God is holy, loving God with all one's heart and one's neighbor as oneself, being filled with the fruit of the Spirit, doing all in the name of the Lord Jesus, doing the will of God on earth as it is in heaven,[146] purity of intention, devoting all of our lives to God, having our heart circumcised from all inward and outward pollution, and being renewed in the image of God.[147]

He acknowledged that a babe in Christ can live without outward sin, but the perfection of which he spoke also frees us from inner sins, such as evil thoughts and desires.[148] It is possible, but unlikely, that a new Christian will be totally resigned to God's will, be gentle without any tinge of anger, love God without the smallest love for self, exclude all pride, love others without jealousy or rash judgment, and be temperate in all things. What every Christian needs, therefore, is to experience the crisis of entire sanctification. He observed that for most Christians, if it occurred at all, it happened a little before death, after a lifetime of gradual sanctification. But Wesley reasoned that God can cut short this time and do in a week, day, or moment what might otherwise take many years. Therefore, after regeneration there is usually a gradual work in the heart (death to sin and growth in grace), and for those who pursue it, a moment of entire sanctification, followed by continued gradual sanctification. What Wesley pressed is that this moment need not wait for the last years of our earthly life, but can occur much earlier for those who are earnest, seek God with all their hearts, and by faith allow God to graciously cleanse them of all sin and love him with all their heart.[149]

145. Wesley, *Plain Account*, 15.
146. Ibid., 36–37.
147. Ibid., 117.
148. Ibid., 25–26.
149. Ibid., 89–90.

The perfection thus described, however, does not produce an absolute type of perfection. We cannot become perfect in knowledge or free of mistakes. We still may be slow to understand, and may display other infirmities and weaknesses. All these things Wesley described as involuntarily transgressions, due to our finiteness and mortality. Others may call these sins, but Wesley does not.[150]

This perfection is also something that can be lost and regained. Wesley observed persons that displayed all the evidence of entire sanctification (fruit of the Spirit and the Spirit's witness to the experience) and subsequently lost it. In fact it is common for persons to lose and regain it more than once.[151] There is no height of holiness that it is impossible to fall from, therefore Wesley gave advice to those who wish to avoid spiritual stumbling. He advised entirely sanctified Christians to: 1) watch and pray against pride, 2) beware of enthusiasm (overemphasis on dreams, visions, voices, revelations; expecting growth in knowledge and grace without study or spiritual discipline), 3) not make void the law of God through faith, 4) beware of sins of omission (instead do all the good you possibly can), 5) beware of desiring anything but God, 6) beware of disunity within the church (instead, have reciprocal love for one another), 7) be exemplary in all things, as a light shining in darkness.[152]

Randy Maddox summarizes the emphasis of Wesley over his ministry career:

> ... Wesley was convinced that the Christian life did not have to remain a life of continual struggle. He believed that both Scripture and Christian tradition attested that God's loving grace can transform our lives to the point where our own love for God and others becomes a "natural" response.... To deny this possibility would be to deny the sufficiency of God's empowering grace—to make the power of sin greater than that of grace.... [W]hile the affirmation of the possibility of entire sanctification may have been the *distinctive* of Wesley, the conception of sanctification (as a whole) as the progressive journey in responsive co-operation with God's empowering grace was most *characteristic* of Wesley.[153]

---

150. Ibid., 54.
151. Ibid., 94.
152. Ibid., 95–105.
153. Maddox, *Responsible Grace*, 90.

Modern Wesleyanism

Modern Wesleyan denominations closely approximate Wesley's views when framing their own descriptions of sanctification. Negatively, modern theologians make it more explicit that it is the effects of the inbred sin (inherited depravity) that we all have received from Adam (original sin), which are eliminated in entire sanctification. The entirely sanctified can still be tempted, but not from this internal source. Wiley states that this carnal mind, which has an affinity toward sinful indulgences, has been crucified and cleansed.[154] Positively, there is the infilling of the Holy Spirit. Up until the point of entire sanctification the Christian has the Holy Spirit residing within, but now the Spirit totally fills the person with God's love. Wesleyans also call this infilling the baptism with the Holy Spirit.[155]

STONE-CAMPBELL MOVEMENT

The Stone-Campbell Movement, sometimes called the Restoration Movement,[156] originated in the late 1800s in the eastern United States. Its goal was to restore primitive Christianity in belief in practice. It does not define itself as Protestant, but has many doctrines similar to Protestantism. However, a difference that *is* obvious relates to the influence of Adam's sin on subsequent humanity. They hold that humanity was indirectly affected by the environment of sin in the world, but not as a direct result of Adam's sin. We retain the image of God, though sin has tarnished it. Humans are depraved, but not totally; they retain their essential moral freedom even though it was abused. Their writers do not speak of the effects of Adam's "original sin" and would deny any inherited guilt from it. Therefore there is no need for a supernatural infusion of divine grace in order for persons to turn to God or respond to the gospel. Grace is inherent in humankind's existing free will. Consequently, before sinning persons are in the same moral condition as Adam before the fall. This means infants have no taint of sin since sin is an act and not some sort of infection blighting human nature.[157]

---

154. Wiley, *Christian Theology*, 488.

155. Ibid., 491, 495. The Church of the Nazarene statement of faith (Article X) contains a modern Wesleyan expression of the progressive and entire sanctification doctrine. See http://www.nazarene.org.

156. Stone-Campbell churches include Disciples of Christ, Christian Churches, and Churches of Christ.

157. Foster, et al., *Encyclopedia of the Stone-Campbell*, 29–30.

Holiness and Sanctification

The two founders of the movement, Barton Stone and Thomas Campbell, made definitive remarks on holiness. Robert Rea summarizes their definitions, saying that they affirmed holiness to be "a life entirely devoted to God, thankfully surrendered in heart, mind, and behavior to the will of God, resulting in increasing conformity of personal attitude, desire, and will to the nature of God."[158]

How does holiness develop? This purity of heart is a work of the Holy Spirit. Alexander Campbell, Thomas Campbell's son, described it simply as: facts, testimony, faith, feeling, and action. This means, "[o]ne hears testimony of the scriptural facts and believes, producing corresponding feelings or states of mind, called repentance. This is the working of the Holy Spirit, who is personally clothed in truth and thereby actively convinces a believer to make good decisions. The new heart acts in holiness, producing increasing degrees of conformity to the divine nature"[159]

Summarizing their doctrine, Stone-Campbell churches see sanctification as both an instantaneous work of God at conversion and a progressive work throughout the Christian life. In the instantaneous aspect, God sets the Christian apart through salvation; this is a change of *state*. The progressive aspect, detailed above, involves the transformative work of the indwelling Holy Spirit whereby both affections and behavior change, thus cultivating a holy life and an overcoming of sin. The believer aids the process as he or she utilizes the spiritual disciplines, such as prayer and Bible-reading.[160]

The holiness lifestyle was a high priority from the beginning of the movement with early leaders avowing that holiness, or a life entirely devoted to God, was the very purpose of Christianity. Alexander Campbell declared that they valued nothing that didn't directly or indirectly foster the purity and perfection of the heart.[161] The early founders believed the purpose of the Church was to promote personal holiness, without which no Christian would be saved. Corporate holiness was an extension of personal holiness and was a manifestation of the unity Christ described in his prayers of John 17. This unity is essential for effective evangelism and is necessary for every aspect of the Great Commission.[162]

---

158. Rea, "'Holiness' in the Writings," 185.
159. Ibid., 178.
160. Foster, et al., *Encyclopedia of the Stone-Campbell*, 667–68.
161. Rea, "'Holiness' in the Writings," 166.
162. Ibid., 169.

NEO-ORTHODOX, LIBERATION, AND CONTEMPORARY CATHOLIC THEOLOGIES

This modern grouping of views is quite broad although they share some common thoughts regarding sin and holiness. Neo-orthodoxy's prime representatives were Karl Barth, Emil Brunner, and Reinhold Niebuhr, who took Adam and Eve to be non-historical figures. Though sin is universal, Adam is not to blame for bringing any harmful effects onto humanity. The Adam-figure represents the sinful actions which all humans have done. Sin is freely chosen rebellion against God, a supreme desire to be the "God" of one's own life that results in guilt and death. Niebuhr believed the primary sin was self-love or pride.[163]

Liberation theology includes ideas from theologians such as Gustavo Gutiérrez, James Cone, and C. S. Song. Sin is a personal and free act rejecting God and his love but it is very social. It is lack of love towards others and other social groups, creating alienation, injustice, and exploitation. When we don't love others we cannot identify with their needs and suffering and we develop sinful societal structures. Jesus illustrated this attitude in the parable of the rich man and Lazarus. "Holiness" in this theology would be closely linked to fostering solutions to these sins by freeing those oppressed, identifying with and ministering to those who suffer, and making positive changes in social or political structures.[164]

Contemporary Catholic theologians, like Karl Rahner, believe sin is consciously saying "no" to God. Since Adam and Eve were not historical persons, original sin expresses something else—the historical accumulation of human sin into which all are now born. This situation precedes us and negatively affects our free choices.[165] Rahner believed in discipleship and in the love of neighbor as the best fundamental option in responding to God's love toward us. This neighbor love does not keep records and expects no returns. The choice to love is basically a choice to die and thereafter to live "theonomously." Theonomous death is a surrender to the mystery of God and is behind every positive moral choice. It is made possible by Christ's death and is therefore from grace; we die with Christ, die to self, and live our lives in obedience to God and neighbor-love. A primary guide to determine what are good and bad moral choices is conscience, something humans have always possessed. To submit to objective moral standards, even those of the Roman Catholic Church, without filtering them through conscience

---

163. Smith, *With Willful Intent*, 114–22.
164. Ibid., 134–38.
165. Ibid., 143–45.

is demeaning to God and persons. Though disagreement between the two would be rare, the process must be followed, even if painful. It is a form of dying with Christ and is central to Rahner's elevation of discernment in making moral decisions.[166]

SUMMARY

This survey shows the variety of Christian views on our subject matter. Regarding original sin, modern theologies saw no effects from original sin, since Adam and Eve are not historical. Judaism, Roman Catholicism, Eastern Orthodoxy, some Wesleyan-Arminian, and the Stone-Campbell movement saw Adam's legacy as an influence toward sin with no guilt attached. They defined sin as an intentional breaking of God's commands or a disobedience of his laws, substituting supreme self-gratification as a guiding life goal.

Some Wesleyan-Arminian and Reformed Protestants saw Adam's effect as a very strong influence or a cause of personal sin with guilt attached. Sin was defined similarly as above, but sin acts were the result of a previous state of sinful bondage or depravity called original sin.

Though impossible to represent every denominational view exactly, the following stick figures illustrate some of the major options available:

---

166. Marmion and Hines, *Cambridge Companion*, 161–69.

Pelagianism	Semi-Pelagianism	Augustinianism
The flesh, world, and Satan's influence toward sin is roughly on a par with God's pull toward obedience.	The negative influence of the world, Satan, and the flesh makes obeying spiritual light difficult but possible.	Original sin and the flesh make it impossible not to sin against spiritual light.

Figure 2. The human condition when facing the first moral decision at the age of accountability. S=sin and H=holiness.

SECTION I

What Do the Scriptures Say about Sin, Its Source, and Its Consequences?

Section I will follow the plan developed in the Introduction to analyze and synthesize the various Scriptures related to sin. Each chapter will interpret the texts in biblical order (NIV 2011 translation). Chapter 2 discusses texts that help define what sin is and from what source it springs. Chapter 3 examines Scriptures related to the consequences of sin, both Adam's sin on his posterity and the effects of our own sin on ourselves and those around us. Chapter 4 delves into the source and effects of the flesh/sinful nature on our behavior. The chapter will conclude with a summary of the findings of this section.

2

What Is Sin?

SIN IS A CONCEPT that comes from God. No mere human can decide was sin is or isn't, therefore, we must go to God's special revelation, the biblical account, to understand it. The first recorded human sin was Eve's, followed by Adam's, both disobeying the one command God gave them—to not eat from the tree of the knowledge of good and evil in the middle of the Garden of Eden (Gen 2:17, 3:6–7). The gist of sin for them was disobeying what they knew God wanted them to do. In our study we will see that this basic foundation remains.

How should we approach the study of sin? Erickson's tack seems appropriate since he begins with the biblical terminology for sin and then observes the varying concepts that emerge. By doing this we can see the nuances of sin as well as distill what are its core features.[1]

This chapter will begin with a word study on sin and related words; notice the context of these words in biblical passages; seek to develop both a comprehensive and brief definition of sin; investigate sin's nature, source, and motives; and conclude with an interaction with historical sin definitions.[2]

---

1. Erickson, *Christian Theology*, 583.

2. It is not this chapter's purpose to provide a full-blown discussion of sin, but to provide a definition and nature of sin that can be then related to the topics of original sin, the flesh, and holiness. Such tasks have been adequately done by other authors. For example, see Smith, *With Willful Intent*, Sections II, III.

WORD STUDY

There are a number of Hebrew and Greek words that the biblical writers use to define sin and each adds to a fuller understanding of it. We will look at the most prevalent and significant words used. However, words by themselves, to use a baseball analogy, will only get us in the ballpark on what sin is. Context is necessary to get an accurate meaning. If we look at sentences and paragraphs with these words we have more context; we could say we have made it to first base. Finally, if we exegete key passages, looking broadly to get a *tota Scriptura* view, we can find recurring themes or explicit examples and therefore get the big picture of our topic—we have hopefully made it to home base. This pattern will be followed in this and subsequent chapters.[3]

Hebrew Words

ra (adj, 8273)[4], *rāʿâ* (v. or n. 8288).

This word group is used over six hundred times in the Old Testament (OT). When referring to human behavior, they mean bad, evil, wicked, or ethically disagreeable to God. What is sinful is also evil or wicked. Erickson notes that this word refers to anything that has gone bad and become harmful—food, animal behavior, or human moral behavior. There can also be the connotation that the state of badness or evilness is a consequence of sinning.[5]

> *The Lord saw how great the* wickedness *of the human race had become on the earth, and that every inclination of the thoughts of the human heart was only* evil *all the time.* (Gen 6:5)

> When responding to the men who wanted to have sex with the men in his home:
> *Lot went outside to meet them and shut the door behind him and said, "No, my friends. Don't do this* wicked *thing.* (Gen 19:6–7)

---

3. In this chapter we can arrive at a broad definition of sin without exegeting numerous passages, therefore the last level of inquiry is omitted.

4. Each transliterated Hebrew or Greek word will be listed in descending order of frequency. Each will include the Goodrick/Kohlenberger numbers for reference, have the translated English words used in the NIV, and the definition. See Goodrick and Kohlenberger, *Strongest NIV*. In the Bible verse quotes, the corresponding English word will be set off by using regular text.

5. Erickson, *Christian Theology*, 593–94.

WHAT IS SIN?

> *Ahab son of Omri did more* evil *in the eyes of the Lord than any of those before him.* (1 Kgs 16:30)

> *Whoever plots* evil *will be known as a schemer.* (Prov 24:8)

ḥāṭā' (v. 2627), noun and adjective forms (2628–2633).

These words are used over three hundred times and are frequently translated as: to sin, sin(s), or sin offering. Their literal meaning is to "miss the mark," as in a target,[6] or "miss the way," as in a walking path. Millard Erickson clarifies, noting that these words suggest a mistake, but in reality are willfully chosen sins. These are decisions to purposely miss by aiming at a wrong moral target or by deliberately following the wrong ethical path.[7] John Goldingay concurs, noting that missing the mark does not imply trying to hit God's moral target and missing none-the-less. Failure is active and is a refusal to hit God's target. Therefore, it is akin to the willfulness of transgression which flouts God's law. Behind this disobedience is wrong desire.[8]

> *He* [Jeroboam] *committed all the* sins *his father had done before him; his heart was not fully devoted to the Lord his God, as the heart of David his forefather had been.* (1 Kgs 15:3)

> *Wash away all my iniquity and cleanse me from my* sin. (Ps 51:2)

> *But your iniquities have separated you from your God; your* sins *have hidden his face from you, so that he will not hear.* (Isa 59:2)

> *But if a righteous person turns from their righteousness and commits sin and does the same detestable things the wicked person does, will they live? None of the righteous things that person has done will be remembered. Because of the unfaithfulness they are guilty of and because of the* sins *they have committed, they will die.* (Ezek 18:24)

rāsāʿ (adj. 8401) (v., n. 8399, 8400).

This Hebrew word-group is also used over three hundred times and is most frequently translated as wicked, wickedness, act wickedly, to condemn, or to do wrong.

---

6. In very rare cases, such as Judges 20:16, this word does mean missing an actual target while slinging a stone.

7. Erickson, *Christian Theology*, 586.

8. Goldingay, *Old Testament*, 257.

The Lord examines the righteous, but the wicked, those who love violence, he hates with a passion. (Ps 11:5)

Even from birth the wicked go astray; from the womb they are wayward, spreading lies. (Ps 58:3)

After Ezra had read the whole book of the Law, the Levites confess the sins of Israel to God:
33In all that has happened to us, you have remained righteous; you have acted faithfully, while we acted wickedly. 34Our kings, our leaders, our priests and our ancestors did not follow your law; they did not pay attention to your commands or the statutes you warned them to keep. 35Even while they were in their kingdom, enjoying your great goodness to them in the spacious and fertile land you gave them, they did not serve you or turn from their evil ways. (Neh 9:33–35)

. . . we have sinned and done wrong. We have been wicked and have rebelled; we have turned away from your commands and laws. (Dan 9:5)

'āwōn (n. 6411), (v. 6390).
These words, used over two hundred times, signify sin, wickedness, and iniquity; often focusing on the guilt, liability, and punishment that follows. The verb form is frequently translated as "to do wrong or pervert." Like pervert, the base of the verb implies aspects of being crooked, warped, twisted, or ruined in the moral sense.

Cain said to the Lord, "My punishment is more than I can bear." (Gen 4:13)

David was conscience-stricken after he had counted the fighting men, and he said to the Lord, "I have sinned greatly in what I have done. Now, Lord, I beg you, take away the guilt of your servant. I have done a very foolish thing." (2 Sam 24:10)

A person is praised according to their prudence, and one with a warped mind is despised. (Prov 12:8)

Then I acknowledged my sin to you and did not cover up my iniquity. I said, "I will confess my transgressions to the Lord." And you forgave the guilt of my sin. (Ps 32:5)

> *A cry is heard on the barren heights, the weeping and pleading of the people of Israel, because they have* perverted *their ways and have forgotten the Lord their God.* (Jer 3:21)

pešaʿ (n. 7322), (v. 7321).

These two words occur over one hundred times and are often translated as sins, offense, rebellion, transgression, and to rebel or revolt against human or divine authority.

> *After Ahab's death, Moab* rebelled *against Israel.* (2 Kgs 1:1)

> *Declare them guilty, O God! Let their intrigues be their downfall. Banish them for their many* sins, *for they have rebelled against you.* (Ps 5:10)

> *You have neither heard nor understood; from of old your ears have not been open. Well do I know how treacherous you are; you were called a* rebel *from birth.* (Isa 48:8)

> *He said: "Son of man, I am sending you to the Israelites, to a rebellious nation that has rebelled against me; they and their ancestors have* been in revolt *against me to this very day.* (Ezek 2:3)

> *Rid yourselves of all the* offenses *you have committed, and get a new heart and a new spirit. Why will you die, people of Israel?* (Ezek 18:31)

> *For I know how many are your* offenses *and how great your sins. There are those who oppress the innocent and take bribes and deprive the poor of justice in the courts.* (Amos 5:12)

ʾāšām (v. 870), (n., adj. 871/873, 872).

Together used over one hundred times, these cognates signal being guilty and by implication committing an offense or trespass. The noun frequently refers to a guilt offering.

> *It is a* guilt offering; *they have been* guilty of wrongdoing *against the Lord."* (Lev 5:19)

> *Declare them guilty, O God! Let their intrigues be their downfall. Banish them for their many sins, for they have rebelled against you.* (Ps 5:10)

> The people of Samaria must bear their guilt, *because they have rebelled against their God. They will fall by the sword; their little ones will be dashed to the ground, their pregnant women ripped open.*" (Hos 13:16)

māʿal (v. 5085), (n. 5086).

Used over sixty times, these words depict a breach of faith or being unfaithful, committing treachery, either against another person or God.

> 12"*Speak to the Israelites and say to them: 'If a man's wife goes astray and is* unfaithful *to him 13so that another man has sexual relations with her* . . . (Num 5:12–13a)

> *Our parents were* unfaithful; *they did evil in the eyes of the Lord our God and forsook him. They turned their faces away from the Lord's dwelling place and turned their backs on him.* (2 Chr 29:6)

> *But the Israelites were* unfaithful *in regard to the devoted things; Achan son of Karmi, the son of Zimri, the son of Zerah, of the tribe of Judah, took some of them. So the Lord's anger burned against Israel.* (Josh 7:1)

ʿāwal (v. 6401) and cognates (n. 6404, 6405, 6406).

Together used over fifty times, the verb means to do evil or act wrongly with the noun signifying wrong, evil, sin, injustice, moral perversion, or doing what is against the right.

> "'*Do not* pervert justice; *do not show partiality to the poor or favoritism to the great, but judge your neighbor fairly.*'" (Lev 19:15)

> *The fool says in his heart, "There is no God." They are corrupt, and their ways are vile; there is no one who does good.* (Ps 53:1)

> *But if a righteous person turns from their righteousness and* commits sin *and does the same detestable things the wicked person does, will they live? None of the righteous things that person has done will be remembered. Because of the unfaithfulness they are guilty of and because of the sins they have committed, they will die.* (Ezek 18:24)

tāʿâ (v. 9494).

This verb, used over fifty times, is translated in the religious or moral arena as to lead or go astray, wander or cause to wander, be wayward, to err. The straying regards God, his truth, his law, or what is good. The non-religious use means to wander, as from a path, or to reel or stagger, as when drunk.

One of the seven deadly sins, sloth, is related to this word. It implies wandering due to lack of trying, therefore suggesting moral indolence, laziness, or inertia. One wants to be left alone by God and to avoid obligations to others. It is the same desire of Israel to avoid the challenge of taking the Promised Land. Many wanted to go back to Egypt—even though they were slaves, life there was predictable.[9]

> *Even from birth the wicked* go astray; *from the womb they are wayward, spreading lies.* (Ps 58:3)
>
> *For forty years I was angry with that generation; I said, "They are a people whose hearts* go astray, *and they have not known my ways."* (Ps 95:10)
>
> *The righteous choose their friends carefully, but the way of the wicked* leads *them* astray. (Prov 12:26)
>
> *We all, like sheep, have* gone astray, *each of us has turned to our own way; and the Lord has laid on him the iniquity of us all.* (Isa 53:6)

The use of *tāʿâ* in the sense of "causing to stray" warrants special attention since it relates to the cause of sin.

> *But Manasseh* led *Judah and the people of Jerusalem* astray, *so that they did more evil than the nations the Lord had destroyed before the Israelites.* (2 Chr 33:9)
>
> *So the Lord will cut off from Israel both head and tail, both palm branch and reed in a single day; the elders and dignitaries are the head, the prophets who teach lies are the tail. Those who guide this people* mislead *them, and those who are guided are* led astray. *Therefore the Lord will take no pleasure in the young men, nor will he pity the fatherless and widow, for everyone is ungodly and wicked, every mouth speaks folly.* (Isa 9:14–17)

The "causing" is done by those who lead Israel—kings, prophets, priests, elders, and civil leaders (see also Jer 23:9–40, Jer 50:6, Mic 3:5). Most of the instances of this refer to the actions of the wicked king Jeroboam and his effect on the nation of Israel recorded in 1 and 2 Kings.[10] Is this "causing" or "making" in the same sense as we have defined earlier—a compelling or coercion? The context of these passages suggests not. This is a leading or a drawing into. The people were not innocent in being led into sin. As the

---

9. Goldingay, *Old Testament*, 257–58.
10. VanGemeren, *New International*, vol. 1, 91.

above passage from Isaiah states, the people themselves were ungodly and wicked. In another example, 2 Kings 17:21 declares that "Jeroboam enticed Israel away from following the Lord and caused them to commit a great sin. The Israelites persisted in all the sins of Jeroboam and did not turn away from them until the Lord removed them from his presence . . ." This affirms that both Jeroboam and the people were guilty before God. Jeroboam as a leader sinned and the people followed in his steps.

In an unusual verse, Isaiah 63:10 states that even God makes his people wander. This suggests hyperbole since Isaiah is distraught with the waywardness of Israel and knows that God is now judging them, fighting against them like an enemy. In his anguish, Isaiah asks why God has made his people to wander and hardened their hearts. Isaiah's question does not mean that God *is* doing this, but apparently that Isaiah feels as if he has. The alternative is that God actually does coerce his people to wander into sin, which is a concept totally opposed by God's self-description in the rest of Scripture. Contrarily, God commands his people *not* to wander and tries to get his people to obey his commands.

shagah (v. 8704, 8706), (n. 8705).

Shagah and its cognates are used approximately fifty times in the OT and are analogous to *ta'â*, suggesting to stray or to cause to stray, mislead, or mistake. They can also refer to acts done unintentionally. When used literally, they can refer to animals or drunken persons who stray or stumble. The figurative sense is frequently used morally, to describe those who have erred and are therefore culpable.[11]

> *I seek you with all my heart;* do not let *me* stray *from your commands.* (Ps 119:10)

> *If the whole Israelite community* sins unintentionally *and does what is forbidden in any of the Lord's commands, even though the community is unaware of the matter, when they realize their guilt 14and the sin they committed becomes known, the assembly must bring a young bull as a sin offering and present it before the tent of meeting.* (Lev 4:13–14)

> *Then Saul said, "I have sinned. Come back, David my son. Because you considered my life precious today, I will not try to harm you again. Surely I have acted like a fool and* have been terribly wrong." (1 Sam 26:21)

---

11. Erickson, *Christian Theology*, 584.

Greek Words

Similar to *ḥāṭā'* is the Greek word, *hamartano* (v. 279, with noun and adjective forms 280, 281, 283), which is the most commonly used NT word group for sin, used over three hundred times. They are translated as: sin (something contrary to the will and law of God), to sin, sinful, sinner, to do wrong. They mean to miss the mark in the same way that *ḥāṭā'* did. Erickson again gives clarity on the interpretation of these words:

> This sin is always sin against God, since it is failure to hit the mark he has set, his standard, of perfect love of God and perfect obedience to him. We miss the mark and sin against God when, for example, we fail to love our brother, since love of brother would inevitably follow if we truly loved God. Similarly, sinning against one's own body is mistreatment of God's temple (1 Cor 3:16–17) and therefore a sin against God.
>
> Some additional observations are needed. One is that the idea of blameworthiness is clearly attached to missing the mark. Whatever antecedents may have led to the act of sin, it is culpable behavior. The fact that . . . *ḥāṭā'* is often found in confessions indicates that the sinner senses responsibility. A further point is the teleological association of the concept. One has a goal or purpose and has failed to achieve it. While some protest that this is a Greek way of thinking, it is found in both testaments.[12]

Then Peter came to Jesus and asked, "Lord, how many times shall I forgive my brother or sister who sins *against me? Up to seven times?"* (Matt 18:21)

The prodigal son's words to himself:
I will set out and go back to my father and say to him: Father, I have sinned *against heaven and against you.* (Luke 15:18)

Paul negates any moral distinction between Jews and Greeks:
. . . for all have sinned *and fall short of the glory of God.* (Rom 3:23)

Therefore, just as sin *entered the world through one man, and death through* sin, *and in this way death came to all people, because all* sinned. (Rom 5:12)

---

12. Erickson, *Christian Theology*, 587.

> *No one who lives in him* keeps on sinning. *No one who* continues to sin *has either seen him or known him.* (1 John 3:6)

ponēros (adj. 4505), (n. 4504).

Used over eighty times, these two words are translated as evil, wicked, or bad. They suggest a negative moral quality that is opposed to God and his goodness. Similar in meaning is the noun *kakos* and it cognates, which are used fifty times in the NT. The previously discussed Hebrew adjective, *ra*, has a comparable meaning.

> *Blessed are you when people insult you, persecute you and falsely say all kinds of* evil *against you because of me.* (Matt 5:11)

> *All these* evils *come from inside and defile a person.* (Mark 7:23)

> *Then the Lord said to him, "Now then, you Pharisees clean the outside of the cup and dish, but inside you are full of greed and* wickedness.*"* (Luke 11:39)

> *They have become filled with every kind of wickedness,* evil, *greed and depravity. They are full of envy, murder, strife, deceit and malice.* (Rom 1:29)

adikia (n. 94, v. 92, and cognates 93, 96, 97).

These words appear approximately seventy times and mean unrighteousness, injustice, to act unjustly, or to cause harm to people. They are generally less specific and more varied in their meaning than *hamartia*. *Adikia* suggests the outward and visible characteristics of sin, such as injustice toward others (cf. the unjust steward, Luke 16:9).

> *But he will reply, "I don't know you or where you come from. Away from me, all you* evildoers!*"* (Luke 13:27)

> *The wrath of God is being revealed from heaven against all the godlessness and* wickedness *of people, who suppress the truth by their* wickedness . . . (Rom 1:18)

> *If we confess our sins, he is faithful and just and will forgive us our sins and purify us from all* unrighteousness. (1 John 1:9)

> *All* wrongdoing *is sin, and there is sin that does not lead to death.* (1 John 5:17)

planaō (v. 4414, cognates 4415, 4416, 4417).

This word group is used over fifty times in active and passive forms. The active form refers to leading astray, as by false teachers. The passive form indicates being led astray, usually by being deceived. These have a similar meaning to the Hebrew *tā'â* and *shagah*.

> *In fact, everyone who wants to live a godly life in Christ Jesus will be persecuted, while evildoers and impostors will go from bad to worse,* deceiving *and* being deceived. (2 Tim 3:13)

> *He is able to deal gently with those who are ignorant and are going astray, since he himself is subject to weakness.* (Heb 5:2)

> *My brothers and sisters, if one of you should* wander *from the truth and someone should bring that person back, remember this: Whoever turns a sinner from the error of their way will save them from death and cover over a multitude of sins.* (Jas 5:19–20)

> *Jesus said to them: "Watch out that no one* deceives *you. Many will come in my name, claiming, 'I am he,' and* will deceive *many."* (Mark 13:5–6)

> *That is why I was angry with that generation; I said, "Their hearts are always going astray, and they have not known my ways."* (Heb 3:10)

Erickson notes that the passive form still implied that persons could have avoided the error, otherwise God would not have warned them to not be deceived. Similarly, some of the sins described by *planaō* are involuntary through ignorance or mistake, but still had consequences. Why was this so? He elaborates:

> . . . acts like involuntary manslaughter are more in the nature of accidents than the result of willful ignorance. In most cases, however, what the Bible terms errors simply ought not to have occurred: the person should have known better, and was responsible to so inform himself. While these sins are less heinous than the deliberate and rebellious type of wrongdoing, the individual is still responsible for them, and therefore penalty attaches to them.[13]

paraptōma (n. 4183), (v. 4178).

These cognates are used twenty times in Scripture and carry the meaning of: to trespass, transgression, to sin by failing to keep a command, to step out of the bounds of God's law, to fall away. These meanings are similar

---

13. Erickson, *Christian Theology*, 585.

to the Hebrew *peša'* and *mā'al*. In both testaments the implication is that a covenant between God and his people has been broken. There is the sense of betrayal, infidelity, and treachery.[14]

> *For if you forgive other people when they* sin *against you, your heavenly Father will also forgive you.* (Matt 6:14)

> *But the gift is not like the* trespass. *For if the many died by the* trespass *of the one man, how much more did God's grace and the gift that came by the grace of the one man, Jesus Christ, overflow to the many! 16Nor can the gift of God be compared with the result of one man's sin: The judgment followed one sin and brought condemnation, but the gift followed many* trespasses *and brought justification. 17For if, by the* trespass *of the one man, death reigned through that one man, how much more will those who receive God's abundant provision of grace and of the gift of righteousness reign in life through the one man, Jesus Christ! 18Consequently, just as one* trespass *resulted in condemnation for all people, so also one righteous act resulted in justification and life for all people.* (Rom 5:15–18)

> *4It is impossible for those who have once been enlightened, who have tasted the heavenly gift, who have shared in the Holy Spirit, 5who have tasted the goodness of the word of God and the powers of the coming age 6and who have* fallen away, *to be brought back to repentance. To their loss they are crucifying the Son of God all over again and subjecting him to public disgrace.* (Heb 6:4–6)

KNOWLEDGE AND SIN

Several NT passages further define the nature of sin, some using the word sin and others not.

> Speaking about the Jews' rejection of him, Jesus said:
> *If I had not come and spoken to them, they would not be guilty of sin; but now they have no excuse for their sin. Whoever hates me hates my Father as well. If I had not done among them the works no one else did, they would not be guilty of sin. As it is, they have seen, and yet they have hated both me and my Father.* (John 15:22–24)

---

14. Ibid., 592.

WHAT IS SIN?

Paul defends the law to the Romans:
What shall we say, then? Is the law sinful? Certainly not! Nevertheless, I would not have known what sin was had it not been for the law. For I would not have known what coveting really was if the law had not said, "You shall not covet." (Rom 7:7)

Jesus responds to the blind man he had healed earlier and some Pharisees:
Jesus heard that they had thrown him out, and when he found him, he said, "Do you believe in the Son of Man?" "Who is he, sir?" the man asked. "Tell me so that I may believe in him."

Jesus said, "You have now seen him; in fact, he is the one speaking with you."

Then the man said, "Lord, I believe," and he worshiped him.

Jesus said, "For judgment I have come into this world, so that the blind will see and those who see will become blind."

Some Pharisees who were with him heard him say this and asked, "What? Are we blind too?"

Jesus said, "If you were blind, you would not be guilty of sin; but now that you claim you can see, your guilt remains. (John 9:35–41)

If anyone, then, knows the good they ought to do and doesn't do it, it is sin for them. (Jas 4:17)

The next two verses are Paul talking about his earlier persecution of the Church:
I too was convinced that I ought to do all that was possible to oppose the name of Jesus of Nazareth. (Acts 26:9)

Even though I was once a blasphemer and a persecutor and a violent man, I was shown mercy because I acted in ignorance and unbelief. (1 Tim 1:13)

The first four passages stress the need for knowledge of who God is and what his commands are before sin can be assigned. To sin against God, we need to know something of who he is, even if it is only from general revelation. To break a law or fail to do what is good, we need to know what each is first. This leads to the last two verses, which describe the zealous Pharisee Paul and his pre-conversion persecution of Christians. Was Paul "not guilty" of persecuting Christ-followers because of his ignorance that Jesus was the Christ? Paul doesn't directly say, but states this is why he was shown mercy. Two verses later, he lets Timothy know he considered himself the chief of sinners. Whether that applied to his early persecutions is unknown. Surely he regretted it; it seems reasonable to believe he thought even when done in ignorance, this was sin against God. David queried, "... who can discern their own errors? Forgive me my hidden faults" (Ps 19:12). These suggest that when we *do* become aware that our past actions were sinful, we need to confess and repent. If we do not, we will likely not receive the level of mercy Paul did. Our knowledge has increased, as has our responsibility.

THE NATURE OF SIN

Further attempts to define sin have explored what is called the "nature of sin." What is its bedrock nature or foundation? Theologians list several aspects:

1. Sensuality, which is supremely following our physical or sensual desires (food, sex, drugs, pleasure, anything that gratifies the senses).

2. Selfishness (loving oneself more than God and others). Self is on the throne of the heart.

3. Rebellion (turning away from whatever God wants or commands). Consider the sordid history of Israel and the condemnation Paul lays on all, including Gentiles, who spurn what God and his creation have revealed about himself (see Rom 1:18–32).

4. Idolatry (putting anything in the supreme place God should have in our hearts). Consider the First Commandment, which targeted other gods Israel might worship. Later, Paul chastised those who worshipped such gods (Rom 1:23). Idols are frequently personal (a god), physical (an object), or ideological (a principle or way of life), but can include whatever we worship.

5. Unbelief, which is rejecting God's revelation through his acts, incarnation, personal revelations, and written word. Agreeing with this is Jesus's description of sin (John 12:48, 16:9) and the Apostle John's charge that all who disbelieve in Christ are condemned (John 3:16, 18).[15]

These are all accurate but partial descriptions of what sinners do. Some words describe the sinner turning from or against God (unbelief and rebellion) and others what the sinner is turning to (sensuality, selfishness,

---

15. Erickson, *Christian Theology*, 595–98; and Smith, *With Willful Intent*, 314–26. See these references for more detailed discussion of these concepts.

idolatry). In either case, God is dethroned and is not loved as he should be. Something else, something lesser, is enthroned in the heart.

Temptation and Sin

The Bible words we have studied make clear the intentionality necessary for sin to occur. However, sometimes it is difficult to determine in our own hearts when temptation ends and sin begins. The Bible is again a great help in determining this point.[16] Jesus made distinctions between temptation and sin in the Lord's Prayer—we are to pray for forgiveness for trespasses and seek deliverance from temptation (evil or the evil one). Jesus himself was tempted, but didn't sin (Heb 4:15). Jesus's brother, James, also emphasized the difference, noting that desire can lead to temptation, sin, and death (Jas 1:14–15); each is a further step in the progression.

The difference between temptation and sin matters because we humans sometimes confuse the two. Some people believe they are constantly sinning because they regularly feel fleshly desires rise up, thinking the mere presence of an initial thought or feeling is sinful. Men see a beautiful woman and feel attracted; people see a sumptuous meal and want to splurge; those that come home from work tired wish their family would not put immediate demands on their time; we want to tell someone off in anger when he or she disappoints us repeatedly. However, these are manifestations of the world, the flesh, and the devil working on our hearts; they are means of temptation and not sin itself. If the man above continues to gaze at a beautiful woman and then chooses to fantasize what she looks like naked and imagines having sex with her, then he has crossed over into lust and sin (see Matt 5:28). If the disappointed person lets go a flurry of angry words, disregarding more appropriate responses, he or she has likely sinned. In each case the critical point is what we do with the initial thought or feeling, many of which are involuntary. It is the next step that determines the holiness or sinfulness of our response. There is no need for guilt for feeling tempted; guilt rightly attaches only when we give in to the temptation.

Distinguishing the difference also encourages us to be good fighters. We can be encouraged that we can be as God asks us to be, which is holy. We know we are in a spiritual battle and need to raise our shield and fight back. If that first thought or feeling is already a sin we are tempted to despair. Why fight the battle if there is nothing we can do to stop the first bullet from piercing our armor? This is wrongheaded. Let's keeping praying for strength

---

16. The scriptures and train of thought for this section is taken from Kevin DeYoung, "Temptation is Not the Same as Sin."

and for God to lead us away from temptation. If we do sin, let's also be quick to repent and get back on the track of following God into the good life he has for us.

A DEFINITION

We saw that Adam and Eve's disobedience to God's command was the hallmark of the first human sins. Our word study and discussion of sin's nature helped flesh out that beginning. Like the first sins, we saw that that God and the biblical authors described sin as *disobedience and rebellion against him*—sinners have set themselves up as their own little gods, acting for their own good supremely. Sin involved *breaking or transgressing the good laws God established* and setting up our own priorities in their place. John says as much in one of his letters: "Everyone who sins breaks the law; in fact, sin is lawlessness" (1 John 3:4). Sin also has a personal aspect; we have acting *unfaithfully and treacherously toward God* and *unjustly toward others*, thereby harming them in some way. Implied in all of our definitions is sin's *intentionality—it is done on purpose*. We aim at the wrong moral target or twist God's laws for our own ends. As a result of all this there is *moral liability—guilt and punishment*. If sin is engaged in repeatedly, it produces a character that the Bible describes as *evil* or *wicked*; such people have gone bad or have become broken.

There are some categories of OT sin that are deemed unintentional or done in ignorance and God required a sin offering for these. Whether these persons *ought* to have known the laws or not is not stated. Humans, and especially the Israelites who were in covenant with God, should be diligent to know God's ways. Though sincere Israelites could sin inadvertently, there is likely neglect and laziness that accounts for much of this; they failed to inform themselves regarding God's requirements.

A further nuance suggested by these "sin" words is neglect. If we allow ourselves to stray or wander little by little from God and his will, our life ends up in the same place that more blatant or severe sins would take us. These things that get in between us and God harken to the first three soils in the parable of the Sower. The people described there have allowed other things to take the most cherished spot in their heart. They have failed to obey the two Great Commandments.[17]

---

17. These were first commanded by God through Moses in Deut 6:5 and Lev 19:18 and are apt summaries of the Ten Commandments in Exod 20. Jesus put them together and calls them the two greatest commandments in Matt 22:37, saying all the law and the prophets hang on these.

WHAT IS SIN?

This section has not offered a succinct definition of sin, because sin has several facets. However, if one sentence could describe it, it might be that sin is violating the two Great Commandments and any more-specific commands God has established.

THE SOURCE OF SIN

We have defined sin, and this is a good beginning when trying to understand it. We also examined its nature—what base motives undergird it? This is also very illuminating. Another key issue is its source. What is the root (or roots) beneath it? From what does it spring? Using our definition of cause—what is the ultimate cause of sin? Is it our physical body, emotions, will, thoughts, soul, spirit, Satan?[18]

The Heart

God and the Bible's authors label the source of sin (and goodness) as the heart. This, of course, does not refer to the organ that pumps blood throughout our body but to the inner person. It is the seat or core of our inner nature, which includes:

Emotions:

> The Israelites were "joyful and glad in heart[19] *for all the good things the Lord had done . . ."* (1 Kgs 8:66)
>
> . . . *Oh, the* agony of my heart! (Jer 4:19)
>
> . . . *I* groan in anguish of heart. (Ps 38:8)

Thinking:

> *The* discerning heart *seeks knowledge . . .* (Prov 15:14)
>
> *For the word of the Lord . . . judges the* thoughts and attitudes of the heart. (Heb 4:12)

---

18. The "flesh" is mentioned by Paul as a source of sin and will be given special treatment in chapter 4.
19. Plain text phrases relate to the faculty being illustrated.

> *For God . . . made his* light shine in our hearts to give us the light of the knowledge of God's glory . . . (2 Cor 4:6)

and Willing:[20]

> *But if your* heart turns away and you are not obedient . . . (Deut 30:17)
>
> "Even now," declares the Lord, "return to me with all your heart," . . . (Joel 2:12)
>
> . . . *Asa's* heart was fully committed *to the Lord all his life.* (1 Kgs 18:14)
>
> *For it is* with the heart that you believe *and are justified* . . . (Rom 10:10)

It frequently means the person working as a whole with all his or her character and abilities, and not an isolated function:

> . . . *People look at the outward appearance but the Lord looks on the heart.* (1 Sam 16:7)
>
> *So we rebuilt the wall till all of it reached half its height, for the people worked with all their heart.* (Neh 4:6)
>
> *You will seek me and find me when you seek me with all your heart.* (Jer 29:13)

This totality of human personhood, the heart, is responsible to God.[21] It was the bad heart of the Pharisees that provoked such an angry response from Jesus and motivated him to warn them of their condemnation to hell if they didn't repent (Matt 23:33, see whole chapter).

Various Scriptures affirm that this "heart" is the source of sin.

> *Above all else, guard your heart, for everything you do flows from it.* (Prov 4:23)
>
> *Make a tree good and its fruit will be good, or make a tree bad, and its fruit will be bad. For a tree is recognized by its fruit. You brood of vipers, how can you who are evil say anything good? For the mouth speaks what the heart is full of. A good man brings*

---

20. Brown, *New International*, vol. 2, 181–82.
21. Ibid., 182.

WHAT IS SIN?

> *good things out of the good stored up in him, and an evil man brings evil things out of the evil stored up in him.* (Matt 12:33–35)

> *But the things that come out of a person's mouth come from the heart, and these defile them. For out of the heart come evil thoughts—murder, adultery, sexual immorality, theft, false testimony, slander. These are what defile a person; but eating with unwashed hands does not defile them."* (Matt 15:18–20)

Jesus said that where your "treasure" is, there your *heart* will be also (Matt 6:21), and follows that by using the eye instead of the heart as a metaphor for our total inner person:

> *The eye is the lamp of the body. If your eyes are healthy, your whole body will be full of light. But if your eyes are unhealthy, your whole body will be full of darkness. If then the light within you is darkness, how great is that darkness!* (Matt 6:22–23)

The heart, then, is not only the source of good (which is applicable to our later discussion of holiness), but evil.

SUMMARY

We have seen that the biblical authors use various words to define sin as a conscious act done against God, his covenant laws, and his rule. In certain cases under the Old Covenant, sins were designated as unintentional or out of ignorance. These were not sins that separated someone from the nation of Israel and the sacrifices required for them were less demanding. Sin is not temptation, but is an active turning from or against God (unbelief and rebellion) and toward sensuality, selfishness, or idolatry. The source of sin is the heart, the center of human personality—the will, intellect, and emotions; both *good and evil* spring from this source.

INTERACTION WITH HISTORICAL DEFINITIONS OF SIN

How does the definition developed in this chapter compare with those produced by the various Christian divisions? Judaism, Eastern Orthodoxy, Roman Catholicism, Reformed Protestantism, Anabaptism, Wesleyan-Arminian Protestantism, the Stone-Campbell movement, and Neo-orthodoxy all emphasize sin as a turning away from God, his will, and law. Although some specifically mention sin as sometimes being unintentional, the basic trait of sin is intentionality and voluntariness; this leads to personal responsibility for sins committed. Protestants seem to emphasize the attitude behind sin—selfishness or lack of faith—but it is hard to imagine any of the others disagreeing that motive is a critical part of sin. In line with their tradition, Eastern Orthodox center on sin as disunion with God. The Reformed underline original sin as part of their definition.

The biblical and historic Christian definitions of sin seem to be very close. The biblical words do stress more the "straying" or "wandering" aspect of sin and the source of sin being the heart—the total human will, thoughts, and emotions.

Many Christian theologians throughout history have attributed the ultimate source of human sin not to the heart but to Adam's first sin. It is affirmed that the result of his original sin brought upon humanity an irresistible urge to sin. Adherents believe this is how persons develop an evil heart—their sinfulness comes from the direct fall-out of Adam's sin. This topic will be taken up next in chapter 3.

3

What Are the Consequences of Adam's Sin?

CHAPTER 2 EXAMINED THE definition and source of sin. Many Christian theologians link the ultimate cause of sin to something we have inherited from our first parents—Adam and Eve. This cause is called original sin, a sinful nature, human depravity, or the flesh. The topic of the "flesh," a biblical word used by Paul in his treatment of sin, warrants its own discussion in chapter 4. In this chapter we will seek to accurately interpret both Old and New Testament passages that relate to original sin, determine what the direct and indirect consequences of this sin are, and delineate the consequences of subsequent human sin, including our own.

We have already defined two key phrases, "original sin" and "the fall" in chapter 1. They are used in theology to discuss the effects of Adam's sin on his posterity. They are not biblical words, but incorporate concepts suggested by some Scriptures. Thomas Noble elaborates on our definition by developing a list of ten facets or metaphors that describe the meaning of original sin as commonly used. These words/phrases are either denoted or connoted by many authors who write on this subject. Understanding these meanings will prove very helpful as our discussion progresses.

1. Universal sin is implied in the term original sin; everyone sins.
2. The fall refers to Adam's (and Eve's) eating the forbidden fruit in the Garden. They both "fell" from the original good and obedient relationship they had with God. Sometimes original sin is implied in the use of this word, but is surely implied in the next term—fallenness.

3. To be fallen is to be sinful. The details of what fallenness entails is discussed in points 4–10.

4. Original sin sometimes implies original guilt. This concept has Augustinian roots and states that all humans sinned when Adam sinned and are therefore legally guilty for his sin. For some Christian groups this guilt is removed by water baptism.

5. Disease is another frequently implied concept. This disease state, sometimes called our "sinful nature," means we do not possess Adam and Eve's original righteous standing with God. A similar word to disease is the word depravity, which implies crookedness. Our spiritual nature is now out of sync with God. Further, the phrase "total depravity" is commonly used to say that every facet of humanity is crooked—our physical nature, intellect, emotions, relationships, and even the creation itself. The crookedness means we are totally unable to save ourselves or even respond positively to God's call to salvation without God's grace.

6. The concept of heredity is implied in many of the preceding phrases. Guilt, a sin tendency, and the disease of sin are somehow bestowed on all subsequent humans. How this heredity works is unknown but all born into this world inherit these negative effects of Adam's sin.

7. A commonly included result of Adam's sin is a bent/tendency/inclination toward sin. Augustine called this concupiscence. It sometimes connotes sexual desire but frequently is more broadly construed to include self-centered desire or covetousness. It is misdirected love, a love toward self and against God, his desires, commands, our fellow humans, and the creation.

8. Noble lists sin propagated through sexual desire as a facet of original sin but this aspect has waned in prominence. Most Christians see sexual relations and desires as good and only bad when they are perverted and go outside God's boundaries.

9. The Greek word *sarx*, translated in many Bible versions as "flesh," is a very common facet that Paul uses prominently in his epistles and with several meanings. The first two are merely physical—meaning our physical body/existence or the human race as a whole ("all flesh"). The other two meanings are spiritual or moral and are distinctive Pauline; these are the meanings that many scholars relate to original sin. Flesh can refer to a "mind set on the flesh," which means we put our trust in the things of this world. It can also mean a power within us that conflicts with the wishes of the Spirit. This does not mean our flesh or

body is inherently evil, although some branches of Protestantism seem to suggest this. The power is a self-centered disposition to live only for human or earthly values. This power is sometimes referred to as the "desires of the flesh." As suggested under a bent toward sin and fallenness, these desires are selfish, out of control, and against God.

10. Corporateness is the final concept. There is a solidarity in human sinfulness.[1]

When writers are quoted in this book, these facets of original sin are likely implied unless he or she makes a disclaimer to that effect. The validity of the concept of original sin will be evaluated as this chapter goes along, but for now this author fully accepts point one above, that sin is universal. There are several direct scriptural statements that make this point:

> *Indeed, there is no one on earth who is righteous, no one who does what is right and never sins.* (Eccl 7:20)

> *All of us have become like one who is unclean, and all our righteous acts are like filthy rags; we all shrivel up like a leaf, and like the wind our sins sweep us away.* (Isa 64:6)

> *Everyone has turned away, all have become corrupt; there is no one who does good, not even one.* (Ps 53:3)

> In Romans 3:9–18, Paul assembles several OT passages to make the point that all (Jews and Gentiles) have sinned and are unrighteous, referencing Ps 14:1–3, 5:9, 140:3, 10:7; Isa 59:7–8; and Ps 36:1.

> *There is no difference between Jew and Gentile, for all have sinned and fall short of the glory of God.* (Rom 3:22b–23a)

> *If we claim to be without sin, we deceive ourselves and the truth is not in us.* (1 John 1:8)

UNIVERSALITY AND PERSISTENCE OF SIN

As we have just seen, the universality and persistence of sin is admitted up front by God and many of the biblical writers. However, they spend little

---

1. Noble, "Prolegomena."

time trying to account for it beyond affirming that sin comes from the human heart. They spend more time exhorting all humans to give it up. For example, Israel's godly leaders and prophets chastise them for living in sin and urge them to abandon it. God does the same, sometimes wooing Israel (consider the book of Hosea) and sometimes threatening them with punishment and promising forgiveness and restoration if they repent (much of the OT).

In the OT, God's reaction to sin's universality is akin to puzzlement, sadness, and anger. John Goldingay describes the puzzlement aspect—God might not be surprised if the heathen exchanged one god for another, but is surprised when his chosen people exchanged him, the only true God, for a non-god (an idol)! They gave up a spring of living water for a broken leaky cistern (Jer 2:13) and sought cures for their spiritual sickness and sores from fake doctors instead of the true Physician (Hos 5:13–14).[2] God compared his people to a choice grapevine that was specially selected and cared for but later produced worthless grapes (Isa 5:1–7, Jer 2:21). He asks rhetorically, "What more could have been done for my vineyard than I have done for it" (Isa 5:4)? He marvels again: "Inquire among the nations: Who has ever heard anything like this? A most horrible thing has been done by Virgin Israel. Does the snow of Lebanon ever vanish from its rocky slopes? Do its cool waters from distant sources ever stop flowing? Yet my people have forgotten me; they burn incense to worthless idols, which made them stumble in their ways, in the ancient paths" (Jer 18:13–14).

A further mystery to God is why his people *persisted* on this dead-end track. In Jeremiah, God asks logically: If people fall down, don't they get back up? If people discover they're going the wrong way, don't they turn around? But my people refuse to turn, refuse to repent, and instead run toward sin like a horse charging into battle (Jer 8:4–7). In Isaiah 1:1–7, God speaks to his people, who have been judged for their sin and had their land laid waste by sword and fire. They are like a stubborn and defiant child who grits his teeth when punished. God probes: "Why should you be beaten anymore? Why do you persist in your rebellion? Your whole head is injured, your whole heart afflicted. From the sole of your foot to the top of your head there is no soundness—only wounds and welts and open sores, not cleansed or bandaged or soothed with olive oil" (Isa 1:5–6). When Israel habitually burned incense to and worshipped other gods God sent his prophets to warn them of coming judgment. He asks why they bring disaster upon themselves and leave themselves without a remnant. Do they want to be a curse and reproach among the nations? Have they forgotten the wickedness

---

2. Goldingay, *Old Testament*, 274.

of their previous kings and ancestors (Jer 44:1–10)? Goldingay concludes that God is marveling at the mystery of human stupidity and expressing his frustration and anger at a people who knew better and could do better.[3]

Likewise in the NT, Jesus taught in his hometown of Nazareth and perceived the local's questioning of his Messiahship—after all, isn't he just a carpenter, the son of Joseph and Mary (Mark 6:1–6)? In spite of his supernatural wisdom and miracles, they wouldn't believe in him, therefore he "was amazed at their lack of faith" (Mark 6:6). Similarly, he was deeply saddened by Israel's rejection of him, "Jerusalem, Jerusalem, you who kill the prophets and stone those sent to you, how often I have longed to gather your children together, as a hen gathers her chicks under her wings, and you were unwilling" (Luke 13:34). He was even frustrated with his own disciples, who were unable to heal a demon-possessed boy, "You undeserving and perverse generation," Jesus replied, "how long shall I stay with you? How long shall I put up with you? Bring the boy to me" (Matt 17:17).

It seems a quest to understand the "why" of universal and persistent sin will lead no further than God's own puzzlement, anger, and sadness. He made obedience and love toward him eminently possible but was consistently disappointed with his creatures' turning away to lesser gods. Therefore, it is Noble's points four through ten that will be generally evaluated in the Scriptures below.

PASSAGES RELATING TO ORIGINAL SIN

This section contains scriptural passages that suggest in what moral state post-Adamic humankind is created. Because our theological method includes the ingredients of historical/cultural and literary context, a brief context will frequently precede passages. Texts will be exegeted and interpreted according to the method described and comments made regarding their effect on the doctrine of original sin.

Genesis 3:14–24

Several passages come from the book of Genesis. Genesis is the first of the five books of the OT, called the Pentateuch. The Jewish and Christian traditions have selected Moses as the likely author or compiler of these books. The theme of Genesis is beginnings and it discusses the creation of the universe and all life on earth. The first two humans, Adam and Eve, are

---

3. Ibid., 275–78.

created and placed in a paradise, the Garden of Eden. Their first actions, and the actions of the serpent, who seems to be a corporeal manifestation of Satan, are portrayed. Adam and Eve disobey by eating forbidden fruit and experience their sins' consequences, to include their family's subsequent life outside the Garden.

Leading up to Genesis 3:14–24 the serpent has tempted Adam and Eve to eat of the tree of the knowledge of good and evil and they have both eaten the fruit. They have hidden themselves from God and covered their bodies with fig leaves. God confronts all three of them:

> *14So the Lord God said to the serpent, "Because you have done this, "Cursed are you above all livestock and all wild animals! You will crawl on your belly and you will eat dust all the days of your life. 15And I will put enmity between you and the woman, and between your offspring and hers; he will crush your head, and you will strike his heel."*
>
> *16To the woman he said, "I will make your pains in childbearing very severe;*
> *with painful labor you will give birth to children. Your desire will be for your husband, and he will rule over you."*
>
> *17To Adam he said, "Because you listened to your wife and ate fruit from the tree about which I commanded you, 'You must not eat from it,' "Cursed is the ground because of you; through painful toil you will eat food from it all the days of your life. 18It will produce thorns and thistles for you, and you will eat the plants of the field. 19By the sweat of your brow you will eat your food until you return to the ground, since from it you were taken; for dust you are and to dust you will return."*
>
> *20Adam named his wife Eve, because she would become the mother of all the living.*
>
> *21The Lord God made garments of skin for Adam and his wife and clothed them. 22And the Lord God said, "The man has now become like one of us, knowing good and evil. He must not be allowed to reach out his hand and take also from the tree of life and eat, and live forever." 23So the Lord God banished him from the Garden of Eden to work the ground from which he had been taken. 24After he drove the man out, he placed on the east side of the Garden of Eden cherubim and a flaming sword flashing back and forth to guard the way to the tree of life.*

This passage lists the consequences of the serpent's temptation and Adam and Eve's sins. Two things are cursed—the serpent and the ground; the serpent is cursed because of his own actions and the ground is cursed due to Adam's sin. Gordon Wenham notes that neither the man nor the woman are cursed, however they are punished and their appointed roles are made difficult (by implication and by subsequent human experience the roles of all to follow them are negatively altered). The man must now toil to work the ground for food, continually fighting weeds. The woman will have more severe pain in childbirth and her relationship with her husband will be strained. The man's penalty correlates with his sin (eating forbidden fruit) as he must now undergo painful toil for food. The originally pleasant work in the Garden is gone. Likewise, the woman's fundamental role of mother and wife will be afflicted with pain.

Wenham notes commentators disagree about "returning to dust" as a direct punishment for sin. He believes since Adam and Eve are now banned from the Garden and do not have access to the tree of life that the return to dust (physical death) is inevitable. Conclusions are difficult since direct references to life and death are missing.[4] Victor Hamilton also observes that death is not mentioned in verses 17–19. The penalty for the pair's disobedience is not death but expulsion from the pleasantness and security of the Garden and exposure to pain in living out one's identity (worker and mother/wife).[5] Although some Christians believe physical death would have occurred regardless of human sin, the most likely conclusion is that it is either a direct or indirect consequence of sin.

This passage does not describe any direct long-term moral consequences from Adam and Eve's sins. Original sin, by definition, affects human moral choices. If any passage should describe original sin, it should be this one, since its purpose is to define the effects of the fall. However, it is silent in this regard. It is usually a fallacy to argue from a lack of evidence (a negative argument), but in this case the lack of any mention of original sin in the exact place it should be preeminent contains some evidence against it.

Genesis 4:7

This verse is part of God's response to Cain's unfavorable offering. Cain is angry and downcast because of this.

> 7 If you do what is right, will you not be accepted? But if you do not do what is right, sin is crouching at your door; it desires to have you, but you must rule over it.

---

4. Wenham, *Genesis 1–15*, 81–83.
5. Hamilton, *Book of Genesis*, 204.

Commentators agree that the use of unclear terms and grammatical improprieties make this verse difficult to interpret. Nevertheless, Wenham notes that five commentators suggest a very plausible rendering is, "Is there not forgiveness of sin, if you do well? If you do not do well, the croucher is at the door. Its desire is for you but you must rule over it." Sin is personified as a demon that is crouching like a wild beast at Cain's doorstep.[6] Dwight Swanson provides evidence for a different nuance to the nature of sin here. He notes the participle here, *robets*, is used of animals lying down at rest, much like the "lying down in green pastures" of Psalm 23. So, sin is less an animal waiting in ambush than a domestic pet sitting inside the doorway. This fits well with the tone of Genesis 3, where the serpent is having a civil conversation with the woman.[7] This interpretation is possible but is less important for our purposes than the next verse, the crux of which regards sin's mastery. Hamilton informs us that the Hebrew sense of the phrase could be either "you *shall* master it, you *must* master it, or you *may* master it." Each option implies Cain has a choice:

> He is not so deeply embedded in sin, either inherited or actual, that his further sin is determined and inevitable. The emphasis here is not on Cain as a constitutional sinner, one utterly depraved, but on Cain as one who has a free choice.... Otherwise, God's words to him about "doing well" would be meaningless and comic. Should he so desire, Cain is able to overcome this creature who now confronts him. The text makes Cain's personal responsibility even more focused by its use of the initial emphatic pronoun: "*you*, you are to master it."[8]

This strongly suggests God expected Cain to conquer sin and there is no suggestion there was anything beyond Cain's choice that impeded that action. Hence, this verse suggests no ill effects in Cain's own being from his father's sin. Moreover, sin is pictured as an external threat, not something originating from within the individual.

Genesis 6:5, 11–13

> 5 The Lord saw how great the wickedness of the human race had become on the earth, and that every inclination of the thoughts of the human heart was only evil all the time.

---

6. Wenham, *Genesis 1–15*, 104–6.
7. Swanson, "Original Sin."
8. Hamilton, *Book of Genesis*, 228.

WHAT ARE THE CONSEQUENCES OF ADAM'S SIN?

> 11Now the earth was corrupt in God's sight and was full of violence. 12God saw how corrupt the earth had become, for all the people on earth had corrupted their ways. 13So God said to Noah, "I am going to put an end to all people, for the earth is filled with violence because of them. I am surely going to destroy both them and the earth."

Verse 5 notes that humankind's wickedness *had become* great, this now being the time of Noah. This verb selection suggests it had not always been so. Wenham expounds on the meaning of certain words in verse 5, saying that the plans of the mind are things thought about ahead of time. The "mind" in the Hebrew means literally "heart," which is the center of our human personality and will. Humankind's plans are generally evil, and evil continually.[9] Hamilton also adds that "inclination of the thoughts of the human heart" refers to things thought about beforehand; synonyms could be "imaginations" or "schemes." Like the potter fashions a pot, humans fashion their own thoughts and these thoughts are chronically evil.[10]

Verses 11–13 continue this theme. Because humankind has corrupted or ruined itself until it is irredeemable, God decides to destroy all life. The Hebrew word translated "violence" suggests acts that are un-neighborly, antisocial, and oppressive. They involve aspects of brute force or the exploitation of the have-nots by the haves.[11] All this leads the Genesis author to write in verse 12 that when God viewed the earth, that *indeed!* or *behold!*, it was corrupt! These words are not in the NIV, but are included in the KJV, RSV, NASB, and NET Bible. Hamilton suggests that, as it does in other contexts, this word means humanity's total rebellion and crookedness was surprising to God.[12] God had expected better!

This total ruin that humanity had worked its way into could provide good support for the idea that all humans are born with an innate sinful depravity that causes them to sin. However, several things mitigate against this interpretation. First, verse 5 says humanity *had become* corrupt, signaling a time when they weren't, or were less so. Second, God's apparent surprise at how his creatures had behaved, considering how he had made them. He was shocked, filled with regret, grieved, and troubled. If they possessed an irresistible sin nature, there would be no surprise. The rampant sin of that era would have been expected.

---

9. Wenham, *Genesis 1–15*, 144.
10. Hamilton, *Book of Genesis*, 273.
11. Wenham, *Genesis 1–15*, 171.
12. Hamilton, *Book of Genesis*, 278.

God's act of unilaterally stepping in if sin advances too far reveals a pattern evident several times in Genesis. It has already occurred with Adam and Eve being expelled from the Garden, so they could not eat of the tree of life and live in that sinful condition forever. Now, God steps in again with the flood. Soon, he will confuse the languages of the earth at the tower of Babel because human power and pride had become too great. Later, he will reign down fire on Sodom and Gomorrah, destroying the sinners there (Gen 19; 2 Pet 2:4–9). Later still, God wanted to destroy all Israel over the golden calf idolatry, but his mercy prevailed (Exod 32:9–10). All these actions lessen the influence of sin, but they are drastic and occasional.

So, what was God's purpose in unilaterally stepping in, sometimes even to kill rebellious groups? It is obvious that God's purging of corrupt humans didn't remove the possibility of sin—consider Noah's later inebriation and Ham's reaction. However, sin had become too dominant and God was lessening its impact, not removing its possibility. Sin was not something God could remove by force. However, if there was an inherent "sinful nature" that had caused all this trouble in his creatures, here was God's opportunity to unilaterally remove it. But what does he do? He warns them to abandon it or suffer his punishment, strongly suggesting sin was something they could avoid; it was not inevitable or innate.

Genesis 6:8–9

Preceding and following this passage, God laments how pervasive wickedness is on the earth and how everyone has become corrupt. Filled with regret, he contemplates blotting out humanity and all the animals.

> *8But Noah found favor in the eyes of the Lord.*

> *9This is the account of Noah and his family. Noah was a righteous man, blameless among the people of his time, and he walked faithfully with God.*

Let's analyze the important words used to describe Noah—righteous, blameless, and walked faithfully. In the OT the word "righteous" is used over two hundred times and the righteous are frequently contrasted with the wicked. Positively, righteous means "innocent" or "upright" and implies someone has kept God's moral law and done good things to his or her neighbors. It means "acquitted of an offense" when used in legal contexts. Negatively it means a person has not sinned. The word "blameless" is used rarely compared to righteous, and connotes wholeness and completeness, being blemish-free (as were animal sacrifices, for example). Blameless includes the characteristics of righteous. All Israel was commanded to be blameless before God (Deut 18:13), but few appeared to attain it. "Walked with God" is a phrase used only of Noah and Enoch. There seems to be a progression of increasing goodness in the description of Noah—righteous, blameless, walking with God.[13] Hamilton avers that being blameless does not infer sinless, but the Hebrew word for "righteous," *saddiq*, *does* refer to someone who is *habitually* righteous. The biblical idea is that if righteousness exists it cannot be practiced on an occasional basis; one is habitually righteous or habitually sinning.[14] This verse reports that even though most of humanity was evil in Noah's day, Noah and his family were different; they were righteous and pleased God. The idea of an inner sinful bent, a necessity of sinning, or the idea that sin must dominate their lives is not present here.

It was actually the presence of righteousness which prompted God to save Noah and his family and start over. So, the earlier statement in verse 5 that "every inclination" of the heart was evil "all the time" has a degree of hyperbole, since Noah and his family had righteous thoughts and deeds. Moreover, if there was an innate crookedness in human nature, as original sin requires, then it is useless to start over with Noah, since Noah, his family, and all their progeny are still inherently sinful! The problem remains unfixed and sin will, of necessity, occur again. However, starting over with Noah is exactly what God does. This speaks against the doctrine of original sin.

Genesis 8:21 (Job 31:16–18; Ps 22:9–10; Ps 58:3; Isa 48:8; Jer 3:25, 22:21, 32:30)[15]

Genesis 8:21 plus seven other passages will be considered together because they have similar phrases that describe the beginning of either good or evil behavior (from conception/ birth/youth) and are frequently used to defend the doctrine of original sin. It is affirmed that these verses declare that a sinful nature inherited from Adam is present at conception or birth in every person and is the root behind all actual sins. Do the use of these words signal that human sinfulness actually begins at conception/birth/infancy (supporting original sin) or a later time in life (not supporting original sin)? We will survey these multiple verses and decide which time of life they refer to.

---

13. Wenham, *Genesis 1–15*, 169–70.
14. Hamilton, *Book of Genesis*, 277.
15. Psalm 51:3–6 fits in this category, but because of its prominent use in defending original sin, it will be discussed separately later.

Our first text, Genesis 8:21, occurs after the flood, in which Noah has come out of the ark. Noah has built an altar to the Lord and offered a burnt offering.

> 21 The Lord smelled the pleasing aroma and said in his heart: "Never again will I curse the ground because of humans, even though every inclination of the human heart is evil from childhood. And never again will I destroy all living creatures, as I have done.

The Hebrew word that the NIV translates as "childhood" is translated "youth" in the NASB, NRSV, and ESV. The Hebrew phrase is transliterated as *minna'arav* (from his youth) and is used numerous times in the OT. Dwight Swanson gives a helpful array of texts that correlate various activities that took place during this time in a person's life:

> This biblical phrase can refer to a girl before marriageable age, but old enough to make vows of her own which can stand with legal validity (Lev 22; Num 3); or to the age at which a youngster begins to be a warrior/leader (1 Sam 12:2, 17:33); or to the age at which a male may already be married (Prov 5; Ps 127) and a female a bride (all of Jeremiah and Ezekiel references to Israel as Yahweh's bride). 'Youth,' then, is an age at which one is ready for responsibility, and can be culpable for sins (Job 13:20; Ps 25), and yet is not wholly adult. This refers, not to a child, but to a young adolescent.[16]

Therefore it seems reasonable to conclude that "from childhood/youth" suggests a timeframe of early adolescence, and hence the evil people God is referring to started their sinful ways at that time, not conception or birth, as is suggested by the doctrine of original sin.

Job 31:16–18, 22

Job speaks positively about himself here and seems to be giving either a monolog directed to himself or a prayer toward God. A prayer seems most likely; it is a lament in which Job is rehearsing the evils that have beset him and defending his life and actions before God. He is presenting his case before God and waiting for God's reply (31:35), which does come in chapters 39–41.[17]

---

16. Swanson, "Original Sin," 196.
17. Clines, *Job 31–37*, 978–79.

> *16"If I have denied the desires of the poor or let the eyes of the widow grow weary, 17if I have kept my bread to myself, not sharing it with the fatherless—*
>
> *18but from my youth I reared them as a father would, and from my birth I guided the widow—*
>
> *22then let my arm fall from the shoulder, let it be broken off at the joint.*

David Cline concludes there is more than a little hyperbole in verse 18 since Job says he has been a father to the fatherless from his youth and a guide to the widow from birth.[18] These are actions that an adult performs, not an infant or a newborn. The use of these words suggests Job is using them to affirm that from his earliest ability to do these kind actions, he has done them. He did not do them literally from birth.

Psalm 22:9–10

These are also positive verses and yet fit in the category of lament. They are thought to have likely been part of a liturgy for persons who were very sick or near death. In any case the person laments God's silence and the scorn of others in the face of a grave difficulty. The supplicant hopes there will be a positive response from God, so that he or she can praise God for his kindness (vv. 22–31).[19]

> *9Yet you brought me out of the womb; you made me trust in you, even at my mother's breast.*
>
> *10From birth I was cast on you; from my mother's womb you have been my God.*

These two verses are parallels, a common device in the Psalms. They depict the psalmist as trusting God and as being the God he worshiped from the very first (birth/my mother's breast). It is very unlikely that a newborn could trust in or worship God. Jewish tradition suggests that minor children who were mentally fit were allowed to participate in religious ceremonies, to include reading the Torah or using the Tfillin.[20] They were encouraged, but not required, to begin learning the commandments and

---

18. Ibid., 1023.
19. Craigie, *Psalms 1–50*, 198.
20. Tfillin are translated "phylacteries" in Greek and designate two boxes containing Scripture passages that dangled from an Israelite male's forehead and his left forearm. They were attached with leather straps and were to guard the wearer from evil thoughts during prayer. See Gerhard Falk, "Bar Mitzvah—Bat Mitzvah."

other adult requirements. The Mishnah of the Talmud first mentioned when young Hebrews *were* required to know and obey the commandments, and this occurred at age 13 for males (earliest record in third century AD). In the last several hundred years this male "age of commandment" marker, or "*bar mitzvah*," was added for girls at age 12 (*bat mitzvah*). At this age these young adults were obligated to obey the commandments and participate in adult religious life. Neither was a ceremony required or mentioned in the Talmud, but was added around the fifteenth century AD to mark the occasion.[21] These are the best insights into when Hebrew children could make religious commitments and do not suggest these type of commitments could be made as newborns. Again, Ps 22:9–10 seems to exhibit hyperbole, tracing the beginning of the psalmist's relationship with God to the earliest possible moment, likely the school-age or adolescent stage.

Psalm 58:3

Psalm 58 is directed against evil rulers and the wicked in general. The psalmist lists their evil deeds and calls for God's vengeance and judgment upon them.

> 3*Even from birth the wicked go astray; from the womb they are wayward, spreading lies.*

Verse 3 forms a parallel, describing the wicked (faithless) as going astray from birth and speaking lies. Goldingay believes this phrase implies they are dishonest from the very beginning of their lives and up until the present. However, he notes that since the verse describes only the faithless that it does not relate to the question of the original sin of humanity.[22] Further evidence in Psalm 58 bolsters the idea that the psalmist is talking about current evil rulers and not the behavior they exhibited shortly after birth due to original sin. The common observations of infants reveals that they do not devise injustice, mete out violence, speak lies and other venomous words, and not listen to advice. Therefore, we are not tempted to break their teeth or bathe in their blood (v. 6, 10). The most likely meaning of "from the womb" is that these rulers have done these evil deeds from the very beginning of their time as rulers, or possibly even from an earlier time in their adult life, but not from the time they exited the womb as a testimony to their inherited depravity.

---

21. Rich, "Bar Mitzvah, Bat Mitzvah"; and Schauss, "History."
22. Goldingay, *Psalms 42–89*, 205.

Isaiah 48:8

Isaiah, like all the prophets, condemns Israel's idolatry and stubbornness and exhorts them to listen to God's words so they can be restored to right standing. This verse contains both elements:

> 8 You have neither heard nor understood; from of old your ears have not been open.
> Well do I know how treacherous you are; you were called a rebel from birth.

Commentator Gary Smith explains that "treacherous" often refers to unfaithfulness in violating a loyalty agreement, betrayal of a spouse, breaking a treaty with another nation, or breaking a covenant with God. Because of this type of unfaithfulness, God calls Israel a "rebel" from the beginning (metaphorically—from birth or the womb). Ezekiel 2–3, 16, and 23 repeat this charge that Israel has been treacherous from the beginning, the beginning implying the beginning of Israel's existence[23] and not the beginning of an individual's life. John Oswalt suggests that Israel's rebellion is not merely a phase in either Israel's or humanity's existence but is part of their nature.[24] Oswalt seems to go too far in suggesting that "rebel from birth" should refer to humanity as well as Israel. It is not possible for a human from birth to act treacherously as the word has been defined; those actions are reserved for adults. It seems the context refers to the nation of Israel, who from early on in their existence (complaining during the wilderness wandering in the desert, the golden calf incident, and so on) turned away from God to serve their own agenda. It is also unlikely that "from birth" refers to a pre-moral state in which Israel did not know what sin was or what obedience to the covenant entailed.

Jeremiah 3:25, 22:21, and 32:30

The book of Jeremiah declares God's words to his faithless people. First Israel and now Judah have committed spiritual adultery by worshipping foreign gods. In chapter 3 God commissions Jeremiah to speak to Judah to implore them to return to him. Jeremiah preaches, telling them of their idolatry and confessing their sin on their behalf.

---

23. Smith, *Isaiah 40–66*, 322.
24. Oswalt, *Book of Isaiah*, 268.

> 3:25 *Let us lie down in our shame, and let our disgrace cover us. We have sinned against the Lord our God, both we and our ancestors; from our youth till this day we have not obeyed the Lord our God.*
>
> 22:21 *I warned you when you felt secure, but you said, "I will not listen!" This has been your way from your youth; you have not obeyed me.*
>
> 32:30 *"The people of Israel and Judah have done nothing but evil in my sight from their youth; indeed, the people of Israel have done nothing but arouse my anger with what their hands have made, declares the Lord."*

Jack Lundblom remarks that these verses are hyperbole in describing Judah doing evil "from their youth" as individuals. More likely it is the evil which began in their youth as a nation and which has continued until the present, similar to Isaiah 48:8 above. Whether it is kings, priests, prophets, or the people in general, Jerusalem and Judah are contemptuous, casting a deaf ear to God's words of correction.[25] If they refer to individuals, it seems likely this means at least an age at which they knew what the commandments were (again, school-age or older to adolescent at the minimum). It is unlikely that any younger person could anger God by "what their hands have made" (32:30), since this suggests the making of idols.

In conclusion, it seems most likely that the OT phrases "from womb/birth/youth" refer to the beginning of the behaviors the verses describe and not to the beginning of life. First, the context describes moral behaviors that only adolescents or adults have the understanding to commit. Second, the contexts describe both righteous and sinful behaviors. Since this is the case, the positive verses could then support the idea that humans are born "good," which is not supported by Scripture or believed by those who defend the doctrine of original sin. Third, the majority of commentators do not see these behaviors as occurring either before (or soon after) birth. Accordingly, it seems these passages do not support the idea of original sin, but rather support the idea that both good and evil occur after humans can understand what each is, which is beyond the birth or infant stage.[26]

---

25. Lundblom, *Jeremiah 21–36*, 516, 523.

26. This is suggested by the Jewish distinction of bar and bat mitzvah and by the Christian concept of the "age of accountability."

Exodus 20:5–6

The setting for these verses is the nation of Israel waiting for Moses to return from the top of Mount Sinai. God's presence is in a thick dark cloud atop the mountain. Moses returns from talking with God and there is lightning, thunder, and trumpet sounds. God speaks the Ten Commandments to his people and our text is from the Second Commandment. God has told them they must not make idols.

> *5 You shall not bow down to them or worship them; for I, the Lord your God, am a jealous God, punishing the children for the sin of the parents to the third and fourth generation of those who hate me, 6 but showing love to a thousand generations of those who love me and keep my commandments.*

Commentator Douglas Stuart clarifies this verse, noting it is not insinuating that God punishes an innocent generation for the sins of a previous one.[27] It means God will punish succeeding generations (up to the third and fourth generations) for committing the same types of sins as their parents did. Further, "third and fourth generations" is an idiomatic phrase meaning "whatever number" and is a necessary punishment in order to enforce the covenant. On the other hand, God shows his covenant loyalty by being willing to bless much more extravagantly (to a thousand generations) those who obey him. This is what is really on his heart. The words "love" and "hate" are also idiomatic to loyalty or the lack thereof, and do not refer to emotional attitudes.[28]

The historic and modern Jewish interpretations of Exodus 20:5–6 align well with Stuart.[29] Children that "hate God" will receive the same punishment as their disloyal predecessors. This text, then, seems to support the idea that the legacy of sinful behavior affects succeeding generations through children following the pattern established by their parents. It says nothing about an internal sinful nature that is behind generational sins.

Exodus 32: 9–14

These verses are part of God's response to Moses regarding Israel's idolatry with the golden calf.

---

27. This is denoted among the various laws for the Israelites that fathers shall not be put to death for the sins of their children and vice versa (Deut 24:16).
28. Stuart, *Exodus*, 454.
29. Wigoder, *New Encyclopedia*, s. v. "sin."

> *"I have seen these people," the Lord said to Moses, "and they are a stiff-necked people. 10Now leave me alone so that my anger may burn against them and that I may destroy them. Then I will make you into a great nation."*
>
> *11But Moses sought the favor of the Lord his God. "Lord," he said, "why should your anger burn against your people, whom you brought out of Egypt with great power and a mighty hand? 12Why should the Egyptians say, 'It was with evil intent that he brought them out, to kill them in the mountains and to wipe them off the face of the earth'? Turn from your fierce anger; relent and do not bring disaster on your people. 13Remember your servants Abraham, Isaac and Israel, to whom you swore by your own self: 'I will make your descendants as numerous as the stars in the sky and I will give your descendants all this land I promised them, and it will be their inheritance forever.'" 14Then the Lord relented and did not bring on his people the disaster he had threatened.*

This text recounts God's anger with his wayward people and his contemplation of destroying them and starting over with Moses, a righteous man. These verses support a philosophical argument against original sin. The concept of original sin asserts that it is human nature itself that is corrupt and it is something we have no choice about; we are born with it. If that is that case there is no logical reason to start over with Moses. Moses would indeed possess the same sinful nature, and starting over with him would not solve anything—his progeny would still go on sinning. If however, sin originates within the individual heart, then starting over with Moses makes sense—Moses is a righteous man and would start the nation over again from a good spiritual foundation. Practically, if original sin was a fact, God would need to destroy *all* of humanity and redesign the human creature to be less susceptible to sinning. Then he could have a creature that would habitually obey his wishes and not constantly fail. However, that is not what he did here in Moses's (or Noah's) example.[30]

Deuteronomy 1:39

God has just told Moses he will not enter the Promised Land and that he should encourage his successor, Joshua, because he will lead their children to inherit the land.

---

30. Ibid.

> 39And the little ones that you said would be taken captive, your children who do not yet know good from bad—they will enter the land. I will give it to them and they will take possession of it.

This verse suggests that there is a time when Israelite children (and likely all children) will reach a point in their moral development when they distinguish between good and evil (see also Isa 7:15–16). This implies a time before which they are innocent, or not capable of making a moral decision. Christian theology has developed a concept describing the crossing over from innocence to responsibility as the "age of accountability."[31] If these children are considered innocent and should happen to die, there is no inherited sin or guilt that would be laid on their moral account, since God does not punish the innocent (Prov 17:15). However, if these little ones possess Adam's sinful nature, then their sinful state would separate them from God forever (Rev 21:27 declares no impure person shall enter the New Jerusalem). Some stronger determinists suggest that infants and other innocents *are* guilty of Adam's sin and will end up in hell if they die in infancy. However, this is not compatible with either God's mercy *or* justice. Others also believe this but hold that infant baptism will remove original sin and allow them to enter heaven. Still others do not offer infant baptism but propose an *ad hoc* change in the administration of God's government that would allow them to enter heaven. Wesleyans propose that infants have inherited depravity but are not guilty until they commit a sin. In any case, the doctrine of original sin has difficulty handling the fate of the innocent, since they *directly* inherit negative and irresistible consequences due to the sin of another. See the following discussion on Deuteronomy 24:16 and Ezekiel 18 for more commentary.

Deuteronomy 24:16

This verse is part of the miscellaneous laws Moses is reviewing with the Israelites before they enter the Promised Land and is among laws governing treatment of those who are most vulnerable in Israel—aliens, poor neighbors, family, the fatherless and widows, and hired workers.

> 16Parents are not to be put to death for their children, nor children put to death for their parents; each will die for their own sin.

---

31. Swanson, "Original Sin," 195. Discussion on Ps 22:9–10 and the testimony of Jewish history suggests this age is 13 for males and 12 for females. Duane Christensen suggests this age is 20 years, citing Num 14:29–31, rabbinic tradition, and the Dead Sea Scrolls. See Christensen, D., *Deuteronomy*, 32.

The legal court is the setting for the principle put forth in this verse. Immediate family members were not to suffer criminally for actions of another. This principle of individual responsibility was upheld throughout Israel's existence. Moreover, the principle negates collective punishment, in which children were sometimes put to death for crimes of their parents. There is an example where this principle was enacted, found in 2 Kings 14:5–6.[32] King Amaziah put to death the assassins of his father, the then king, but did not put their sons to death.

This verse relates to our topic since it affirms that there is no responsibility, guilt, or punishment for sins done by ancestors or one's children. This does not mean these sins did not *affect* other family members; that surely happened in a negative way, but death here was a punishment for those guilty of a breach of law and God is saying here that punishment and guilt cannot be transferred from one human to another. However, the doctrine of original sin does not want to go back one generation, it wants to go back *many generations* to Adam and lay the spiritual death of all humanity on his doorstep. This contradicts the clear principle elaborated in this verse and speaks against its truthfulness. Further, proponents of original sin do not bring up this verse in their defense of their doctrine. This is the fallacy of suppressed (or selective) evidence, and is another strike against it.

Deuteronomy 30:11–14

At the close of Deuteronomy, Moses finishes his re-telling of the law and reminds Israel of the curses for disobedience and the blessings for obedience (Deut 28). Even though both God (Deut 31:16–22) and Moses (Deut 31:27) could see the Israelites current heart status was rebellious and stiff-necked, Moses offers them life for obedience.

> *11Now what I am commanding you today is not too difficult for you or beyond your reach. 12It is not up in heaven, so that you have to ask, "Who will ascend into heaven to get it and proclaim it to us so we may obey it?" 13Nor is it beyond the sea, so that you have to ask, "Who will cross the sea to get it and proclaim it to us so we may obey it?" 14No, the word is very near you; it is in your mouth and in your heart so you may obey it.* (Deut 30:11–14)

If the Israelites were unable to love and obey God and all the commandments he gave them because of a defective nature, Moses knew nothing of it. Speaking for God, he commanded them to love and obey the Lord,

---

32. Wright, C., *Deuteronomy*, 259–60.

something that was not too difficult for or beyond them. In fact, the word they were to obey was in their mouth and heart! If Israel disobeys, it appears it is not because they are unable, as the theory of original sin affirms.

Joshua 7

> 11 Israel has sinned; they have violated my covenant, which I commanded them to keep. They have taken some of the devoted things; they have stolen, they have lied, they have put them with their own possessions. 12 That is why the Israelites cannot stand against their enemies; they turn their backs and run because they have been made liable to destruction. I will not be with you anymore unless you destroy whatever among you is devoted to destruction. (Josh 7:11–12)

This whole chapter is sometimes used to defend the idea that since the nation of Israel suffered directly and collectively for the sins of one person, Achan, that all humanity suffers the penalty of Adam's sin. Achan hid some of the spoils of war in the Israelite victory over Jericho, burying them under his tent. In the next battle at Ai, three thousand Israelite soldiers were routed by only a small band, losing thirty-six lives in the process. God would not allow them to be victorious until the stolen articles were destroyed and Achan stoned to death (Josh 7). The sin of one man held up an entire nation. This is certainly true—Israel directly suffered on Achan's account—God's blessing was withheld and thirty-six soldiers lost their lives. Israel had no choice in the matter. However, unlike original sin, neither Israel as a nation nor the thirty-six dead were *guilty* of Achan's sin. Further, Achan's *death sentence* was not handed down to Israel; Achan died for his sin and the nation of Israel moved on with God's covering restored. The situations of Achan and original sin have similarities, but only on the surface. Humanity and Israel both suffered at the hands of one man, but that tie is not strong enough to support the doctrine of original sin; guilt and the nature of the consequence do not match across the comparison. This is a case of a "weak or false analogy," which is a subgroup of the weak induction fallacy.[33]

---

33. In a weak analogy there is a comparison between two things, but the similarities are incomplete or not present.

Psalms Background

John Goldingay suggests that the Psalms conceal their origins. While Christian tradition sees the Psalms as the "Psalms of David" and numerous psalms have headings alluding they are "of David," this can be misleading. The Hebrew word translated "of" can also mean "for," "belonging to," "on behalf of," or "about." Furthermore, "David" can refer to King David himself or a king in his line.[34] Goldingay remarks that this illustrates the human tendency to associate writings with someone we know:

> One can see how the references to David in the headings, the emphasis on David as patron of the worship in the temple (see Chronicles), and his reputation as a musician and poet would have made him a natural candidate for identification as author of the Psalter as a whole. This may have encouraged or followed the development of a tradition of linking psalms with incidents in David's life. . . . but they still need not imply his authorship.[35]

Psalm 51's heading, for example, probably linked David's confrontation with Nathan and his sin with Bathsheba to the content of this psalm because of significant similarity. However, the headings may suggest more about the Psalm's use than its origin. There is also evidence of changes or additions made to various psalms. In the current example, Psalm 51:18–19 was probably added at a later date to correspond with occurrences in Israel at that time, since in David's time there was no need to rebuild the walls of Jerusalem.[36] Does this mean David didn't write Psalm 51? No, it means he may have, but evidence suggests it is just as plausible that he didn't.

Psalm 51:3–6[37]

> *3For I know my transgressions, and my sin is always before me.*
> *4Against you, you only, have I sinned and done what is evil in your sight;*
> *so you are right in your verdict and justified when you judge.*
> *5Surely I was sinful at birth, sinful from the time my mother conceived me.*

---

34. Goldingay, *Psalms 1–41*, 25–27.
35. Ibid., 27–28.
36. Ibid., 29.
37. Though this psalm could have been discussed under the "from birth/youth" category beginning with Genesis 8:21, it is discussed separately due to its ubiquitous use as a defense of original sin.

WHAT ARE THE CONSEQUENCES OF ADAM'S SIN?

> *6Yet you desired faithfulness even in the womb; you taught me wisdom in that secret place.*

Psalm 51 is classified as a penitential prayer since it is directed toward God and the content regards personal sins. The writer is confessing sin and guilt and asking for personal forgiveness, cleansing, and restoration to purity and joy.[38]

The main concern for our purposes is verse 5. Commentator Marvin Tate believes that in verse 5, the writer is confessing his own human condition and inheritance as a sinner since human life has always involved sin and guilt. Tate also sees the social view, which holds that the writer was born into a world of sin and is adversely affected by his surroundings.[39] Hans-Joachim Kraus has a similar view, seeing the psalm as recognizing the power of sin to corrupt from the beginnings of life. Sin has the element of personal action and its corresponding responsibility, but also that of fate, which affects all humanity. Therefore all humans are fallen and guilty.[40] They are totally depraved from the beginning.[41]

John Goldingay does not go as far as these commentators. He concludes the meaning of this verse is compatible with the idea that sinning is natural for humans, however sinfulness is not transmitted genetically. The verse is making a personal statement about the writer's life and it is unknown whether his confession applies to all humans, but the verse does assume all are somehow affected by sin.[42] Similar to Goldingay, The IVP Bible Background Commentary sees the psalm as a confession of a penitent and less a statement of a doctrine:

> Although this psalm has been used by some commentators to bolster the doctrine of "original sin," it seems a more appropriate interpretation to see it as part of the general confession of the penitent. . . . The Israelites would have agreed with that theology in that they would have acknowledged a general inclination to sin that was characteristic of all people. They do not go the next step of Christian theology by seeing Adam's sin imputed to people.[43]

---

38. Tate, *Psalms 51–100*, 8, 12.
39. Ibid., 19.
40. Kraus, *Theology of the Psalms*, 157.
41. Kraus, *Psalms 1–59*, 503.
42. Goldingay, *Psalms 42–89*, 129–30.
43. Walton, et al., *Psalm 51:5*.

Gordon Thomas correctly sees the psalmist as trying to incriminate rather than exonerate himself; he is not looking for an alibi or mitigating circumstance (by implying a doctrine of original sin). Further, the genre of the psalm is penitential and the psalmist here releases an emotional wave of guilt through confession and appeal for forgiveness; this is not intended as a theological discussion of sin! Hence, this is likely the familiar Jewish use of hyperbole, similar to Jesus's use of "planks in eyes," "camels going through eyes of needles," or Paul's self-description as the "chief of sinners." Each is maximizing effect through hyperbole, which is quite prominent in the lament psalms.[44]

Verse 6 does hint at some human action "in the womb" and in "the secret place," but commentators agree this passage is difficult to understand and are not confident regarding any proposed meaning.

To conclude, although Psalm 51:5 is routinely used as a defense for the doctrine of original sin, close scrutiny reveals meager evidence. First, the psalmist is centered on current and actual sins that are "always before me" and "evil in your sight," sins that are impossible for him to have committed when he was conceived or born. Second, there is no hint the author feels these sins came from a pre-existing sinful state. Third, commentators who see original sin in this verse provide little evidence that this personal statement can be generalized to the rest of humanity; it appears to be a fallacy of composition.[45] The context suggests the author refers to his earliest existence as a way to highlight the depth of his guilt for his current sins; in his distress he is using hyperbole. He currently sees no good within himself and is pouring out his heart to God in hopes of receiving forgiveness and cleansing.

Ecclesiastes 7:29

29 This only have I found: God created mankind upright, but they have gone in search of many schemes."

The writer of Ecclesiastes, called the Teacher, is seeking for wisdom and to understand the stupidity of wickedness and folly in verses 25–29. His search for wisdom has turned up little. In the end all he can conclude is that humans were made "straight" (not crooked), the connotation being in the

---

44. Thomas, "Old Testament," 209–10.

45. Composition is an informal fallacy of logic in which an attribute of a part is wrongly transferred to the whole, in this case the sin of the psalmist is transferred to meaning the sin of humanity.

moral or religious sense. This echoes Genesis 1, when God saw the humans he had created and that they were "very good."[46] Tremper Longman III also sees this as humanity being created virtuous and morally upright (not just Adam and Eve).[47] If this is the case with humans, how did they end up sinning? The end of verse 29, in which the Hebrew word *hisbonot* is translated "schemes," "devices," or "inventions," suggests an answer. This word refers to humanly conceived inventions that are wrong, ineffective, or evil.[48] William Brown calls these inventions destructive "accountings" of life.[49] This failed scheming started in the Garden with Adam and Eve desiring knowledge they shouldn't have had, scheming that continued to the Teacher's day. Bartholomew suggests the use of *hisbonot* and *hesbot* (meaning an explanation, which is what the Teacher is seeking) is a pun on his search for wisdom. The Teacher is engaging in his own ironic scheme—he is searching for wisdom and certainty through his unaided reason and discovers he cannot find it. His personal experience and observations are not enough; his autonomous search for the meaning of life is hopelessly inadequate. This crooked approach is at the heart of human folly—humans who seek wisdom on their own terms and do not depend on God always fail. Moreover, humans are not crooked because God made them so, they have used their free will to assert their own agendas.[50] This verse contradicts the idea of original sin by asserting that we humans have been made upright, but we have taken that good beginning and devised schemes of our own making to lead us. Those defending original sin do not discuss this verse, or if they do, do not relate it to any discussion of the doctrine. This is therefore another example of the logical fallacy of suppressed or selective evidence.

Isaiah 5:1–7 and Jeremiah 2:21

> 1I will sing for the one I love a song about his vineyard: My loved one had a vineyard on a fertile hillside. 2He dug it up and cleared it of stones and planted it with the choicest vines. He built a watchtower in it and cut out a winepress as well. Then he looked for a crop of good grapes, but it yielded only bad fruit. 3"Now you dwellers in Jerusalem and people of Judah, judge between me and my vineyard. 4What more

---

46. Bartholomew, *Ecclesiastes*, 268.
47. Longman, *Book of Ecclesiastes*, 207.
48. Bartholomew, *Ecclesiastes*, 268.
49. Brown, *Ecclesiastes*, 84.
50. Bartholomew, *Ecclesiastes*, 268–69, 274–75.

> *could have been done for my vineyard than I have done for it? When I looked for good grapes, why did it yield only bad? 5Now I will tell you what I am going to do to my vineyard: I will take away its hedge, and it will be destroyed; I will break down its wall, and it will be trampled. 6I will make it a wasteland, neither pruned nor cultivated, and briers and thorns will grow there. I will command the clouds not to rain on it." 7The vineyard of the Lord Almighty is the nation of Israel, and the people of Judah are the vines he delighted in. And he looked for justice, but saw bloodshed; for righteousness, but heard cries of distress.* (Isa 5:1–7)

> *21I had planted you like a choice vine of sound and reliable stock. How then did you turn against me into a corrupt, wild vine?* (Jer 2:21)

Both of these prophets are describing the nations of Israel and Judah as vines. Isaiah describes their situation in a love song, which is in parable format. Isaiah reflects on the tender care God took to establish his vine, how he dug up stones, tilled the fertile soil, and planted the choicest vines. Isaiah asks what more God could have done for their good. Much like Nathan confronting David, Isaiah sets the reader up to side with God against such a poor vine, finally revealing that the vine is the wayward house of Israel and Judah (v. 7), especially the powerful and wealthy (vv. 8–24). God expected good and great things from them but was severely disappointed.[51] Similarly, Jeremiah 2:21 describes Judah, a nation that is offering pagan sacrifices on every high hill (v. 20). He planted them as a choice vine (*soreq*[52] in Hebrew), but they have turned wild and rotten.

What can we conclude about the origins of the Hebrew nation? God describes them as good from the beginning. They are compared to a very desirable grapevine, valuable and fruitful. However, they have become worthless, not because of any lack in how they started, but what they have become. They have gone after foreign gods and angered the true God. God expected much better from them.

How does this relate to original sin? These verses imply that Israel's origins were only good. They were "choice vines" of "good and reliable stock." There is no hint of any spiritual lack or inherent sinfulness in their make-up, personally or as a nation. If that were the case, God surely would not have been so dismayed since they would then be only living out the inferior and sinful way they were made. He questions them curtly about why they have

---

51. Smith, *Isaiah 1–39*, 164–65, 168.

52. This type of grapevine was very desirable, bearing reddish fruit, and good for winemaking.

betrayed him (rest of Jer 2). This does not sound like a God who knows his people are destined to sin due to a sinful nature. Consequently, God does not blame Adam for Israel's woes, he blames them and their wicked ways. He *expected* them to do better.

Ezekiel 18

> 1 The word of the Lord came to me: 2 "What do you people mean by quoting this proverb about the land of Israel:
>
> > "'The parents eat sour grapes,
> > and the children's teeth are set on edge'?
>
> 3 "As surely as I live, declares the Sovereign Lord, you will no longer quote this proverb in Israel. 4 For everyone belongs to me, the parent as well as the child—both alike belong to me. The one who sins is the one who will die.
>
> 5 "Suppose there is a righteous man who does what is just and right. 6 He does not eat at the mountain shrines or look to the idols of Israel. He does not defile his neighbor's wife or have sexual relations with a woman during her period. 7 He does not oppress anyone, but returns what he took in pledge for a loan. He does not commit robbery but gives his food to the hungry and provides clothing for the naked. 8 He does not lend to them at interest or take a profit from them. He withholds his hand from doing wrong and judges fairly between two parties. 9 He follows my decrees and faithfully keeps my laws. That man is righteous; he will surely live, declares the Sovereign Lord.
>
> 10 "Suppose he has a violent son, who sheds blood or does any of these other things 11 (though the father has done none of them):
>
> > "He eats at the mountain shrines. He defiles his neighbor's wife. 12 He oppresses the poor and needy. He commits robbery. He does not return what he took in pledge. He looks to the idols. He does detestable things. 13 He lends at interest and takes a profit. Will such a man live? He will not! Because he has done all these detestable things, he is to be put to death; his blood will be on his own head.
>
> 14 "But suppose this son has a son who sees all the sins his father commits, and though he sees them, he does not do such things:
>
> 15 "He does not eat at the mountain shrines or look to the idols of Israel. He does not defile his neighbor's wife. 16 He does not

oppress anyone or require a pledge for a loan. He does not commit robbery but gives his food to the hungry and provides clothing for the naked. 17He withholds his hand from mistreating the poor and takes no interest or profit from them. He keeps my laws and follows my decrees. He will not die for his father's sin; he will surely live. 18But his father will die for his own sin, because he practiced extortion, robbed his brother and did what was wrong among his people.

19 "Yet you ask, 'Why does the son not share the guilt of his father?' Since the son has done what is just and right and has been careful to keep all my decrees, he will surely live. 20The one who sins is the one who will die. The child will not share the guilt of the parent, nor will the parent share the guilt of the child. The righteousness of the righteous will be credited to them, and the wickedness of the wicked will be charged against them.

21 "But if a wicked person turns away from all the sins they have committed and keeps all my decrees and does what is just and right, that person will surely live; they will not die. 22None of the offenses they have committed will be remembered against them. Because of the righteous things they have done, they will live. 23Do I take any pleasure in the death of the wicked? declares the Sovereign Lord. Rather, am I not pleased when they turn from their ways and live?

24 "But if a righteous person turns from their righteousness and commits sin and does the same detestable things the wicked person does, will they live? None of the righteous things that person has done will be remembered. Because of the unfaithfulness they are guilty of and because of the sins they have committed, they will die.

25 "Yet you say, 'The way of the Lord is not just.' Hear, you Israelites: Is my way unjust? Is it not your ways that are unjust? 26If a righteous person turns from their righteousness and commits sin, they will die for it; because of the sin they have committed they will die. 27But if a wicked person turns away from the wickedness they have committed and does what is just and right, they will save their life. 28Because they consider all the offenses they have committed and turn away from them, that person will surely live; they will not die. 29Yet the Israelites say, 'The way of the Lord is not just.' Are my ways unjust, people of Israel? Is it not your ways that are unjust?

30 "Therefore, you Israelites, I will judge each of you according to your own ways, declares the Sovereign Lord. Repent! Turn away from all your offenses; then sin will not be your downfall. 31Rid yourselves of all the offenses you have committed, and get a new

> *heart and a new spirit. Why will you die, people of Israel? 32For I take no pleasure in the death of anyone, declares the Sovereign Lord. Repent and live!*

This extensive passage responds to the proverb that some Israelites were apparently using as an excuse for their behavior, blaming their parents as the source for their predicament in exile. They were now in Babylon and looking back and trying to figure out the causes for the fate they were experiencing. They could have picked up this proverb from neighboring nations, since the idea of transgenerational accountability was well known in the Ancient Near East. Whatever the source, the response from God implies they were using the proverb as an excuse for their *own* sins, saying "It's our parents who are to blame and we couldn't have done anything to stop our exile!"[53] Ezekiel counters this fatalism by responding that the actions of one generation do not determine the fate of another. This was not a new teaching for the Israelites; verse 20 closely follows the pattern and meaning of a chronologically earlier verse, Deuteronomy 24:16.[54]

Commentator Daniel Block asserts that Ezekiel is making two counterclaims to the proverb: 1) All persons belong to him. No one is the victim of cosmic laws outside God's control.[55] Each person's destiny is safely protected by God from outside forces. 2) There is a direct relationship between guilt and punishment, sin and retribution—it is only the person who sins who will die. Ezekiel's declaration is repeated in Ezekiel 33:12–16 and Jeremiah 31:29–30 as Jeremiah looked forward to the New Covenant (31:31–34); Ezekiel 33 makes it plain the proverb didn't apply then and Jeremiah declares it won't apply in the future either. Block concludes that Ezekiel 18 teaches four central truths (that relate to our discussion of original sin): 1) Each person is the master of his or her own destiny. 2) Any idea of eternal security or damnation that holds a person captive to the decisions of their past is repudiated. 3) God cannot be accused of being capricious but runs his universe on moral laws of accountability. 4) God does not prefer to execute judgment but wants to withhold judgment and offer chances for life.[56]

---

53. Block, *Book of Ezekiel*, 558–60.
54. Ibid., 581.
55. Ibid., 562.
56. Ibid., 589–90. Lamar Cooper Sr. sees much in Block's comments to agree with. However, he disagrees with central truth number 2 above and concludes that Ezekiel 18 (especially verses 24 and 26) is not primarily concerned with impermanent salvation or the idea that salvation can be lost. He interprets Ezekiel's use of judgmental language, such as "will die," as a chastening of those who are true believers. He believes if salvation could be lost, chastening has no meaning. Cooper, *Ezekiel*, 186, 192.

Ezekiel 18 and Jeremiah 31 relate to original sin in that they repudiate the idea that persons can somehow be held responsible or suffer directly for the moral decisions of others. Their point is that children are not judged for or do not *directly* receive the consequences of the sins of their fathers (and vice versa).[57] However, the doctrine of original sin goes even farther than this and directly links the sin of our first father, Adam, with *all* his posterity. Original sin concludes that humans are born into a condition (spiritual separation or death) in which they are enslaved to sin due to the decision of another—Adam; they can do nothing *but* sin. They had no choice about receiving a sinful nature from him, a nature for which some Protestants teach all persons are held guilty (see Noble's list of 10). This doctrine is the opposite of what Ezekiel and Jeremiah are teaching—it is those who commit actual sins who will die. However, original sin teaches that all persons are spiritually dead starting at birth, even before they have committed actual sins. Ironically, the proverb Ezekiel condemns is similar to the tenets of original sin. "The parents eat sour grapes" correlates with Adam and Eve's sin. "The children's teeth are set on edge" correlates with descendants suffering direct personal harm from their sins!

Ezekiel doesn't condemn his fellow Israelites for inheriting a sinful nature (a state), but challenges them to stop their own personal and corporate sins (actions)—to repent and live! Original sin claims we are sinners at birth (and beyond). However, this leaves us unable to follow Ezekiel's, Jeremiah's, and God's command; we cannot change the state we were born into; we cannot repent of original sin! Consequently, Ezekiel 18 and Jeremiah 31 both weaken the truth claim and coherence of this doctrine.[58]

Romans 5:12–19

In the book of Romans, Paul[59] is writing to the Jewish and Gentile believers in Rome, having not yet visited them at the time of this letter. He writes that

---

57. The word "directly" here denotes that there are no consequences that immediately follow and that are experienced in their being, such as occurs with original sin. There were surely "indirect" consequences to the sins of fathers or children in Ezekiel's and Jeremiah's day—sinful examples make it more likely others will follow suit.

58. Proponents of original sin rarely discuss this important chapter and fail to deal with how it negatively impacts their doctrine. This is again, as with Deut 24:16, a fallacy of suppressed or selective evidence.

59. Paul, a confessed Pharisee (Phil 3:5, Acts 23:6), was likely influenced in his Christian theology by his Pharisaic training. N. T. Wright makes a good case that Paul was part of the more conservative branch of Phariseeism that existed in the first century, which followed the teachings of Shammai. Shammai, along with another

he is intending to go on to Jerusalem to deliver much needed monies from mostly Gentile churches to the poor and needy Jewish saints in Judea (Rom 15:23–33). He hopes the gift will be favorably received, likely because that kind of reception would help cement the relationship between the Gentile and Jewish churches, churches that have significant social and theological differences.[60] He does, however, hope to stop in Rome on his way to Spain.

The ethnic and theological mix of the Roman church was no doubt affected by Claudius's expulsion of all Jews (Jewish Christians included) in approximately 49 AD, who were also likely to have returned soon after his death in 54 AD. Gentile converts would have become a greater percentage of the church and would have had to reintegrate the influx of banished Jewish believers, all of whom seemed to meet in house churches (Rom 16). A good guess on the dating of Paul's Letter to the Romans is 57 AD.[61]

The main portion of the book is a sustained treatise on the relation of law and gospel, Jew and Gentile. This then lays a good foundation for his appeal for unity (Rom 14–15) and for his emphasis—to persuade Jews of the law-free gospel so they can join the Gentiles and form one church and to remind Gentiles that Jews are not to be scorned since they are the root of the church. Paul is explaining the gospel as part of God's large salvation plan that has operated continuously through the ages. His treatise is universal since it addresses the sin and needs of all humanity, our salvation in Christ, our need for a holy life, and our comfort in times of suffering.[62] Moo summarizes:

> The bulk of Romans focuses on how God has acted in Christ to bring the *individual* sinner into a new relationship with himself (chaps. 1–4), to provide for that *individual's* eternal life in glory (chaps. 5–8), and to transform that *individual's* life on earth

---

influential teacher, Hillel, developed two schools of thought as they interpreted the Hebrew Scriptures. Hillel is generally observed to be the more lenient in his views on the law, Jewish religious practice, personal piety, and Israel's political agenda, and Shammai the stricter. During Paul's life there appeared to be considerable controversy between the two schools, something Paul would obviously have been aware of. As a Pharisee, Paul states that his religious training was under the teacher Gamaliel, who was a noted Hillelite. This is curious, since Paul's zeal for the law and his persecution and arresting of Christ-followers (Acts 7:60, 22:1–5) are more in line with the ways of Shammai. Gamaliel's more tolerant views are noted in his speech before the Sanhedrin in Acts 5, where he cautions the Sanhedrin to let Peter and the apostles go rather than kill them. Paul, then, seems to have both lenient and strict influences in his religious training. See Wright, N., *What Saint Paul Really Said*, 26–31.

60. Moo, *Epistle to the Romans*, 2–3.
61. Ibid., 3–5.
62. Ibid., 14, 21–22.

now (12:1—15:13). Since it is essential to Paul's message that God acts, in a way that he has not previously, to include on an equal basis both Jew and Gentile in this transforming operation, Paul must pay constant attention to the implications of this new equality of treatment. He must explain how his message of individual transformation relates to God's focus on Israel in the OT. This explanation thus becomes a constant motif in the letter and occupies an important section of the letter (chaps. 9–11) in its own right. But it remains the background as Paul presents in the foreground the way in which God has acted to transform rebellious sinners into obedient saints.[63]

> *12Therefore, just as sin entered the world through one man, and death through sin, and in this way death came to all people, because all sinned—*
>
> *13To be sure, sin was in the world before the law was given, but sin is not charged against anyone's account where there is no law. 14Nevertheless, death reigned from the time of Adam to the time of Moses, even over those who did not sin by breaking a command, as did Adam, who is a pattern of the one to come.*
>
> *15But the gift is not like the trespass. For if the many died by the trespass of the one man, how much more did God's grace and the gift that came by the grace of the one man, Jesus Christ, overflow to the many! 16Nor can the gift of God be compared with the result of one man's sin: The judgment followed one sin and brought condemnation, but the gift followed many trespasses and brought justification. 17For if, by the trespass of the one man, death reigned through that one man, how much more will those who receive God's abundant provision of grace and of the gift of righteousness reign in life through the one man, Jesus Christ!*
>
> *18Consequently, just as one trespass resulted in condemnation for all people, so also one righteous act resulted in justification and life for all people. 19For just as through the disobedience of the one man the many were made sinners, so also through the obedience of the one man the many will be made righteous.*

This classic passage, frequently applied to original sin discussions, centers on the comparison between the effects of Adam and Jesus Christ on human destiny. The critical verses are 12, 18, and 19. The other verses are of less concern or redundant and will be discussed more briefly.

---

63. Ibid., 28.

Verse 12

One of the most debated verses is verse 12 and its four clauses. The verse is clear in 12a that sin entered the world through one man, and it is reasonably inferred that this one man is Adam.

Verse 12b states that death was the result of sin. This brings us to the first disagreement among commentators, which is what kind of death Paul is referring to. Sanday and Headlam think it is limited to physical death because of Paul's reference to physical death in verse 14 and his probable allusions to Genesis 2:17 and 3:19.[64] Douglas Moo suggests death's meaning is broader, including physical and spiritual.[65] Paul's reference to eternal life in verse 21 and his use of "condemnation" in verses 16 and 18 suggest his meaning is spiritual death. Moreover, Paul frequently uses the word "death" to include both physical and spiritual aspects—the total penalty due to sin. Physical death is just the outward expression of this total death. Thomas Schreiner agrees and refers to additional evidence suggested by Genesis 2:17, which states Adam will die "on the day," or soon following a transgression of God's command. Since Adam did not physically die on that day or even shortly after, the connotation is more than physical death. The death he likely experienced was spiritual, since he was immediately separated from God. His and Eve's hiding combined with their expulsion from the Garden suggest this.[66] It seems Schreiner and Moo's conclusions fit the context best. Paul doesn't seem too intent on emphasizing only one consequence for sin, but goes back and forth to highlight the various negatives sin has brought.

Verses 12c and 12d move on, saying that in this same way death comes to all, because all sinned. Moo and Cranfield see a chiasm[67] here:

> A sin enters the world (12a)
>   B death results from sin (12b)
>   B' all die (12c)
> A' because all sin (12d)

---

64. Sanday and Headlam, *Epistle to the Romans*, 132.
65. Moo, *Epistle to the Romans*, 320.
66. Schreiner, *Romans*, 272.
67. A chiasm is a literary technique used in the Bible and other ancient literature in which there are corresponding parallel statements. The first line parallels the last, the second the second-to-last, and so on. In our verse, A and A' are parallels and B and B' are parallels. If there is a single middle statement, it is usually the central point of the chiasm.

The meaning is that since sin is universal, then death is universal; all die because all sinned.[68] However, there has been great disagreement over the years as to the proper rendering of the last clause, especially the transliterated Greek phrase *eph' ho*. Cranfield lists and critiques the options that have been proposed by scholars:

1. In this way death came to all, *with the result that* all sinned. Cranfield believes this interpretation is difficult and forced and that the grammatical structure points to one of the other interpretations below.

2. In this way death came to all, *in whom (Adam)* they all sinned. This was Augustine's interpretation, basing it on what we know today was a Latin Vulgate mistranslation (in whom or in Adam). This interpretation is also unlikely because the first mention of Adam (one man) is too far back in the sentence to be referring to him. Another version of this interpretation uses *because of whom* in place of *in Adam*, but it suffers from the same critique.

3. In this way death came to all, *because in Adam* all sinned. This means all sinned collectively in Adam's first transgression. This interpretation highlights the parallel Paul uses between Adam and Christ, and this requires that since Christ alone is responsible for our salvation, Adam alone is responsible for our sin. We all sinned collectively in Adam's sin; his sin was ours. Cranfield counters that the parallel is not equal between the two and the best that can be said is that each produced far-reaching consequences for all persons that followed. Furthermore, Paul's use of the word for sin clearly refers to actual sins and does not fit well when trying to say we sinned in Adam's sin.

4. In this way death came to all, because all sinned *by imitating Adam*. This is unlikely because there is no grammatical evidence suggesting Paul meant to say we sin by imitating Adam. It negates the strength of the analogy of Adam and Christ and the solidarity of all persons with Adam we see in verses 18–19 and 1 Cor 15:22.

5. In this way death came to all, because all sinned *voluntarily in their own persons, but as the result of inheriting Adam's corrupt nature*. This interpretation states we sinned not only externally, but due to an internal depravity and corruption we inherited. We sin in solidarity with Adam and as a result of his transgression. Cranfield asserts that this interpretation weakens the existing parallel—Christ alone is responsible for our salvation and Adam alone is responsible for our sin. However,

---

68. Moo, *Epistle to the Romans*, 321. See also Cranfield, *Epistle to the Romans*, 274.

WHAT ARE THE CONSEQUENCES OF ADAM'S SIN?

as mentioned under number 3, the word Paul uses for sin refers to actual sins and it seems best to say that we all sinned voluntarily and the most likely reason is that we possess a corrupt nature. To Cranfield, this is the best interpretation.[69] It follows the general import of the Genesis account and agrees with later Jewish teachings about the cause of sin—Adam and individual humans both contribute to human death.[70]

Schreiner gives more credence to number 1 than Cranfield, a preference also favored by Joseph Fitzmyer, who championed that view. *Eph' ho* is then seen as a consecutive rather than a causal conjunction and thus can be translated as "upon the basis of which." In this case, the immediately preceding word "death" is the word the phrase is referring to. However, Schreiner notes that *eph' ho* is an idiom and need not point to any particular antecedent, as in 2 Corinthians 5:4, Philippians 3:12, and Philippians 4:10. He does not give up the connection, however. The context should determine the conclusion, and he believes the logical connection between the two propositions is expressed in something like, "On the basis of death entering the world through Adam all people sinned."[71] Schreiner believes "original death" is more the idea of this passage than original sin. Death is a power that reigns over us (Rom 5:14, 17) and ends in physical death. We are born separated from God (spiritually dead) due to Adam's sin. Our sins don't cause us to die; our spiritually dead state causes us to sin.[72] Option 1 is also the Eastern Orthodox view. Orthodox scholar John Romanides believes the grammar determines that *eph' ho* can only refer to death.[73] Likewise, Frank Matera concludes that the overall meaning of Romans 5:12 is that as a consequence of Adam's sin death spread to all humans. All subsequent human sin resulted from that death.[74] Schreiner also critiques Cranfield's preference for number 5, contending he squeezes in the idea of a corrupt nature behind the word "sinned." Whether referring to a corrupt nature or sins committed "in Adam," Schreiner notes that the word used for sin refers regularly to voluntary sins committed by people in their own persons. However, to suggest a Pelagian conclusion (number 4) goes too far for Schreiner.

---

69. Cranfield, *Epistle to the Romans*, 274–79.
70. Ibid., 280.
71. Schreiner, *Romans*, 273–74.
72. Ibid., 276.
73. Romanides, "*Original Sin According to St. Paul.*"
74. Matera, *Romans*, 127.

He believes verses 15–19 and the Adam–Christ parallel rule out this kind of conclusion.[75]

Moo, like Cranfield's interpretations 3 and 4, views *eph' ho* as a causal conjunction—"because." This is the most preferred interpretation by both the majority of commentators and modern English Bible translators, although other variations of "because" include "from which it follows," "with the result that," and "inasmuch as." Paul uses *eph' ho* in other epistles (2 Cor 5:4, Phil 3:12, and Phil 4:10) and it is best translated as "because" in those cases; it seems to fit the context of Romans 5:12, too.[76] Brendan Byrne agrees, believing that Paul's whole argument is that sin causes death and not vice versa.[77]

What can we conclude from Romans 5:12?

Dunn reminds us that the verse is too ambiguous to try to pull definitive conclusions out of it regarding the relation of Adam's sin, our sin, and death. He believes the verse would probably have been ambiguous to the Romans as well. The best we can do is conclude that death is the consequence of sin and all die because all sin. Death dominates because of Adam's sin and sin is perpetuated in all who follow him.[78] Moo reiterates this viewpoint since Paul says nothing about *how* Adam's sin led to the death of all or the connection between his sin and ours. The clear conclusion is that sin led to death for Adam and we have all repeated that scenario.[79]

Others remind us that Paul's purpose in Romans 5:12–21 is not to tell his readers anything new about Adam, but to emphasize the supremacy of Christ.

> [Paul's] attention is firmly centered on Christ, and Adam is only mentioned in order to bring out more clearly the nature of the work of Christ. The purpose of the comparison is to make clear the universal range of what Christ has done. Though Paul does elsewhere refer by implication to the glory which was Adam's before the fall (3:23), he is here concerned with Adam only as that man who has affected all other men disastrously but whose

---

75. Schreiner, *Romans*, 275.

76. Moo, *Epistle to the Romans*, 322. This conclusion is also that of Brown, *New International*, vol. 1, 1194.

77. Byrne, *Romans*, 183.

78. Dunn, *Romans 1–8*, 290.

79. Moo, *Epistle to the Romans*, 323.

effectiveness for ill has been far surpassed by Christ's effectiveness for good.[80]

This author's conclusion is similar to Moo and Dunn above. All Paul has said is that all die because all sin and Adam began the process. People do not sin expressly by imitating Adam since many who sin know nothing of Adam; they sin nonetheless. Paul does not discuss or hint at infants here, so the claim that these young persons, who are incapable of voluntary sins yet, and who still die, must therefore have some residual Adamic effect causing their death, is a moot point.[81] If Paul had wanted to directly implicate Adam in our sin he surely could have said so. His main point is otherwise—all sin leads to death. It seems a version of number 5 is most correct—*in this way death came to all because all committed actual sins* (implying voluntarily in their own persons).

Verses 13–14

Paul here is likely taking a side journey from his initial statement in verse 12. He continues, "*just as* sin entered the world through one man, and death through sin . . ." Many commentators believe he finishes his thought in verses 18–19, "*so also* one righteous act resulted in justification and life for all people." and the context suggests this is likely. In this aside, verses 13–14 remind the hearers that sin was in the world before the law of Moses existed. Paul made this plain earlier when he remarked that the Gentiles, who had no law, had the law written on their hearts and their consciences either approved or disapproved of their conduct (Rom 3:12–15). Therefore it is understandable why death reigned since there *was* sin, even if there was no written code on stone. Moo agrees that the law, in one form or another, is universal and when broken, leads to death. People before Moses consciously sinned, though not breaking an express command, which is called a "transgression." To the Roman audience this meant that even Gentiles, without the law (torah), could sin such that it led to death.[82] Moo's reasoning seems plausible.

---

80. Cranfield, *Epistle to the Romans*, 281.
81. Moo, *Epistle to the Romans*, note 58, 327.
82. Ibid., 330–32.

Verses 17–19[83]

Moo believes that the reigns of death and life noted in verse 17 have different characters—death is a fate and is not a consciously chosen condition, whereas life is experienced through human choice. God's gift of righteousness is for those who respond positively to God.[84] Dunn is not quite so deterministic, asserting that the participants in both Adam and Christ have a say in the matter.[85] Similarly, Byrne notes that the Adam/Christ parallel is not totally synonymous, requiring a positive human response to God's grace. Balanced with this is the responsibility for sin on the negative side since "all sinned" (v. 12d).[86] Byrne's point is critical since Paul has already stated that all died because all sinned. Moo seems to forget this viable option in his interpretation, going directly to the idea that death is a "fate" and not a choice, but does not provide any evidence to favor his conclusion. Taking verse 17 alone, one could value Moo's conclusion, but verse 12d adds the human participation side.

Paul adds two final comparison/contrasts of Adam and Christ in verses 18–19 and seems to finish the point he started in verse 12. Let's look at them:

18Consequently, just as one trespass resulted in condemnation for all people,	so also one righteous act resulted in justification and life for all people.
19For just as through the disobedience of the one man the many were made sinners,	so also through the obedience of the one man the many will be made righteous.

These two parallel verses are synonymous, saying the same thing in similar ways. An important key to their meaning is understanding Paul's use of "all" and "many." Moo argues that Paul's two uses of "all" in verse 18 do not mean these words describe a coextensive (the same) group of people. He believes all humans are "in Adam" according to verses 12d and 14, but only those who "receive the gift" are "in Christ" (v. 17). Likewise, in verse 19 all humans are made sinners by Adam's act being their act but only *believers* who choose Christ are made righteous by him.[87]

---

83. Verses 15–16 are elaborated on in vv. 17–19, so we limit our discussion to the latter passage.
84. Moo, *Epistle to the Romans*, 340.
85. Dunn, *Romans 1–8*, 295.
86. Byrne, *Romans*, 185.
87. Moo, *Epistle to the Romans*, 343–45.

Therefore, Moo believes in verse 18b that "justification and life for all people" refers to believers only, but admits that the text says "for all people." He defends his view by saying: 1) that Paul uses justification language only for those who have experienced it, 2) verse 18a describes all people as condemned and therefore the parallel is broken if justification is a mere "offer," 3) that Paul's point is that there can be an assurance of justification and life just as there is assurance of condemnation. Christ has not just made justification available, but has secured it for those who belong to Christ.[88]

There are weaknesses in Moo's assertions. First, he contends that "justification and life for all people" must refer only to believers since they have already experienced it. This is unlikely, for we know that justification and life are "*for* all people" (v. 18) (cf. John 3:16, 1 John 4:14, Rom 5:10) and not just for a select few. His premise is false. God wants the whole world to be justified and to experience eternal life. Second, Moo suggests the parallel is broken if justification is just an offer. However, this is the only way the parallel is maintained. If literally "all" are condemned and only those who respond are saved, *he* breaks the parallel. Third, he asserts there must be assurance for justification and life for those who belong to Christ. This is a true statement, but such assurance is not the subject of these verses; Moo is bringing in content that Paul does not address. If Moo wants to maintain the parallel, then all humans condemned by Adam's transgression are also saved by Christ's righteous act (universalism). Since Moo doesn't believe in universalism, his explanation is incoherent.

Schreiner agrees generally with Moo, adding that there is no reason to bring Adam into the parallel if people die only because of their own sin; the parallel is maintained if they die because of Adam's sin. But how is Adam's sin reckoned to all who follow him? Schreiner describes two views, the realist and representative. The *realist view* states when Adam sinned we were in a sense "in his loins," as Hebrews 7:9–10 suggests. When Adam sinned, we *really* sinned at the same time. The *representative view* suggests Adam functioned as the head of the human race and that whatever he did, he did as our representative. When he sinned we sinned in corporate solidarity with him; his sin was imputed to us. Schreiner believes the representative view best explains the text's repeated statement that Adam's one sin leads to death for all people.[89] However, his explanation merely gives a hypothetical "how" to Adam's effect and it suffers the same critique as Moo's above.

Schreiner attempts to counter several objections to his views. First, some objectors will say we should enter the world as Adam did and not

---

88. Ibid., 342–43.
89. Schreiner, *Romans*, 288–89.

begin by being alienated from God. Schreiner contends that we are all affected by the sins of our parents and ancestors and the doctrine of original sin is the only viable explanation to explain why sin is universal. Second, some say these verses teach universalism, since to be consistent in the parallel the "all" and "many" must refer to the same groups of people—all are sinners through Adam and all will be saved through Christ. Schreiner counters by referring back to verse 17 to echo Moo; that only those who receive the gift will reign in life. Like Moo, he also affirms that "all" and "many" are not the same across the parallel—those condemned are universal but those who are justified are those who belong to Christ.[90]

Let's evaluate Schreiner's responses to objectors. His first response includes premises and conclusions that are either weak or false. He argues that:

Premise 1: All are affected by the sins of ancestors.

Premise 2: All human beings enter the world in a state of spiritual death as descendants of Adam.

Conclusion 1: All people inevitably sin because they enter the world alienated from God (spiritually dead).

Conclusion 2: Only the doctrine of original sin satisfactorily explains universal sin.[91]

It is hard to deny Premise 1—experience teaches us that our parents' and ancestors' sins do negatively affect us, albeit in an indirect way. They don't directly *cause* us to sin or to be good—they *influence* us. Premise 2 has been shown to be weak throughout this whole chapter. Conclusion 1 is part of an unsound argument since the premises are suspect. Conclusion 2 goes beyond the parameters of his two premises. First, Premise 1 has to do with human influence. He claims, however, that original sin acts as a *cause*. His analogy doesn't fit (fallacy of a weak analogy). If he would make the case that parental and ancestral sins *influence* our moral acts and that original sin *influences* us toward sin, then that fits better with the scriptural evidence and is a better analogy. Second, Premise's 1 and 2 do not support that original sin is the *only* viable explanation for universal sin. *He hasn't dealt with any other contending explanations, so he cannot make the claim it is the only viable option!* This is the fallacy of *ignoratio elenchi* or *missing the point* (see Appendix).

90. Ibid., 290–92.
91. Ibid., 290.

There is other evidence against Conclusion 2. If a sinful nature acquired through original sin is the only explanation for 100 percent of people post-Adam sinning, then what is the explanation for 100 percent of people without a sinful nature sinning (as is the case of Adam and Eve)? Consider:

Percent of people born without any proposed sinful nature (Adam and Eve) who sin: 100%

Percent of people born with a proposed sinful nature (rest of humanity) who sin: 100%

Sin was already universal before the proposed original sin nature could take effect!

Schreiner's Conclusion 2 is contradicted by Adam and Eve's own experience—why did 100 percent of people without a sinful nature commit sins? Is it not likely that the reason they both sinned is the same reason the rest of us have sinned—we give in to temptation? Schreiner never considers this. All in all he has weak or false premises, which make Conclusions 1 and 2 also weak or false. Philosophically, his arguments are unsound. Conclusions 1 and 2 could still be true, but Schreiner has not made a good case for them. The reasonableness of these conclusions will be evaluated more fully by the end of this chapter.

Schreiner's counter to the second objection is also weak. He believes we are made sinners by Adam's act, he being our representative. This is a weak theological inference, is not denoted in Scripture, and is critiqued by many of the passages interpreted in the rest of this chapter. However, if he believes that doctrine, would he also conclude that if Adam *hadn't* sinned we would have inherited a pure standing before God, or Adam's righteousness? Would we then have possessed "original righteousness" by default and not "original sin"? Would it then be inevitable, since we possessed a pure nature, that we would be made righteous and incapable of sinning? If Adam was truly our deterministic representative, then the second option is just as viable. However, I doubt either Moo or Schreiner would swallow that conclusion. Even if they would, it doesn't prove their point; they are making up the representative idea to fit their theological system and not because they find it in Scripture.

There is also no justification for either Moo or Schreiner to claim that the words "all" or "many" do not refer to the same group of humans (are "coextensive"). Paul describes them as the same group. The burden of proof is on them and they provide no exegetical evidence for us to think of them differently. Their already questionable theological interpretation of verses 12–14 is their justification, which has been evaluated above. Mark

Rapinchuk also negatively critiques their view, noting that there are no contextual clues that change the scope of Paul's designation. The group affected by Adam's sin is the same one affected by Christ's act of righteousness. If all are condemned by Adam (original sin), then all are saved by Christ (universalism).[92] This is not a true conclusion, since we know all will not be saved. Then what does Paul mean? It seems more likely that *all who respond* to temptation like Adam will die, and as God promises, *all who respond* to God in faith and love are accepted, justified, and given life (as is affirmed in John 1:12, 6:37). This maintains the parallel without contradicting known facts.

Rapinchuk gives further evidence on the exact intent of Paul's use of "all" and "many." He makes a convincing case that they refer to "both Jews and Gentiles, without any ethnic distinction."[93] This has been Paul's point all along in Romans. The gospel is the power of salvation for Jew or Gentile, for all who believe (Rom 1:16). Likewise, both Gentiles (Rom 1:18–32) and Jews (Rom 2:1–5, 17–24) are sinners and will be judged by God (Rom 3:9). God is truly God of both (Rom 3:29, 10:12) and the promise is by faith to all (Jews and Gentiles, Rom 4:16, 9:6–8, 11:13–24). All have sinned (both Jews and Gentiles, Rom 3:23) and brought death on themselves (Rom 5:12, 11:32). Paul's point is that all, without ethnic distinction, have put themselves under the power of sin and death and all can freely partake of Christ's righteousness.[94] What is clearer is that inherited sin is not in view. Paul is describing sin's universal nature—it affects all peoples. He is not speculating about sin's transmission or imputation, and Rapinchuk believes scholars should reconsider seeing Rom 5:12–21 as an exposition on original or inherited sin. Such a position leads to hermeneutical wrangling on universalism.[95] His conclusion is a preferable alternative to Schreiner's and Moo's interpretation since it accounts for the universal wording Paul uses without divorcing it from human participation, which is another of Paul's emphases.

Dunn also discusses the parallelism of these verses. Are the "all" and the "many" universal? He believes Paul could not object if the Romans (and all who would read it thereafter) took these words to mean the whole human race, no matter which side is referred to. If that is the case, did Paul want his readers to believe that the members of each epoch (sinners or righteous) were made such before any choice on their part? Or, did he assume

---

92. Rapinchuk, "Universal Sin," 430.

93. For further distinction on how Paul uses the word "all" in Romans, see Rapinchuk, "Universal Sin," 434–36.

94. Ibid., 436–40.

95. Ibid., 440–41.

his readers understood that a choice must be made to enter each group? Dunn believes Paul's verb choice, which we translate as "made" or "appoint," is ambiguous. Paul might even have purposely chosen an imprecise verb to leave the link between the one act and the many's destiny unclear.[96] He concludes, "Here, as elsewhere, Paul refuses to be drawn into a more rigorously defined and consistent systematization of his theology, thus leaving space both for the diversity of opinion and the silence of agnosticism on more than one contentious issue."[97] It seems Dunn has taken a wise course by not making claims that some doctrine exists without a preponderance of evidence.

In light of this discussion, how should verses 18–19 be interpreted? The most plausible alternative, that is consistent with the context of Romans, seems that neither Adam nor Christ cause/coerce/constrain people into a spiritual condition of death or life. Adam is *the occasion* for the condemnation and death *of all* (both Jews and Gentiles). To experience these, we must personally sin, as Adam did before us.[98] Likewise, Christ is *the occasion* for justification and life *for all* (Jews and Gentiles). To experience life, we must enter a relationship with God by faith; we must receive the gift. Paul qualifies his absolute words in these verses with verses 12d and 17, and the parallel between Adam and Christ is affirmed. We need not resort to either condemning all humanity because of Adam's sin or saving them all through Christ's redemption, ideas which have considerable evidence against them.

Galatians 3:22–25 (cf. Rom 3:9, Rom 11:32)

> 22*But Scripture has locked up everything under the control of sin, so that what was promised, being given through faith in Jesus Christ, might be given to those who believe.* 23*Before the coming of this faith, we were held in custody under the law, locked up until the faith that was to come would be revealed.* 24*So the law was our guardian until Christ came that we might be justified by faith.* 25*Now that this faith has come, we are no longer under a guardian.* (Gal 3:22–25)

---

96. Dunn, *Romans 1–8*, 297.
97. Ibid., 298.
98. If condemnation occurs without our choice, then the fate of infants and the mentally/morally incompetent who die is likewise hellish. Both Schreiner and Moo do not follow their theological conclusions to their logical end, which is that if these persons should die in their current state, then Adam's sin condemns them eternally—they cannot make the choice to follow Christ as described in v. 17.

> 9 What shall we conclude then? Do we have any advantage? Not at all! For we have already made the charge that Jews and Gentiles alike are all under the power of sin. (Rom 3:9)

> 32 For God has bound everyone over to disobedience so that he may have mercy on them all. (Rom 11:32)

Several words in Galatians 3:22–25 have proved difficult for translators to decipher—Scripture, locked up, and everything—and the meaning of the whole passage hinges on the meaning of each. Schreiner suggests that since Paul's use of "Scripture" (singular) always contains reference to an individual verse, then Deuteronomy 27:26 is the likely referent of verse 22, which states that cursed is anyone who does not carry out the law. Schreiner believes "Scripture" personalizes God, connoting that God wills that all be imprisoned under sin. Sin can imprison because it is a power that wields its control over humans. Other scholars see it as a reference to the Scripture in general or to the law.[99] Fee thinks because there is no specific reference in sight that it is impossible to tell which it is. Further, Paul uses the law in general when he picks up the idea in the next verses, so it likely refers to the Scripture in general.[100] It seems Fee's conclusion is most probable.

"Everything" or "all things" can refer to persons or to the world and its powers at large. Longenecker thinks it refers to all people without distinction and that therefore this suggests the main function of the law was to bring everyone under its curse. The law brought or increased the knowledge and conviction of sin.[101] Fee sees it as likely meaning both Jews and Gentiles, as suggested by Romans 3:23 and 11:32.

"Locked up" is the verb used here, and Fee believes it is used in the sense of being "hemmed in by," referring to the work of the law to outwardly reign in those who were "under the control of sin." Now that faith in Christ has appeared (v. 22–23), that function of the law is not necessary. The law could not impart righteousness, but it was imparted through the promise to those who have faith in Christ. Fee believes the meaning of the whole metaphor is best understood by further verses, such as Galatians 4:3 and 4:8. Paul changes the metaphor to the slave/master form there and this helps us understand that before salvation his hearers were slaves under the elemental spirits of the world and slaves to gods who were not gods at all.[102] Romans 3:9 and 11:32 are also both still talking about Jews and Gentiles

---

99. Schreiner, *Galatians*, 244.
100. Fee, *Galatians*, 133.
101. Longenecker, *Galatians*, 144.
102. Fee, *Galatians*, 133–34.

together but use slightly different verb phrases—"are all under the power of sin" and "bound everyone over to disobedience" to convey the point that sin is universal and enslaving to both Jews and Greeks.

Fee's plausible conclusions counter adequately the views of some, like Schreiner, who see God willfully imprisoning everyone in sin! This imprisonment is frequently seen as a manifestation of original sin. In like manner, some interpreters use the first part of Romans 11:32 to say God unilaterally and by force condemns all of humanity. However, this is against his whole purpose—he does not wish to imprison us or force us all to be disobedient, but to free all from the penalty and power of sin. Others use Romans 11:32 in the opposite vein to make the point that since God has bound all over to disobedience he will then save them all ("he may have mercy on them all"), resulting in universalism. Both of these pendulum swings have been critiqued above in our discussion of Romans 5:18–19. The use of these verses as a defense for original sin is therefore unwarranted.

Ephesians 2:1–3

> *1As for you, you were dead in your transgressions and sins, 2in which you used to live when you followed the ways of this world and of the ruler of the kingdom of the air, the spirit who is now at work in those who are disobedient. 3All of us also lived among them at one time, gratifying the cravings of our flesh and following its desires and thoughts. Like the rest, we were by nature deserving of wrath.*

In Ephesians, Paul is writing to those in Ephesus and likely other cities in Asia Minor, so that they may better understand God's eternal purposes and the grace he has given them. The passage here reminds these Christians that they at one time were all spiritually dead because of their sins. Paul highlights the three temptations toward sin we mentioned in the beginning of this chapter—the world, the devil, and the flesh. Before becoming believers, the Ephesians supremely satisfied their fleshly desires and were like every sinner, "by nature deserving of [or destined for] wrath," or as some other modern translations put it, "by nature children of wrath."

The most common modern interpretation of this last phrase is that "by nature" signifies by birth. We have inherited this status (spiritual death) by being born.[103] Andrew Lincoln believes this phrase connotes the doctrine of original sin since it describes our innate Adamic sinful nature received

---

103. Arnold, C., *Ephesians*, 134.

as a consequence of the fall and therefore deserving of God's judgment and wrath.[104] Peter O'Brien concurs, describing our nature as the result of the three "evil, determining influences"[105] aforementioned. Although he uses the word "influences" (suggesting persuasive as opposed to coercive), he uses "determinative" with it, so it is unclear what the nature of these factors is for him.

The key word is "nature," a translation of the Greek word *physis*, which is frequently associated with physical nature, the origin of things, and the usual way something is.[106] The most likely meaning options from a theological dictionary would be:

1. By birth or physical origin.
2. A mode of feeling and acting which by long habit has become nature.
3. The sum of innate properties and powers.[107]

The phrase "by nature" is used three other times by Paul for: those who were "Jews by birth and not sinful Gentiles" (Gal 2:15, and suggesting definition 1 above), those gods the Galatians were slaves to, who "by nature [in reality] are not gods" (Gal 4:8, suggesting definition 3), "Gentiles, who do not have the law, do by nature things required by the law, they are a law for themselves, even though they do not have the law. They show that the requirements of the law are written on their hearts . . ." (Rom 2:14–15a, suggesting definition 2 or 3).[108]

If Ephesians 2:1–3 was the only passage describing how humans are "by nature," these three commentators' interpretation would be most likely. However, the other Pauline passages noted above betray other likelihoods. Paul uses "by nature" in Galatians 2:15 to actually distinguish that Jews were born with a *more privileged status* than Gentile sinners; they were born as the people of God, of the "natural" olive tree (Rom 11:21), with all the privileges that entailed (sonship, glory, covenants, law, worship, promises, patriarchs, Messiah; Rom 9:4–5). Therefore their "nature" is different from Gentiles, suggesting they were not created like Gentile "sinners" and counters the idea all are born sinners.

In Romans 2:14–15a, Paul describes a positive view of Gentiles, as possessing anti-sin qualities—they have the requirements of the law written

---

104. Lincoln, *Ephesians*, 99.
105. O'Brien, *Letter to the Ephesians*, 163.
106. Brown, *New International*, vol. 2, 656–57, 660–61.
107. Kittel and Friedrich, *Theological Dictionary*, vol. 9, 251.
108. Lincoln, *Ephesians*, 99.

on their hearts and can do "by nature" what the law requires! This sounds opposite of being born with an Adamic sinful nature. They have an inborn understanding of the law's requirements and can fulfill that law "by nature." This natural ability could reasonably refer to either definitions 2 or 3 above; in either case it mitigates against the Ephesians 2:1–3 interpretation of our three commentators.

Relatedly, Peter describes Christians as having received God's precious promises, through which we participate in the "divine nature" (*physis*), "having escaped the corruption in the world caused by evil desires" (2 Pet 1:4). No interpreters conclude that this divine nature causes us to be holy without the cooperation of our own person. We are not forever sinless because we are new creations and filled with God's divine Spirit. The sinful "nature" that is said to be from original sin, however, is described as being irresistible. Does this mean a nature foreign to Adam and Eve's created condition that allegedly became part of all humans is more powerful than God's new Spirit-creation inside us? This is the logical conclusion from such a theology. It seems more faithful to God's power and 2 Peter 1:4 that "nature" is not coercive.

Looking again directly at Ephesians 2:1–3, Meyer avers that the context points towards a produced and not an inborn state of guilt and sin. The passage speaks of transgressions (acts against the known law of God) and of living in a fleshly manner under the power of the world and the devil.[109] However a newborn, which according to original sin has a sinful nature, cannot transgress—a baby doesn't know the law of God and could not engage in the sins Paul describes in verses 1–3. Moreover, Paul affirms repeatedly that it is for actual sins that God's wrath falls[110] (godless truth-suppressors in Rom 1:18; immoral, impure, greedy, idolatrous, and disobedient in Eph 5:6; the sexually immoral in Col 3:6), not for being in a state inherited by birth.

These factors mitigate against the idea that Paul is saying here that people are destined for wrath by birth (original sin). His whole point is that the Ephesians, and everyone else, were dead because of their actual sins and transgressions. They had succumbed to the influence of the world, Satan, and the flesh; their way of life and identity were sinful (suggesting definition 2 above). The path they were on was destined for God's wrath.[111]

109. Meyer, *Ephesians 2:3*.

110. Ibid.

111. To mitigate the predicament of the newborn, some Christian groups baptize them in order to remove the sinful nature. However, is one's eternal fate dictated by the actions of one's parents? This is never witnessed in Scripture. Other theologians counter that God's grace covers these young ones' sinful status. However, there is no biblical

Hebrews 2:17

> 17For this reason he had to be made like them, fully human in every way, in order that he might become a merciful and faithful high priest in service to God, and that he might make atonement for the sins of the people.

The writer of Hebrews begins the book declaring Jesus's superiority over angels and the prophet Moses (chapters 1 and 3). In chapter 2 he remarks why Jesus had to share human form—so he could die their death and therefore free them from death (2:9, 14–15), suffer like they did, and therefore help them in their suffering (2:18). Verse 17 states Jesus had to be made like his brothers and sisters in every way. How complete was his identification with humanity? William Lane notes that the phrase "in every respect" is telling. It is emphatic and denotes Jesus's temptation and suffering were like ours, but it likely extends to encompass all qualities that make us truly human.[112] Peter O'Brien agrees, concluding that the verb "to be like" can be interpreted in a weakened sense, but because of the inclusion of "in every way," the likeness is complete. Giving more detail, Hebrews 2:14 says Jesus shared our flesh and blood nature and 2:17 notes that he shares our trying experiences. The only difference is seen in Hebrews 4:15, where Jesus is tempted in every way we are but never sinned.[113] Verse 17 suggests that the only way Jesus, as our high priest, could adequately represent us was to be just like us. To offer the sacrifice of atonement for our sins he had to embody both God and man.

How does this bear on original sin? Those who support the doctrine affirm that Jesus was like us *except* he didn't possess any inherited depravity.[114] However, the general declaration of complete "sameness" in these verses in Hebrews, and no mention of *not* being like us in any way, does not support this exception.

---

evidence this ever occurs. The witness of Scripture is that God condemns only those who sin, not those who are merely born. A further complication arises if we interpret this passage as referring to original sin. Like Romans 5:18–19 and 11:32, universalists will logically conclude that if Ephesians 2:1–3 speaks of original sin, to keep the parallel true, Eph 2:4–5 must mean all will be saved—"But because of his great love for us, God, who is rich in mercy, made us alive with Christ even when we were dead in transgressions—it is by grace you have been saved."

112. Lane, *Hebrews 1–8*, 64.
113. O'Brien, *Letter to the Hebrews*, 118–19.
114. Roman Catholics would expand this to include the Virgin Mary.

DIRECT AND INDIRECT CONSEQUENCES OF ADAM'S SIN

The foregoing biblical exposition suggests that there are both direct and indirect results of Adam and Eve's first sins.

Direct Effects of Adam's Sin

Genesis 3:14–24 revealed the direct consequences of the original couple's sin—curse of the serpent, human expulsion from the Garden of Eden, added pain in a woman's childbirth, a changed marital relationship, and a cursed ground with resultant wearisome toil. These consequences are obvious as we live in today's world.

Death is also frequently added as a consequence of the fall. The connection of sin and death is strong in the Bible, however the kind of death implied is not always clear. The concept of death for the biblical writers seems to be comprehensive, encompassing physical, spiritual, and eternal aspects, especially in the writings of the apostle Paul.[115] Some passages insinuate physical death (Rom 8:23, 1 Cor 15:54–55) and others spiritual death (1 John 3:14). The context determines the meaning.

The idea of a link between sin and death reaches back to the first book of the Bible. There is a hint in Genesis 3:19 that human mortality is included in the curse of the ground. God says to Adam, "By the sweat of your brow you will eat your food until you return to the ground, since from it you were taken; for dust you are and to dust you will return." Thus, human mortality seems to be a new condition now that Adam and Eve are expelled from the Garden.

One of the clearest links between sin and death is Romans 5:12–19, a passage that has already been discussed. We concluded that Paul's link between sin and death was less likely between Adam's sin and the spiritual death of all his progeny as between an individual's sin (Adam's and ours) and personal spiritual death.[116] The personal sin-death link was first mentioned in Genesis 2:17, where Adam and Eve were warned that if they eat from the forbidden tree they will surely die. Some translations use the phrase "in the day" you eat of it, suggesting the very same day. The Hebrew verb translated here suggests promptness of action,[117] but the emphasis is less on chronol-

---

115. Erickson, *Christian Theology*, 630.

116. If anything else could possibly be concluded from this passage, it is that Adam brought *physical* death to humanity by his transgression.

117. Wenham, *Genesis 1–15*, 68.

ogy than certainty. In other OT passages this same verb threatens physical death to individuals, who were known to live on after that day (1 Kgs 2:37, 42; Exod 10:28). What the form of the verb does convey more clearly is that it is God who will bring the death. The death, therefore, could be physical or spiritual.[118] Schreiner made an earlier case that the type of death experienced "on the day" is spiritual death, testified to by Adam and Eve hiding and clothing themselves out of guilt. This is possible, but whether it is delayed physical death or immediate spiritual death is difficult to determine. In either case the death sentence is directed toward Adam and Eve, and nothing is said in Genesis 2:17 about subsequent humanity.

A further nuance is that sin *deserves* death. The writer of Proverbs 10:16 remarks that "the wages of the righteous is life, but the earnings of the wicked are sin and death." Paul comes very close to the same wording in Romans 6:23. This seems to attach to the individual sinner and not to all humanity. There is no indication that we deserve death by being conceived or born. This concept of the individual bearing the guilt of personal sin was illustrated well by our discussion of Deuteronomy 24:16 and Ezekiel 18. It is only the soul that sins that will die. Similarly, James 1:15 states that death is the result of sin when it has become full-grown in a person's life. Sin is also associated with a life cut short; Psalm 55:23 avers that the wicked, who are bloodthirsty and deceitful, will live less than half their days. A link between the sin of Adam and the decay of the physical world is probably alluded to by Paul in Romans 8:20–22:

> *For the creation was subject to frustration, not by its own choice, but by the will of the one who subjected it, in hope that the creation itself will be liberated from its bondage to decay and brought into the freedom and glory of the children of God. We know that the whole creation has been groaning as in the pains of childbirth right up to the present time.*

The ground was cursed by God in Genesis, and apparently the creation as a whole will be liberated when the children of God are finally revealed.

In conclusion, there is evidence Adam's sin is linked to physical death and the physical decay in the creation. This connection with physical death could further explain the death of innocents, such as the preborn, infants, and the mentally challenged; they are not capable of sinning yet and experience the general fate of all humans. Any other direct consequences have meager support.

---

118. Hamilton, *Book of Genesis*, 172–74.

Theologizing on Adam's Sin and the Atonement

If the theory of original sin is to be believed, then there should be some indication that the direct consequences of Adam's sin on subsequent humanity were remedied by Christ's atonement. If: 1) original sin means we must commit actual sins due to an inherited sinful nature, and 2) we are guilty for his sin (according to some who espouse the theory), then there should be some answer to these problems through the atonement. However, it is nowhere stated that any purpose of the atonement was to undo the effects of Adam and Eve's sins on the rest of humanity. Some Christian divisions say baptism or entire sanctification removes original sin's effects, but they offer no convincing biblical support for this connection. There is also no mention of this issue with the OT sacrifices.[119] NT passages that discuss the purpose of the atonement do not discuss it (see John 1:29; Rom 1, 2, 5; 1 John 2:2, 3:8).

Furthermore, God has never asked any person to *repent* for the sin of Adam, only for his or her own sins (Jer 18:11; Mark 3:2; Acts 2:38). Likewise, God has never asked anyone to give an account for Adam's sin or has *judged them* for Adam's sin, only their own (Ezek 18; Matt 12:36; Rev 20:11–15). If original sin is as theologically important and far-reaching in its effects as proponents maintain, then there should be evidence of a remedy. Proponents are making a positive case, therefore there must be positive evidence. However, none is seen.

Indirect Effects of Adam's Sin

One thing is clear—since we are all now "east of Eden," we do experience the *indirect* effects of Adam's sin. This means we do not enjoy Eden's protection and therefore experience toil in working the ground for food, extra pain in childbirth, and distorted marriage relationship tendencies. We develop from infancy with our physical and emotional desires dominating.[120] Our parents likely met our physical needs whenever we cried; we were tuned into our own needs and wants and were not required to think of others. Our creature comforts were satisfied before we developed a concept of the

---

119. The substitutionary sacrifices described in Leviticus are for personal sins. The guilt transferred was the guilt for personal sins or the accumulated personal sins of Israel in general—not for Adam's sin (burnt offerings Lev 1:3–4, 16:21–22; sin offerings Lev 4:1—5:13, 6:24–30, 8:14–17, 16:3–22; guilt offerings Lev 5:14—6:7, 7:1–6).

120. If Adam and Eve had been obedient, and in that state raised children, would our self-oriented physical and emotional desires described here have been less? Probably, but the answer is unknown.

value of others and their needs/wants. When our wants conflicted with our parents or our brothers and sisters, our tendency was to meet ours first. That is the way human growth has been so far. This is not bad or evil, it is just the way life is. Moreover, many of us grew up in a family that was unchristian with a push toward looking after ourselves first. This is what we saw modeled and we assumed this was the way life should operate. If we grew up in a Christian family, life was better. We witnessed unselfish behavior more than not, and learned the importance of loving others.

No matter our family's Christian persuasion, in family life and school we discover others can be loving or unloving. For example, others sometimes make fun of us and we sometimes make fun of them. If we are the recipient, we feel hurt and wronged. If we were the perpetrator, our conscience bothers us and we feel guilty. On the other hand, if we see others behave in an unselfish, loving way, we see the benefits. If it is us, we frequently get respect or praise by helping others or doing what we know pleases others, especially those in charge. This makes us feel good; we sense this is the way things ought to be. All of the foregoing defends the idea that the effect of ancestors, parents, siblings, friends, others, social institutions, and culture on our decision-making is large. This description of the indirect effects of sin could be multiplied by many paragraphs and the effects seen in every person's life. These effects push us all toward sin.

The biblical writers sometimes refer to this negative influence of who and what is around is as "the world." This is the current worldly system dominated by sin and can include culture, social systems, and in general the negative influence from non-Christians. This idea is clearest in the Apostle John's writings. He describes it thus:

> *Do not love the world or anything in the world. If anyone loves the world, love for the Father is not in them. For everything in the world—the lust of the flesh, the lust of the eyes, and the pride of life—comes not from the Father but from the world. The world and its desires pass away, but whoever does the will of God lives forever.* (1 John 2:15–17)

John reminds us that this world is under the control of the evil one, Satan (1 John 5:19). Therefore James says we should not be friends with it (Jas 4:4) or allow ourselves to be polluted by it (Jas 1:27). Its friends are enemies of God. And, looking back, it was Adam and Eve who opened the door for it to enter God's paradise.

The Personal Consequences of Our Own Sin

The consequences for our own sins have been partially discussed above. Spiritual death is an obvious consequence; we are estranged from God and frequently from those around us. Isaiah illustrates this in his words to the Israelites in Isaiah 59:2: "But your iniquities have separated you from your God; your sins have hidden his face from you, so that he will not hear." Let's look at several other personal consequences.

Shame and Guilt

The consequence of separation, estrangement, and death is vertical (between us and God). Many consequences are horizontal (personal and social). For instance, like Adam and Eve, when our own sin looms in front of our minds, we seek to hide and cover up (Gen 3:7). This is internal shame and a sense of personal guilt. A frequent follow-up is blame—it's someone else's fault for what I did (Gen 3:12, 13); this is social.

The guilt that follows sin was even inherent in some of the Hebrew "sin" words we studied. For them, legal guilt is intricately tied in. James highlights this by declaring that he who offends the law in one point is guilty of breaking all of it (Jas 2:10). Again, this kind of guilt is legal—it carries a moral debt to God. The sin and guilt offerings of the OT dealt with such things and restored fellowship with God and with those who were sinned against. Thankfully, those in Christ are justified or declared "not guilty" because of his gracious atonement.

Restlessness and Trouble

Millard Erickson reminds us that the wicked live agitated lives. All of us can sympathize with this feeling. Sinners are internally uncomfortable and bring discomfort and agitation to those around them.[121] Isaiah says it so well: "But the wicked are like the tossing sea, which cannot rest, whose waves cast up mire and mud. 'There is no peace,' says my God, 'for the wicked'" (Isa 57:20–21). This lack of peace leads to weariness, sorrow, misery, and difficulties.[122] Adam and Eve's story has been discussed at length; they were banished from God's Garden and opened a Pandora's Box that the rest of us have had to deal with ever since. It was Jonah who brought trouble

---

121. Erickson, *Christian Theology*, 594.
122. Ibid., 595.

and calamity to himself, the sailors, and the ship he was on (Jonah 1:8). It was disobedient King Saul who brought trouble onto Israel (1 Sam 14:29). Arrogant King Amaziah brought distress on both himself and his nation, Judah (2 Kgs 14:10). Sin and betrayal tortured the soul of Judas, who finally hanged himself in his remorse (Matt 27:3–5), and Peter, who denied the Lord (Matt 26:69–75). We all bear self-inflected wounds that scar our lives, leaving sin-marks to be healed. Most of our stories also involve sins done against us. Sin surely brings pain and turmoil.

This general heading of "trouble" could be vastly expanded; it is a word that can encompass all the evil that results from sin. But for the purposes of this book a few examples will suffice. In every case, sin causes harm—Godward (death covered Godward harm, and sometimes provokes God to intervene directly to limit sin, punish it, or chastise the sinner; words that could go along with death are alienation, separation, loss of grace, or condemnation), personal, and frequently social. We can sin against our body (gluttony, sloth, any harmful drug usage, adultery) and irreparably harm our bodies, affecting quality and quantity of life, creating financial hardship, producing a bad stewardship witness, and distressing God's heart. If we lie, we neglect our conscience, produce guilt, and harm our reputation when the lie is found out. Lies breed lack of trust from others and harm them when they act on our un-truths. Adultery does similar things—it deeply wounds a life-long bond, leads to guilt—both real and false, breaks up families, frequently provokes financial hardship, jades children's respect for marriage, damages reputations, and so on. Spiritual apathy or lukewarmness lulls people to accept a substandard relationship with God and thwarts God's attempt to mature them. Prayers are ineffective and desire for God wanes; evangelism and discipleship seem optional. Family, children, and others who observe us may be tempted to think this is the normal Christian life and be tempted to follow the pattern. All the while God is ready to spit them out of his mouth (Rev 3:14–19)!

A Hardened Heart and Bondage

If we leave sin unchecked in our lives, we discover it becomes harder and harder to resist and easier and easier to succumb to its desires. If we eventually do wish to turn to God, the journey can be very difficult. How does a hard heart develop? The proverb that says, "sow an act, reap a habit, sow a habit, reap a character, sow a character, reap a destiny," is an illustration of the same truth found in James 1:14–15, ". . . but each person is tempted when they are dragged away by their own evil desire and enticed. Then, after desire has conceived, it gives birth to sin; and sin, when it is full-grown, gives birth to death." A hard heart begins with the thought that whatever sin offers is better than what God does. Sin entices and promises to deliver what will satisfy, but its pleasures are fleeting and incomplete. The "having" is not nearly as good as the "wanting" or the "anticipating." Contentment and fulfillment seem just out of reach, so greater and greater sinning ensues, leading only to disillusionment and bondage. All the while sin has quietly calloused the heart; God's voice has become harder to hear, less important, and less relevant. It is no wonder, then, that the Greek words used to describe this hardness, *sklērynō* (5020), *pōrōsis* (4800), and *pachynō* (4266) suggest "impenetrable, insensitive, blind, and un-teachable." These mind states do not develop overnight, but are the result of habitually neglecting the conscience and the voice of God.[123] This condition is possibly the condition Paul was in when he seemed to self-describe his difficulties with sin in Romans 7:14–23.[124] Paul sees a law of sin warring against the law of his mind, bringing him into captivity. Jesus declared that those who commit sin are *slaves* to sin (John 8:34). One is reminded of Charles Dickens's *A Christmas Carol*, where Jacob Marley staggers under the heavy chains hanging from his neck as he confronts Ebenezer Scrooge's own hard heart. Marley fashioned each link himself, one by one, until he had forged a ponderous length.

This pattern is not new. In the OT, God allowed the Israelites to divorce because their hearts had become hard (Matt 19:8). It was a concession—he worked with the people he had. King Zedekiah hardened his heart (became stiff-necked) toward the Lord. He wouldn't listen to Jeremiah the prophet and as a result, the leaders, priests, and people defiled themselves with idols (2 Chr 36:11–14). All this occurred between age twenty-one and thirty-two (Zedekiah's years of reign). One need not be old to have a hard heart!

Though not meaning the same, it was "hard" for the rich man to enter the kingdom of heaven (Matt 19:23). It was difficult because his heart was already filled with seemingly more important things—power, wealth, possessions, ease. It is difficult for the gospel to break through an exterior that is so preoccupied, so "hardened" to anything else. We can think of our own modern-day examples—in our own lives or those we have observed.

---

123. Ritenbaugh, "What Sin Is," 6–7. Although this author is not in the mainstream of Christian doctrine (a World-Wide Church of God offshoot), his comments on this subject fit a biblical model. To reject his insights would be committing the *ad hominem* (in regard to the person [instead of the argument]) fallacy. Specifically, "poisoning the well," which centers on the trustworthiness of the person making the statement instead of the statement itself. See Appendix.

124. These verses will be discussed in greater detail in chapter 4.

Similarly, there are those who neglect God and therefore don't know anything about him. Frequently, when queried, they admit their ignorance, but when given the opportunity to know more about this God and to know him, they do not care to! It is hard to appeal to them because they are happy in their ignorance. Ignorance has led to a version of hardness. It often takes a crisis to break the crust of their heart and expose a window of opportunity for God to penetrate.

Likewise, Paul reminded the Ephesians that the hardness of Gentiles' hearts led to ignorance (Eph 4:17–19). Their "understanding was darkened" because there was a loss of sensitivity (apparently to what is right and wrong). This led to grosser forms of sexual impurity and greediness—a real downward spiral! This trend was borne out in the nation of Israel, whom God and his servants called "stiff-necked" nineteen times in Scripture. Therefore *they wouldn't listen* (remained in willful ignorance, 2 Kgs 17:14; Neh 9:29) and *forgot* the miracles God did for them (Neh 9:16–17). Is this not the trend of those who turn away from wise parents or good counselors—they refuse to listen to good advice and forget the good that has been done for them?

If left unchecked, sin can lead to eventual apostasy and hell. Eli's sons, Hophni and Phineas, had become so stubborn (scoundrels, 1 Sam 2:12) in not fulfilling their duties as priests that the only recourse was for God to kill them (1 Sam 2:25); they were living out the proverb of swift destruction (Prov 29:1). Such was also the fate of Pharaoh. We see in Exodus that he already had developed a hard heart when God hardened it further and used him to bring judgment on himself and the Egyptian nation (Exod 7–14). It appears there was then no more hope for Pharaoh; his only usefulness to God was as an instrument of judgment and as an object lesson for Israel of what not to become.

Paul warned the Romans about the sins of idolatrous and wicked Gentiles whom he gave over to their sexual desires, homosexuality, greed, and many other vices (Rom 1:29–31). Without repentance they were surely headed for hell. The writer of Hebrews even warns Christians: "See to it, brothers and sisters, that none of you has a sinful, unbelieving heart that turns away from the living God. But encourage one another daily, as long as it is called 'Today,' so that none of you may be hardened by sin's deceitfulness" (Heb 3:12–13). He later warns that eternal destruction is not the fate of pagans only; Christians need to guard their hearts:

> *It is impossible for those who have once been enlightened, who have tasted the heavenly gift, who have shared in the Holy Spirit, who have tasted the goodness of the word of God and the powers of the coming age and who have fallen away, to be brought back*

> to repentance. To their loss they are crucifying the Son of God all over again and subjecting him to public disgrace. Land that drinks in the rain often falling on it and that produces a crop useful to those for whom it is farmed receives the blessing of God. But land that produces thorns and thistles is worthless and is in danger of being cursed. In the end it will be burned. (Heb 6:4–8)

Direct Influences of Our Sin on Others and Others' Influence on Us

Human-to-human influence is very potent and some of this influence was discussed as an indirect result of Adam and Eve's sin (an effect of the "world"). It becomes direct when the source is face-to-face—the people we rub shoulders with. Jesus especially warned his disciples about leading others away from him. He told them, "If anyone causes one of these little ones—those who believe in me—to stumble, it would be better for them to have a large millstone hung around their neck and to be drowned in the depths of the sea. Woe to the world because of the things that cause people to stumble! Such things must come, but woe to the person through whom they come" (Matt 18:6–7)! Eve led Adam astray. Cain killed his brother Abel. Leaders, priests, and kings led Israel off target. Delilah instigated Samson's downfall. We ourselves may be guilty of nudging others toward sin and we all likely can think of instances where others pushed us away from God and toward something evil. Many of us bear the marks of dysfunctional families and neighborhoods. Certainly we humans have great impact on each other and sometimes that impact is toward sin.

CONCLUSION

This chapter's study denotes that the source of sin is neither outside the person nor in an irresistible "something" within us.

This extensive biblical survey and analysis warrants several conclusions:

- There is insufficient support for a negative deposit (original sin) in our persons from Adam. Adam and Eve certainly were the first human sinners and in that sense they are original. They did "fall" in the sense of disobeying an express command of God. However, there is scant evidence for any deposit from them within us that forces us to sin or evidence that we are held guilty for Adam's sin.

- We did not lose our faculties when Adam and Eve sinned. Our willing, thinking, and feeling functions are still intact, though negatively affected.
- It is a reasonable inference that innocents (infants and the mentally incapable) are not morally accountable.
- Actual sinning begins in our youth.
- Persons are responsible only for their own sins and not for those of ancestors or children.
- Once humans sin they become guilty, lose their relationship with God, and become spiritually dead.[125]
- A direct result of Adam's sin is physical death, likely affecting all humanity.
- Indirect effects of Adam's sin are the negative influence of the world and a greater opportunity for Satan to work.
- Our personal sins harm our own selves and negatively affect those around us.
- The sins of others influence us toward sin.

Though some of the conclusions of those who hold to original sin are warranted, our study concludes the following must be rejected:

- Either in reality or as our representative, Adam's sin is our sin. When he fell, we all fell and became sinners. His sin resulted in all his posterity's spiritual death.
- We are guilty for the sin of Adam.
- Humans are unable to respond positively toward God and the gospel.
- Innocents are either: 1) held guilty for original sin, 2) not held guilty when baptized, or 3) not held guilty due to an *ad hoc* administration of God's law.

---

125. This view does not demand that the first moral act of a child be sinful. The fact of universal sin only admits that all humans sin and it does not dictate when that sin must occur.

Philosophical/Theological Analysis—Why would God subvert his own Kingdom?

We know that God is *love*; he creates only good things and loves those in his image. His plan was for all to love him supremely and their neighbor as themselves. He wanted his creatures to become sons and daughters who knew, loved, obeyed, worshipped, and became like him in character. Because of that love, God's goal throughout human history has been to forgive, reconcile, redeem, adopt, and transform us. This thread runs through the promise of the rainbow, the Abrahamic promises, the Mosaic Covenant, the Davidic Covenant, and supremely in the New Covenant. Another inherent attribute of God is *holiness*. God always follows the "right" course of action. He therefore wants those made in his image to be "right" like him—to be holy because he is holy. We also know that God is *free*—he can do whatever he wishes within the constraints of his own character. We humans also have a degree of freedom, a freedom to choose to love God or not, to serve our neighbor or ourselves supremely, and to make other moral and amoral choices. God's freedom means he could have chosen whatever consequences he wanted for the sin of humanity. At the extremes, he could have chosen to destroy every person at sin number one (he almost did destroy humanity several times, but he rejected that as a solution), or at the other extreme he could have forgiven everyone for every sin regardless of repentance, faith, or an atonement (he did not choose that solution either). What consequences *did* fulfill his plan? First, he punished sin, discouraged it, and ultimately separated all who willfully remain in sin to a place away from his presence (hell). He revealed his true character through the wonderful universe he has made and the lengths he went to show his creatures love—a humbling substitutionary atonement. Considering God's love, holiness, and freedom, is it likely he cursed (or allowed Adam to directly curse) his creatures with an irresistible sin-ward force that caused them to do the exact opposite of what he wanted them to do—which is to exude love and holiness? No, this is not consistent with God's character. It would remind one of a kingdom divided against itself. Jesus rejected such an idea when he challenged the Pharisees charge that he was driving out demons by the power of Satan (Matt 12:22–28). If driving out Satan by the power of Satan makes no sense, then driving out God by the power of God (the same as ordaining or allowing ungodliness to forcibly rule his creatures) makes just as little sense! If God freely chooses that we will all possess an irresistible sinful nature, which forces us to obey Satan and our sinful desires as a consequence for the first human sins, then God surely seems to be creating a divided kingdom—a kind of kingdom that Jesus acknowledged would not stand! In this situation

God is guiltier for human sin than humans are, since this indwelling sin is described as the root of all actual sin. This argument is philosophical and not scriptural, but it appears to be a strong analogy. The doctrine of original sin fails both the test of Scripture and the test of God-given reason.

HISTORICAL INTERACTION WITH THE CONCEPT OF ORIGINAL SIN

This chapter's conclusions show agreement and disagreement with traditional original sin dogma, depending on which tradition is referenced. The most agreement is with Judaism, Anabaptism, the Stone-Campbell movement, and some aspects of Eastern Orthodox thought. The agreements include the idea that: 1) the only direct result of Adam's sin is physical death, 2) there were indirect consequences to Adam's sin—the presence of sinful persons and institutions that influence us toward sin (the world) and a greater ability for Satan to use worldly influences to entice persons to sin, 4) the image of God remains intact post-Adam, implying that humans can still choose between good and evil, but also acknowledging the harm done to it by personal sins and sins against us, 5) humans are not held guilty for Adam's sin.

There are disagreements with some tenets of Roman Catholicism and Wesleyan-Arminianism Protestantism and most of Reformed Protestantism. This chapter disagrees with their idea that: 1) Adam's sin resulted directly in spiritual death or separation from God for all subsequent humanity, 2) this separation included a sinful nature/depravity such that this constrains the human will to commit actual sins, 3) the image of God is lost in all post-Adam humans, 4) the nature of Adam's negative effect is through either a realist or representative model, 5) humanity is held morally guilty for Adam's sin. This chapter's conclusions also differ from many modern theologies, which hold that Adam and Eve were not historical persons and therefore could not directly or indirectly affect humanity.

4

What Are Fleshly Desires and How Do They Relate to Sin and Original Sin?

CHRISTIAN TRADITION, BASED ON biblical foundations, says that the three enemies of the soul are the world, the flesh, and the devil. The question of this chapter concerns one of these three, the flesh, or sin-ward evil desire, especially as these words are used by Paul and Peter. Several key questions regarding fleshly desires will occupy us in this chapter. How are these desires acquired and/or developed? How do they operate; what is their nature? Do they act as influences or causes in the non-Christian? In the Christian? Can they become weaker or stronger? (i.e., Can they be greatly weakened in the Christian's life as he or she progresses in Christlikeness and holiness? Can they become stronger through repeated indulgence?) Do they have a relationship to sin and original sin? We will pursue all these important questions in this chapter.

OLD TESTAMENT USES AND WORD STUDY

The OT writers rarely address the area of sinful desires. However, a significant example precedes the first human sin. Genesis 3:6 states:

> When the woman saw that the fruit of the tree was good for food and pleasing to the eye, and also desirable for gaining wisdom, she took some and ate it. She also gave some to her husband, who was with her, and he ate it.

Hamilton remarks that the tree had three appeals. It was good for food, pleasing or delightful to the eye, and desirable for attaining wisdom. The most desirable trait for Eve appears to be wisdom. She wanted it, didn't think she possessed it, and thought it would make her happy.[1] She knew God told her not to eat from the tree, but in her mind the benefits outweighed the negative consequences. Wenham notes that the Hebrew words used here for "pleasing" and "desirable" are from the same roots that mean "to covet" (*chāmad*).[2] Later, Eve's and everyone else's covetousness is addressed by the tenth commandment—"You shall not covet . . ." So, it appears the desire for what is against God's commands or represents an improper/sinful desire *precedes any original sin* and sounds similar to the desire James said led to sin in James 1:14–15, discussed below. Adam and Eve were able to resist these desires, but didn't.[3]

The Hebrew word *ta'wâ* also refers to a desire or craving that can be evil. While wandering forty years in the wilderness the Israelites gave in to their "cravings" and put God to the test (Ps 106:14). Proverbs 21:25–26 instructs that, "The craving of the sluggard will be the death of him, because his hands refuse to work. All day long he craves for more, but the righteous give without sparing." These are desires for ease and for more and more material things.

NEW TESTAMENT USES AND WORD STUDY

The NT describes evil desires much more frequently. James affirms that when we are tempted we are enticed and dragged away by "evil desires." When indulged, these desires lead to sin (Jas 1:14–15). The Greek word used by James for these evil desires is *epithymia* (n., 2123). This noun usually refers to evil desires (35 of 37 uses), as in James's usage, and almost always with Paul and Peter. Jesus used it several times negatively. In the parable of the sower, it is the evil desire for other things that chokes the sown word (Mark 4:19) and the lustful look that equals adultery (Matt 5:28). These evil desires flow from an evil heart (Mark 7:18–23, Luke 6:45). John portrays fleshly desires as coming from the world (1 John 2:16) and the devil (John 8:44). John sees that the human, worldly, anti-God way of life

---

1. Hamilton, *Book of Genesis*, 190.

2. Wenham, *Genesis 1–15*, 75. The Hebrew word *chāmad* (2773) can refer to proper delight or improper covetousness, lust, or desire. See Goodrick and Kohlenberger, *Strongest NIV*, 1405.

3. They were given a direct command by God to obey, had not experienced sin, and were only tempted by the serpent.

and the devil work in concert. They both pull a Christ-follower away from God and toward the indulgence of a worldly or fleshly lifestyle, a lifestyle that deceivingly promises true life. But Satan has always been a liar and a murderer (John 8:44) and those who follow this path are deceived and will die, separated from God. The verb form (*epithymeō*, 2121) is used sixteen times and is used for mostly good, but sometimes evil desires.[4] Jesus used it in a good way, referring to his desire to eat the Passover meal with his disciples (Luke 22:15). Paul says that he who desires to be an overseer desires a good work (1 Tim 3:1). Negatively, the flesh desires what is contrary to the Spirit (Gal 5:17). James told Jewish Christians in the Diaspora that because they "wrongly desire" things and don't get them, that they kill, quarrel, and fight (Jas 4:1–3).

Paul and Peter use these Greek words most frequently. Paul instructs the Roman Christians that they were not to let sin's evil desires rule their mortal bodies (Rom 6:12). In 1 Corinthians, the nation of Israel was a negative example so that the Corinthians would see Israel's errors and not "set their hearts on evil things" (1 Cor 10:6). Peter told Gentile and Jewish believers that they were not to conform to the evil desires they had when they lived in ignorance (1 Pet 1:14); they were to be holy. Later, Peter gives another exhortation to abstain from them since they wage war against the hearers' souls (1 Pet 2:11). Suffering can help, since those who suffer have mortified evil human desires (1 Pet 4:1–2). Moreover, by applying God's promises believers can escape worldly evil desires (2 Pet 1:4). Contrarily, false teachers, who despise God and his truth, follow their own fleshly, corrupt desires and encourage others to also (2 Pet 2:10–18). These types of people will be especially prevalent in the last days (2 Pet 3:3, Jude 16, 18).

These passages that use *epithymia* and *epithymeō* suggest several conclusions. One, both believers and unbelievers are affected by evil desires. Two, they can be resisted. Three, the Christian can substantially overcome them, suggesting they can become weaker as Christian maturity develops. Four, evil desires appear more like influences than causes since there is significant human participation and there are frequent commands to believers to resist them.

WHAT IS THE FLESH?

Paul connects the idea of evil desires to a word with a similar meaning—the "flesh," using the Greek words together to describe the evil desires of the flesh (*epithymian sarkos*) as opposed to the Spirit (Gal 5:16–17). The Greek

---

4. Brown, *New International*, vol. 1, 457.

word behind this English translation of "flesh" is *sarx*, translated by most modern Bibles as "flesh" and sometimes as "sinful nature" (NIV). It is used mostly by Paul and Peter and frequently carries a negative connotation, signifying a sin-ward desire or bent. In several places Paul uses an apparent synonym, the "old self," to describe this tendency. Theologians in the various Christian traditions habitually tie the origins of the flesh to original sin, inherited from Adam, and this is one reason this word is of special importance to our study.

Students of Paul quickly notice that he uses *sarx* to mean several different things.[5] The first four meanings listed below are not as germane to our discussion as the last two—worldly values and a rebellious human nature. However, to get a feel for Paul's varied use of the term, we explain all the meanings.

1: Physical Matter

The context for this meaning suggest Paul means the physical or material part of living humans or animals. For instance, he speaks of the flesh of humans, animals, birds, and fish (1 Cor 15:39) and humans as "flesh and blood" (1 Cor 15:50).

2: The Human Body

Sometimes Paul uses *sarx* as a synonym for *sōma* (body). A man who unites with a prostitute becomes one body (*sōma*) with her and the two are now one flesh (*sarx*, 1 Cor 6:16). Flesh is contrasted with spirit (2 Cor 7:1) and can suffer physical ailments (Gal 3:13–14).

3: The Human Person or Human Race

In several instances Paul uses this word to refer to persons, since it is a person whom God declares righteous (Rom 3:20) and who is not justified by works of the law (Gal 2:16). In the same way the gospel of Matthew states that no one (person) would survive if tribulation would not be cut short (Matt 24:16). Paul describes the nation of Israel as those of his own race (Rom 9:3, 5, 8).

---

5. Hawthorne, et al., "Flesh." These authors describe the following six Pauline uses of *sarx*.

4: Morally Neutral Human Relationships

He uses *sarx* to refer to human life and earthly affairs in general: "the life I now live in the body" (Gal 2:20); "in the body" (Phil 1:22, 24).

5: Morally Negative Worldly or Human Values and Standards

Paul reminds the Corinthians they were not wise by "earthly" or human standards (1 Cor 1:16) and that he didn't live by the standards or values of this world (*kata sarka*, 2 Cor 10:2). These things have human as opposed to godly origins.

6: Rebellious Human Nature

This is Paul's most common use of *sarx* and is found predominantly in Galatians 5–6 and Romans 7–8. For Paul, the acts of the flesh are obvious and include things like "sexual immorality, impurity and debauchery, idolatry and witchcraft, hatred, discord, jealousy, fits of rage, selfish ambition, dissensions, factions and envy, drunkenness, orgies and the like" (Gal 5:19–21). So, it appears these desires take many directions—sexual deviance, religious or worshipful deviance, relational discord, unloving internal thoughts and attitudes, and lack of emotional and bodily control. Colin Brown summarizes that these fleshly desires and acts are of the human self that has given "himself up to his own aims in opposition to God's."[6] It appears then that fleshly desires have led to fleshly acts and to a mindset that is actively against God.

Jewish Paul and the Flesh

The concept of an evil inclination is not new, as we remember that the Jewish rabbinic tradition used the concepts of the *yetzer hatov* (a good inclination) and the *yetzer hara* (an evil inclination). This Jewish idea was not explicit in the OT (its evil side was suggested by Gen 6:5 and 8:21). This teaching developed over time and was present in rabbinic circles at the time of Paul, so Paul would certainly have been aware of it.[7] Is there a relation between this Jewish concept and Paul's use of the "flesh"? W. D. Davies thinks Paul's experience in Romans 7 is probably his fight with his *yetzer hara*, or

---

6. Brown, *New International*, vol. 1, 676.
7. Davies, *Paul and Rabbinic Judaism*, 21.

flesh, which is a manifestation of the heart. Paul, like the rabbis, would have believed sin's power was external but it comes to dwell in the physical flesh and encourages the mind to be set on the flesh (the *yetzer hara*). Davies believes that Paul's apparent self-description likely refers to three time frames in his life or the life of any Jew: 1) A period of innocence during which he was ignorant of the Law (vv. 8–9). 2) An awareness of sinfulness and a lack of power over it. He knows and desires what is right but cannot do it (rest of chapter 7). This is thought to occur at the "age of commandment" or *bar mitzvah*, when a male Jew is expected to obey the commandments. 3) Deliverance from sin through the Spirit (v. 25, chapter 8).[8]

Other scholars see Romans 7 as referring to Israel or to Christians (see the discussion below), but the idea that evil desires lead to sin is the same. Moreover, Paul uses other phrases that seem to be picturesque synonyms for this *yetzer hara*, or flesh—"sin, the old self, the sinful body, this body subject to death, law of sin, mind governed by the flesh, live according to the flesh." Likely this was because there were no good Greek equivalents for *yetzer hara* and it took several Greek phrases to catch the full meaning.[9] Paul's preference for locating the sin-ward tendency in a word that is also used for the body likely reflects the Jewish idea that the *yetzer hara* was present at birth and it sprang to greater life at the *bar mitzvah*. It had a thirteen-year head start and had time to invade all a young person's members, as well as be in the heart.[10]

HOW POWERFUL ARE EVIL DESIRES AND THE FLESH? ROMANS 6-8

A pivotal passage that can help answer our chapter's questions is Romans 6–8. Here Paul instructs the Jewish and Gentile Christians on the law, sin, the flesh, and overcoming sin in the Spirit. In these chapters Paul highlights the strength of fleshly desires by personifying them as a power he calls "sin."[11] He told the Romans that sin used to be their master, but now they

8. Ibid., 23–25.
9. Ibid., 25–26.
10. Ibid., 27.
11. Dunn, *Theology of the Apostle Paul*, n. 120, 125. As Dunn notes, Paul typically uses a kaleidoscope of metaphors for what he is trying to communicate, which are not exactly alike and not exactly like their referent (otherwise they wouldn't be metaphors!). Dunn does not see the flesh as acting as a principle or power. To him, sin abuses the flesh for its own ends. When one lives "according to the flesh," one's highest objective is the satisfaction of human desires and appetites. See Dunn, *Theology of the Apostle Paul*, 67–68.

have offered themselves as obedient slaves to God (Rom 6:14, 16–18). Similarly, later in chapter 7, sin or the "law of sin" is personified as an enemy that used the Mosaic law to deceive and kill him (7:11). Paul, using the pronoun "I," is sold as a slave to sin and is now not the one who does evil, but it is sin itself in him. He wants to do good and in his mind delights in God's law, however the "law of sin" is his master and uses his flesh to make him a prisoner (7:11, 14, 17, 21–23). How strong is this power of sin? That question will be answered more fully at the end of the chapter, but Dunn sees it as "a compulsion or constraint which humans generally experience within themselves or in their social context, a compulsion towards attitudes and actions not always of their own willing or approving. . . . [Sin] draws men and women back from the best and keeps causing them to miss the target."[12]

Romans 7:5–25

Related to this whole discussion, debate has continued over many years regarding Paul's meaning in a specific passage in Romans 6–8, Romans 7:5–25. As we've seen, Paul uses the personal pronoun "I" when describing the struggle with the law and sin. Several questions emerge after reading this passage. First, is he referring to himself, using himself as a hypothetical or dramatic example, or using himself as a synecdoche?[13] Second, if he is referring to himself, is it before his conversion or after? Third, depending on one's answer to the first two questions, what does Paul mean by this passage and what does this imply about the Christian's ability to overcome sin?

Several scholars see this passage as referring to Paul post-conversion. J. I. Packer identifies this interpretation as coinciding with many pillars of the faith—Augustine, Luther, and Calvin. Packer believes Paul is not describing his total moral failure. Even though he claims he is a "wretched man," he is not as bad as he could be but is not as good as he should be. His inability to be a better Christian troubles and distresses him. This attitude is the mark

---

12. Ibid., 112. Dunn uses certain words here—"compulsion, constraint, causing" without defining their nature. Does sin act, referring to our definitions, as a *cause* or an *influence*? He seems to think it is a cause. Dunn also notes that Paul does not say where this sin-power came from. It entered the world when Adam sinned (Rom 5:12) but the guilt for sin only results from conscious and deliberate disobedience of a known command (Rom 5:13, 7:9). See Dunn, *Theology of the Apostle Paul*, 113.

13. A synecdoche, often used in biblical poetry, substitutes a representative part of a whole for the whole. Frequently in the OT, cities or tribes are used to represent Israel (or later, both Israel and Judah). Sometimes body parts (feet, arms, lips) are used to represent the whole person. See Duvall and Hays, *Grasping*, 358. In this particular use, the theory is that Paul uses "I" to represent the whole of humanity.

of a healthy believer who realizes that however good he or she is, there is still indwelling sin throughout this life. Complete deliverance awaits Christ's second coming and the "redemption of our bodies" (8:23).[14] James Dunn agrees that this struggle with sin is still a part of Paul's experience. He is a divided "I," inasmuch as his mind wills the good but sin enslaves the fleshly "I." The combination of the law, flesh, and sin doom the willing "I" to failure. Paul's use of the present tense in 7:14–25 and especially in 7:25b indicates this is an ongoing experience. It is the tension of the "already and not-yet"; Paul has the present experience associated with salvation (already, 7:4–6) but still has the fleshly "I," which is enslaved by sin (7:14, 23). He awaits the final deliverance from sin, the resurrection of the body (the not yet). Until then he is still under the power of sin.[15] C. Cranfield asserts that Paul uses the first person present in this passage to add rhetorical vividness and to refer to humanity in general (himself included) and not any specific group. Paul is being both autobiographical as well as presenting the experience of Christians in general, even the best and most mature.[16] Verse 14 admits that Christians are carnal, but not in the sense of an unbeliever. Because of this carnality, even though the human will wants to do good, sin is in control and the will is not able to carry out the good (vv. 17–18). If a Christian does come near to accomplishing something good, the effort is still stained by selfishness. This is because the self is under the law of sin (vv. 22–23). Sin has the authority and control over the Christian that God's law should have; God's law is usurped. In fact, the more Christians mature the more they see the great distance between what they are and what they want to be. This interpretation is supported by the end of this passage, verse 25b, in which Paul honestly summarizes his true condition,[17] a condition that is "fully congruous with this deep sense of commitment to God's will that this conclusion does not cloak the painful fact of continuing sinfulness, but goes on to acknowledge frankly that the Christian, so long as he remains in this present life, remains in a real sense a slave of sin, since he still has a fallen nature."[18] The deliverance the wretched man is pining after in verse 25a is the deliverance received in the new age. Paul's thought here flows naturally and does not have to be explained as somehow out of place, as opponents of this view contend (who say v. 25b fits better after v. 23).

14. Packer, "The 'Wretched Man,'" 71–77.
15. Dunn, *Theology of the Apostle Paul*, 474–76.
16. Cranfield, *Epistle to the Romans*, 343–44.
17. Ibid., 357, 361, 365–66.
18. Ibid., 370.

These scholars' interpretations suggest that the nature of sin is a cause and not an influence in the unbeliever. Additionally, there is minimal victory over sin for the believer in this lifetime. The war between the Spirit of God and the flesh in the believer wages continually and though the Spirit provides power for Christians to overcome sin, the remnants of Adam's sin, the fleshly desires we possess, the effects of the world, and the lures of Satan are strong and limit how much the Christian ever takes advantage of God's help.

The majority of scholars, however, see this passage as referring to either Paul before his conversion, the Jew in general, or to someone who is not a believer.[19] Moo represents this interpretation, noting that Paul refers to those outside of Christ as "in the flesh" (v. 5).[20] Paul, in verses 7–25, also uses the word "sin" and describes it as the perpetrator that uses God's good law and human fleshly desires to bring forth death in him. This interpretation seems best.

The main difficulty comes when Paul uses the personal pronoun "I" in the past tense (vv. 7–13) and in the present tense (vv. 14–25) when describing the workings of the law, sin, and the flesh. Moo thinks it unlikely that this use of "I" is a rhetorical device, owing to its sustained use in this passage, so it is likely there are some autobiographical references here.[21] The hearers are those "under the law," which refers only to Jews, since Gentiles were never under the law. So, who does that leave? Moo believes the most likely referent for "I" is the people of Israel first and Paul in solidarity with Israel second. Though some have attributed the "I" of verse 9 and 10 to Paul alone (with warrant), Moo believes it more likely that Israel is the target of the phrase "apart from the law," since there were 430 years between Abraham and the giving of the law to Moses. During this time there was sin, but it was not in the form of breaking a commandment from God (i.e., transgressions, see Rom 5:13–14).[22] Moo's view seems reasonable.

Paul begins the last paragraph (vv. 14–25) with the confession that he is "unspiritual, sold as a slave to sin" (v. 14) and a "prisoner to the law of sin"

---

19. Dunn, *Theology of the Apostle Paul*, 472.

20. Moo, *Epistle to the Romans*, 418. Moo sees "in the flesh" in v. 5 as meaning controlled by human and worldly values; the flesh is a power-sphere that the non-Christian lives in. This sphere of the old life and the old age (e.g., sin, the law, death) is not to be seen as part of the person or his or her nature. The NIV's translation of *sarx* as "sinful nature" is thus very misleading.

21. Colin Kruse does see it as a rhetorical or speech-in-character device, believing Paul uses it to depict the plight of the conscience-awakened Jew under the law, but like Moo believes Paul is including his own personal experience. Kruse, *Paul's Letter to the Romans*, 305, 314–21.

22. Moo, *Epistle to the Romans*, 427–28.

(v. 23). Though Christians are certainly influenced by sin and are warned throughout the NT to avoid it,[23] to say this is Paul's present experience goes further and contradicts his previous descriptions of himself and believers in general: we [Paul and his hearers] have died to sin and no longer live in it (6:2); the old self was crucified and the body ruled by sin done away with, that we should no longer be slaves to sin (6:6); count yourselves dead to sin (6:11); sin shall no longer be your master (6:14); you used to be slaves to sin (6:17); you have been set free from sin (6:18); when you were slaves to sin (6:20); but now you have been set free from sin (6:22); we are dying to what bound us and serve in the new way of the Spirit (7:6); us, who do not live according to the flesh but according to the Spirit (8:4); you, however, are not in the realm of the flesh, but are in the realm of the Spirit, if indeed the Spirit of God lives in you. And if anyone does not have the Spirit of Christ, they do not belong to Christ (8:9).[24] This is a description of Paul and the church as they live out a life that is no longer bound by the flesh; it is a life of holiness through the Spirit. Paul exhorts them to *walk* in this Spirit-empowered life, so we cannot remain passive. We can still walk in the flesh if we choose, otherwise Paul's admonitions mean nothing. However, it is a far cry from the wretched, conflicted, bound-by-sin life described in 7:14–25.

Further along, in verse 17, Paul seems to be making a distinction between two sources for failing to keep the law. He has mentioned it before

---

23. Even in Romans, we see Paul encouraging the Romans to not use their freedom to sin but to reap the benefits of holiness—see 6:11–13, 16–19, 8:12). Freedom and victory over sin and becoming slaves to God and righteousness isn't automatic; it must be lived out in daily life with a dependent reliance on the Holy Spirit.

24. As if further evidence is needed that Paul and his hearer's spiritual life surpassed the description in 7:14–25, more is evident in the rest of Romans. Paul's other epistles could be quoted, but the literary context of one book is sufficient. Paul looks negatively upon those who: follow the sinful desires of their hearts (1:24), those Jews who break the law (2:17–24), those who live according to the flesh (8:7–8). Is Paul condemning those who, if 7:14–25 is about the Christian life, act no better than him? Positively, Paul describes his current spiritual state and the state he expects the Romans to emulate: [Paul] *serves God with his whole heart* (1:9), even *Gentiles without the law can be righteous* (2:13–14). If God didn't spare his own son, will he not also *give us all things?* The justifying God, whose son intercedes for us, whose love no external force or demon can separate us from, and from which no suffering or persecution can separate us—*gives us strength to be more than conquerors in all these things* (8:31–39). Paul *sacrificially loves* his fellow Jews (9:1–3, 10:1) and encourages sacrificial and renewed-mind living (12:1–3). Paul gives practical commands to be *virtuous* (12:9–21, 13:1, 8–10) and *not fulfill the desires of the flesh* (13:12–14). Do not offend the conscience of a weaker believer (ch. 14). Paul confesses he, along with others, is *spiritually strong* (15:1). Paul was *fully obedient* to God's commissioning to preach the gospel (15:17–19). He instructed the Romans to *keep away from those who serve their own appetites* (16:17–18). God is *able to establish* the Romans in their spiritual life through the gospel (16:25). These positive verses do not match the person described in Romans 7:14–25.

(vv. 8, 11), but now makes it clearer that it is "sin in me" and not "I" that is breaking the law. What does he mean? Moo suggests Paul is not saying he is not responsible for his actions, but there is something more than the good that his mind approves. This means his good desires (v. 18), his inner being that delights in God's law (v. 22), the law of his mind (v. 23), or his mind, which is a slave to God's law (v. 25b), are not alone.[25] The unspiritual, slavery to sin, doing evil mode is from sin living in him (v. 17, 20), or the flesh (*sarx*, vv. 18, 25b), which wages war against his mind and makes him a prisoner of the law of sin (v. 23). Moo thinks it likely this "indwelling sin" described here has roots in the Jewish concept discussed earlier, the *yetzer hara*. He also believes it has further roots in the sin of Adam (original sin) and is why neither Jew nor Gentile can do what is good.[26] Paul later uses the phrase, the "law of sin," as another way to describe the *sarx*. This law works "in me," or as other translations put it, "in my members" (7:23, also 7:5 NASB, NRSV, ESV). He may even be referring to the flesh more as a reference to the body in 7:18 and 25b where he states no good dwells in his "sinful nature" (again, many modern translations use "flesh").[27] His question then, in verse 24, is who will deliver him from this "body" of death? So, Paul in his inner mind approves of God's law, but cannot outwardly "in his members" do what is good. But, is Paul in verse 24 asking for deliverance for his mortal body at the Second Coming? Some commentators believe so,[28] and note that verse 25b sums up Paul's whole argument by declaring that he is still a slave to the law of sin and the flesh. This interpretation is possible but less likely. The context here is spiritual bondage and both Paul and the Romans are already delivered from this bondage and condemnation. Paul thanks God for this deliverance in verse 25a and reiterates it in 8:2, "because through Christ Jesus the law of the Spirit who gives life has set you free from the law of sin and death."

Summarizing Moo's view, he sees Paul, with God's current revelation, looking back over his personal and his nation's past and recounting how he and his fellow Jews lived under the Mosaic law. This backward look seems to fit the immediate and larger context of this passage. Key contrasts that led to this conclusion are 1) the contrast between the self "sold as a slave to sin" in 7:14b and every believers freedom from sin's power (6:18, 22), and 2) the

---

25. Moo suggests this "law of the mind" is probably the law of Moses. Some consider it the conscience's approval of this same law. Moo, *Epistle to the Romans*, 464.

26. Ibid., 458. Moo's conclusion here has already been evaluated in chapter 3.

27. Ibid., 464.

28. Cranfield, *Epistle to the Romans*, 366–67; and Dunn, *Romans 1–8*, 397.

contrast between the self that is "a prisoner of the law of sin" (7: 23) and the fact that every believer is free from the law of sin and death (8:2).[29]

Who's Responsible?

Paul's wording in this passage has produced some other questions. How should we interpret the part of Paul that approves of the law vs. the fleshly, law of sin-obeying part? Is the "I" a neutral bystander who observes this interior battle between a weaker law-approving mind and a stronger flesh-satisfying law of sin? Dunn does not offer much clarity. To him sin is a "compulsion" or "constraint," that works against the "I" of the mind with the mind being powerless to resist it.[30] Sin, then, uses the "desiring I" or flesh of a person to produce sins. Therefore, the fleshly or desiring "I" is not responsible for sin, but "sin" is.[31] Can a compulsion be a responsible agent? It cannot. Thankfully, Dunn sees the "I" as *somehow* responsible because he claims guilt only follows a deliberate breaking of a command[32] (and sin is not an entity or person who can be held accountable!). Dunn's thinking is muddled. Somewhat differently, Moo interprets Paul's "sin living in me" (7:17) as the ultimate fault of the "I." It is neither the law nor sin, but the fleshly "I" who is responsible. He concludes that it is "'me' and my 'carnality,' my helplessness under sin, which enables sin to do what it does. 'Sin' has invaded my existence and made me a divided person, willing to do what God wants but failing to do it."[33] This is not much better than Dunn—Moo blames the fleshly "I," but declares that this same "I" is helpless under the power of sin. Sin has "invaded" (a word suggesting by force), and "made me a divided person" (this sounds like a causative verb, which certainly downplays any responsibility for sin from the "I"). Moo is likewise unclear as to who or what is responsible for our acts of sin.[34] Let's illustrate their conclusions, with arrows signifying an irresistible causation:

---

29. Moo, *Epistle to the Romans*, 448–49, 454. This is also the general conclusion of Craig Keener and Harold Sweeten. See Keener, *IVP Background Commentary*, Romans 7:7–13; and Sweeten, *Must We Sin*, 134–46.

30. This is odd, since Dunn, when explaining *nous*, the Greek word translated as "mind" in 7:23, 25, affirms that it represents the "rational person, perceiving, thinking, determining 'I,' the 'I' not simply at the mercy of outside powers but able to respond and to act with understanding." See Dunn, *Theology of the Apostle Paul*, 74. Apparently the "I" is not at the mercy of outside powers, but is at the mercy of internal ones.

31. Dunn, *Theology of the Apostle Paul*, 67.

32. Ibid., 113.

33. Moo, *Epistle to the Romans*, 451.

34. Both Dunn and Moo suffer from poorly defined terms, which makes it hard to

> *Dunn*: "sin" → fleshly "desiring I" ("I" of mind is impotent) → acts of sin, breaking of law
>
> *Moo*: Adam's sin → me having "sin in me" → "fleshly I" captive of law of sin ("I" of mind is impotent) → acts of sin, breaking of law

In these models sin is something that happens *to* us. The "fleshly I" is a mere pawn, a passive recipient of these causative forces that inexorably lead us to sin. Moo has linked the force behind sin as original sin from Adam. Therefore if anyone is ultimately responsible in these models it is Adam, or ultimately God, since he decided what the consequences of Adam's sin would be. Can we pass the buck for our sinful desires and acts of sin onto God, Adam, "sin in me," or the "flesh"? No, it seems Moo started on a good track in blaming the "fleshly I" for sin, but ultimately ended by linking "sin in me" back to Adam and causative original sin.

Unfortunately for us, the fleshly "I" is not alone. There is the added sin-ward pull of the world and Satan, both of which try to deepen the sinful ruts we have made for ourselves. However, in one sense, the depth of our sin ruts is immaterial. Whether it was after the first sin or many, the self has no resources to overcome it. Moreover, the self is guilty and can do nothing to erase that guilt and cancel the death that will now follow. Truly, the self is in a spiritual quandary and must do the only thing it *is* able to do—cry out to God for deliverance from the wretchedness.

But who got the "I" into this mess? The better interpretation of our passage, that coheres with the earlier conclusions from Romans 5:12–19, points to the "fleshly I" as responsible for sin. By pre-conversion practice (either shorter or longer), the "I" has been habitually obedient to evil desires, has become deeply self-centered, and as a result is now a slave to the law of sin. In this condition a sinful Jew, like Paul, has a mind that knows what he should do. His conscience and his religious training have done their job. However, in his present bound-by-sin state, he is unable to obey what his mind says is good. His mind hates what he does (v. 15). The "I" or "law" of the mind or the "inner being" is now impotent to carry out the good; it is the "sin in me," the "flesh," the "evil I don't want to do," or the "law of sin" that dominates (v. 17–23). This "I" has walked down a path that has led to bondage. Sin is so strong now it acts like a force or a "law" that requires obedience. A Jew's only hope, Paul being included, is to be rescued through faith in Christ and the work of the Holy Spirit.

In summary, Romans 7:5–25 discusses several phrases pertinent to understanding sinful desires—sinful nature/flesh, sin, and law of sin. Paul

---

understand their points.

considers the non-Christian's way of life as controlled by the flesh. The flesh is powerful and can only be overcome through the Spirit and the life he brings. The Christian should not be, but could be, controlled by the flesh. However, the Christian is exhorted to live in the power of the Spirit and to not gratify the desires of the flesh.

Romans 8

Romans 8:1–13 continues to contrast those "in the flesh" from those "in the Spirit." There is little in this passage that adds to what has already been discussed, except it reinforces that those "in the flesh" are unregenerate and those "in the Spirit" are. One point it emphasizes is that Christians are not obligated to the flesh, but are to live in the Spirit (8:12). This implies that Christians can be affected or influenced by fleshly desires, but they do not live in that realm anymore and have no coercion to live sinfully. Moo provides a helpful analogy: "Like freed slaves who might, out of habit, obey their old masters even after being released—'legally' and 'positionally'—from them, so we Christians can still listen to and heed the voice of that old master of ours, the flesh."[35] Other Pauline passages that discuss the flesh also do not reveal significant clues as to its nature. Galatians 5:13, 16–19, 24, and Colossians 2:11–13, 18, 23 describe followers of Christ as those who have put off the flesh and crucified it with its passions and desires. They are circumcised in Christ, buried with him in baptism, are risen with Christ, and walk by the Spirit. Another similar phrase (old self, new self, Rom 6:6, Eph 4:22, Col 3:9–10) declares that in the believer the old self was crucified, it needs to be put off and the new self put on. This *does* suggest that the new nature does not produce goodness or righteousness by force or by fiat, but the person actively cooperates with the work of the Spirit. This is reinforced by several other passages in which Paul exhorts Christians to clothe themselves with Christ and not think about gratifying the flesh (Rom 13:14), not use their freedom to indulge the flesh (Gal 5:13), to "put off your old self, which is being corrupted by its deceitful desires; to be made new in the attitude of your minds; and to put on the new self, created to be like God in true righteousness and holiness (Eph 4:22). The writer of Hebrews agrees, exhorting Christians to not have a sinful, unbelieving heart and to not be hardened by sin's deceitfulness (Heb 3:12–13).

---

35. Moo, *Epistle to the Romans*, 494.

EXCURSUS: COMPATIBILISM, INCOMPATIBILISM, AND HUMAN FREEDOM[36]

Theologians and philosophers have deliberated on how fleshly desires operate and have inferred differing conceptions of it. The two opposing viewpoints are called compatibilism and incompatibilism (or libertarianism).

The Basics of Compatibilism

A. S. Evans defines compatibilism:

> In philosophy of action, the view that causal determinism is logically compatible with free will. The compatibilist who accepts both determinism and free will is called a soft determinist. Compatibilism usually defines free will as an action that is caused by the individual's own desires or wishes, rather than being coerced by some external power. The alternative possibilities that seem necessary for genuine free will are interpreted by compatibilists as hypothetical in character. For example, the individual who freely gave money to a charity could have refrained from giving the money *if* the individual had wished to do so or *if* the situation had been different.[37]

According to compatibilism, human actions are part of a long historical causal chain that eventually led to the present. The causal chain can include prior events, the laws of nature, or one's previous character, beliefs, and desires. In fact, free acts can only be caused by one's previous character, beliefs, and desires ("states" within a person). This is a "one-way ability" or freedom.[38] This one-way ability is sometimes also called a *hypothetical ability*[39] or freedom. Robert Kane adds that compatibilists would agree that being coerced physically by outside forces or persons would take away freedom (the causal chain has not run through the agent in the right way), but they would deny that determination by heredity, the environment, or the

---

36. Much of this excursus is from Christensen, M., "Description, Comparison, and Critique." The strengths and weaknesses of each view are further discussed by Moreland and Craig, *Philosophical Foundations*, 267–83.

37. Evans, *Pocket Dictionary*, "compatibilism."

38. Moreland and Craig, *Philosophical Foundations*, 268–69, 278.

39. Hypothetical ability is the ability to do otherwise had some "condition" occurred, such as a desire to do so. This ability affirms that we are free to will whatever we desire even though our desires themselves are determined by outside agencies or previous states. Moreland and Craig, *Philosophical Foundations*, 279.

laws of nature raises such an objection[40] (the causal pathway appropriately goes through the agent's prior mental states). Heredity and upbringing may make it inevitable that we choose the actions we do, but intentional actions that spring from these causes are still free.

Millard Erickson described more fully how God fits into a compatibilist scheme. To the Calvinist, God foreordains and therefore foreknows all human decisions and actions. He has rendered it certain how each individual will decide; therefore his plan is not conditioned on human choices. God renders an act certain (a person wills what God chooses) but does not render it necessary (a person cannot act differently than God chooses). God sets limitations on who we are and what we desire and will. He controls all the circumstances that bear on our lives. This is similar to Leibnitz's argument; God knows all possibilities and actualizes one of them. He carefully selects whom he brings into existence and the precise stimuli he will use to produce the free acts he intends. Are humans then free? Erickson asserts that humans do have the ability to choose differently, but they *wouldn't*. The individual could not have *desired* to choose differently. Regarding sin, God's "wish" (his general intention) and his "will" (a specific intention for a situation) may not agree. God wishes there was no sin (generally) but he does permit sin and the eventual destruction of sinners. Why he permits this is unknown—it is a mystery.[41]

Major Ideas in Incompatibilism

Incompatibilism or libertarianism affirms:

> That the freedom necessary for responsible action is not compatible with determinism. Real freedom requires a type of control over one's action—and, more importantly, over one's will—such that, given a choice to do A . . . or B . . . nothing determines that either choice is made. Rather, the agent himself must simply exercise his own *causal powers* and will to do one alternative . . . When an agent acts freely, he is a *first* or *unmoved mover*; no event or efficient cause causes him to act. His desires or beliefs may influence his choice or play an important role in his deliberations, but free acts are not determined or caused by prior events or states in the agent, they are spontaneously done by the agent himself acting as a first mover.[42]

40. Kane, *Free Will*, 6.
41. Erickson, *Christian Theology*, 381–88.
42. Moreland and Craig, *Philosophical Foundations*, 270.

Libertarian freedom does not imply that choices are undetermined (random or by chance), but choices originate in the agent, sometimes called agent causation. Individuals have a *categorical ability* to will and act.[43]

Swinburne concludes that the libertarian type of freedom is the only type that can be the base of moral responsibility and accountability. Persons are only worthy of blame or praise if they are the beginning of their moral choices and their choices are not the inevitable result of other causes. Swinburne also sees that moral beliefs are necessary conditions for moral responsibility, since one must have beliefs before one can act either for or against them.[44]

An additional source of insight into this debate, theology, was used with the compatibilist position and will also be used here. Arminianism agrees substantially with the incompatibilist position by asserting that God's sovereignty is limited by free human acts. Election is based on God's foreknowledge and not his foreordination—he knows what humans will freely choose. Further, God's grace is a prerequisite to exercise saving faith, but humans are free to respond in repentance and faith or to reject God's gracious offer.[45] Evil is explained as the result of humans choosing against God's wishes. Sin is not God's ultimate will and is a distortion of his plan. Open Theism also agrees with incompatibilism and has similar ingredients as Arminianism. However, human acts are not foreknown—except in cases of *non-moral specific sovereignty*,[46] e.g., God unilaterally bringing events to pass that fulfill his purposes (Isa 46:10–11); God hardening Pharaoh's heart (Exod 4:20—15:21); God causing Israel to win in battle (Deut 2:25, 30; Josh 11:20); Nebuchadnezzar's fate (Dan 4); Babylon conquering Israel (Jer 5, 32); and the Persian Cyrus allowing Israel to return to their homeland (Isa 44:24—45:2). God's election is best seen as corporate (he elects a people for his name) rather than individual (selecting individuals to be saved).

---

43. Categorical ability is the ability to want in the first place. The agent has the ability to both want (desire) and will to act, to do act A or refrain from doing act A (dual ability). Previous states (desires, beliefs, character) do not determine present acts, but influence them. Moreland and Craig, *Philosophical Foundations*, 271.

44. Swinburne, *Responsibility and Atonement*, 52.

45. Moreland and Craig, *Philosophical Foundations*, 278–82.

46. Non-moral specific sovereignty or governmental providence is defined as the "abnormal or unusual operation of God's wisdom in inciting men's wills to actions in various particulars through external events or internal persuasion, temporarily setting aside man's normal moral freedom and accountability under a law of cause and effect by coercing or constraining man's will." Olson, *Moral Government*, 24. This mode of action is sometimes confused with God's usual mode of action, which is treating humans as moral agents. When the two are conflated, deterministic views of moral action and salvation can result.

A Comparison and Critique of Both Views

When comparing the two views there are several points of agreement. They both would probably agree some aspects of the human condition are determined, such as our personality type and the outcomes of coerced acts (physical force, the effects of some drugs, some acts of hypnosis, or some uncontrollable forms of mental illness).

However, it seems that the compatibilist's "hypothetical" or "one-way" definition of freedom is no freedom at all; it acts just like hard determinism. In an *ad hoc* fashion, adherents take the traditional libertarian-flavored definition of freedom (a choice to do what one wants, not determined by anything outside of one's being, a choice among alternatives[47]) and change it to a one-way definition.

Soft determinism (compatibilism) is an unsuccessful attempt to marry two concepts that cannot be married. It seems apt to compare compatibilism in humans with instinct in the animal kingdom. For example, birds always instinctively follow their "desire" to migrate; they have only a one-way ability (barring a genetic defect, trauma, human intervention, etc.). One could say that birds "freely" choose to migrate, but would that mean anything?

Let's look next at one-way freedom with God in mind. According to compatibilists, since humans must follow the desires God effectually produces in them, what happens when humans do evil? How does one escape the conclusion that God is the source? Even if compatibilists say God causes only good desires, why doesn't he effactually cause all our desires to be good? Since God always wants good as opposed to evil, then that would result in no evil in the world. The compatibilist mechanism (one-way freedom) and the implications it carries with it do not fit how God acts in the Scriptures, does not fit how humans interact with each other, and does not do justice to God's good character.

Persuasion

For many human acts, what the compatibilist would call a determiner (God or some previous state) the libertarian would call a strong influence (persuader): previous character, beliefs, desires, previous events, psychological habits or preferences (generosity, habitually brushing one's teeth, or liking cheesecake). If the compatibilist is right, then any act of persuasion seems unintelligible. To be consistent, the compatibilist would never use

---

47. See definition of "free" in *American Heritage Dictionary*, *Webster's Ninth*, and the *Oxford Free Online Dictionary*.

persuasion or reason because they have no effect on the causal chain working through the person in the right way. Even if someone acts on reasons, the reasons are in the past or are predetermined for us by God. Preaching, apologetics, or praying (which are designed to affect the mind, emotions, and will) would be assuming an ability to respond we do not possess.

The libertarian's categorical ability to do either/or seems to describe the human situation best. We try to persuade others to change their views or pick a certain option in many areas of life (health, religion, politics, advertising, etc.) because we know they are able to change their behavior. God persuades using love, fear, and rewards and punishments (among others). He does not force moral decisions on us or control our desires from above.

What's New?

Only libertarian agents can cause something new to happen. A compatibilist is a slave to the past or must wait for God's direct intervention. A compatibilist could not have a meaningful debate with a libertarian since it is impossible to change another's mind through present-time discussion. A compatibilist would (could?) never pray for God to change his or her desires because that prayer itself would be determined and desires are only changed by previous states or by God's intervention (a vicious circle!). One must be a libertarian to pray that way and expect a coherent answer from God. The general tone of God's actions toward humanity presumes libertarian agency. He asks us to repent, have faith, obey, and do good works. All God's revelation directs us to cooperate with his plan and to respond to his love. These responses are to come from the "heart." Jesus said good and evil comes from the heart (the seat of our ultimate intentions) (Luke 6:43–45). This implies we need to choose a new course. The compatibilist must look back to past character, beliefs, and values for the present choice. But where did the *past* character, beliefs, desires, and preferences come from? Do we have "original equipment" character or should we look to times before we were born? Neither of these options can be adequately defended.

Moral Responsibility

The issue of causation and agency leads to a discussion of moral responsibility. Libertarians claim they have personal responsibility because they are the originators of their intentions and actions. An originator who has options and can perceive "oughtness" is responsible and therefore worthy of praise or blame. How can the compatibilist be responsible to desires outside their present control? If others put blame or praise on them they must deflect it because they are not the originators of their actions. They may blame or praise their parents, others, or God, but not themselves. They are merely a conduit.

The question naturally arises then, "Who may parents and others blame or praise for *their own* behavior?" One can regress, though not infinitely, since there is a first cause. Christians sometimes look back to Adam and Eve as a first cause. Christians are frequently taught that Adam is the source of sin and that a sinful nature has been passed down from him to all posterity and that this nature causes us to sin. They are taught that *Adam* is the cause and *they* are the cause (coherence?). Some logically see the chain going back to God, since he created Adam and Eve and either foreordained them to sin (and also allowed or determined that all their posterity would bear the consequences of their original sin—a sin-causing fleshly nature, or Calvinism), or foreknew they would sin, but did not prevent it (Arminianism).

Calvinist compatibilists have the hardest time accounting for individual moral responsibility since all human acts are foreordained by God; it is hard to escape the conclusion that God is responsible for evil and hard to show how humans are morally culpable for his foreordaining. Even Arminians have difficulty reconciling God's foreknowing with free human choices. To Erickson, the foreknowledge view suffers, for if God knows what we'll do, then it is certain. If it is certain, then we are "likely" not free.[48] If we are not in control we cannot be responsible. Some theologians, usually found in all doctrinal camps, try to exonerate God and therefore hold the doctrine of *traducianism*, which states that God only created the *souls* of Adam and Eve. All others subsequently *receive their bodies and souls from their parents*, who are then responsible for producing sinful offspring. The Arminian who is also an Open Theist does not contend with foreordination or foreknowledge; the only option for blame is the sinner. The Calvinist compatibilist and the Arminian incompatibilist would agree with this, but their arguments have trouble explaining how lack of control and responsibility coexist and how to exonerate God as the cause of sin.

Conclusion

In conclusion, it seems the view that coheres the best, has the best existential viability, is less *ad hoc*, best accounts for human moral responsibility and moral evil, fits the way God and humans interact with each other, and can exonerate God for the cause of sin, is incompatibilism. Some Christian

---

48. Erickson, *Christian Theology*, 386.

incompatibilists have difficulty explaining the coexistence of free will with God's foreknowledge, others do not. Compatibilists, Christian or not, have weaker arguments and positions on all these issues.

THEOLOGIZING ON THE FLESH

Our discussion of the flesh is not able to pinpoint a source, therefore linking its source to original sin is mere speculation. As we have seen, Adam and Eve displayed desires for food, beauty, and wisdom that they allowed to exceed God's wishes and which the serpent used to entice them to sin. These desires predate their sin, so the conclusion that desires that lead toward sin are a result of the fall is contradicted by Adam and Eve's own experience. In agreement with this, James 1:13–14 confirms that some desires can lead to sin. However, not all our human desires are evil. There seem to be two types—good/ordinate ones and sinful/inordinate ones. First, we all experience certain desires that are appropriate—for food, clothing, shelter, sexual fulfillment, beauty, accomplishment, rest, justice, knowledge, wisdom, to be valued, to love and be loved—these can all be satisfied in a good and God-pleasing way. Second, these ordinate desires can become inordinate, or outside of God's laws and will (think of the seven deadly sins—wrath, greed, sloth, pride, lust, envy, and gluttony—or Paul's vice lists in his epistles). With the seven deadly sins, idolatry perverts the worship of God: greed is an overabundant desire for worldly goods; pride is a selfish overvaluing of our own accomplishments and reputation; wrath is going overboard to satisfy angry feelings, to get revenge, or to cause harm. Paul calls these desires *fleshly* because they pull us toward ultimate self-gratification and sin. Sometimes when Paul speaks of these desires, he assumes they are sinful, implying the person has already given in to them.

Both ordinate and inordinate desires are described in the Bible. Ordinate ones are good. Inordinate ones pervert good desires, and when indulged, step outside God's established boundaries and are necessarily sinful. We have seen that neither God nor Adam force us to possess inordinate or fleshly desires; God always holds us to blame for acquiescing to them.

Testing

The question arises, then, about what possible purpose God had for allowing inordinate desires to exist in his human creations. Some theologians maintain that our time on earth can be described as a "divine probation," with probation defined as "the process or period of testing or observing the character or abilities of a person in a certain role."[49] He does not tempt anyone to sin (Jas 1:13) but wants all people to be holy like him. A plausible answer is that he allows such desires to test and perfect us. God repeatedly tested his people. Initially he tested Adam and Eve. He could have put them in the Garden, let them do as they please, and given them no particular commands. However, he tested their hearts—he gave them one "do not do this" command and allowed a tempter (the serpent) to have access to them. He did not shield them from the serpent's wiles. He allowed them to experience desires that they could overcome if they chose to, all the while watching how they would respond.

This idea of testing can reasonably be linked to the tendency toward evil acknowledged by Jewish teachers (the *yetzer hara*). Scholars have plausibly suggested this is the same factor that Paul calls the "flesh" or "evil desires." Human experience teaches us all that we have pulls toward both good and evil behavior and that many times, especially before some of us became Christians, the evil pull won. As an example, in a recent TV commercial, children were questioned about how they made moral decisions and they talk about a "good voice" and a "bad voice" in their heads.

Whatever one decides to call it, we all sense this internal moral struggle with a sometimes intense pull from the evil side. The biblical authors do not put their finger on a definitive source. We have already discussed the influence of those around us (sometimes called "the world") and have biblical examples of Satan enticing people to sin. Altogether these three combine to be potent influences toward sin and a significant test of what priority we will give God. Several Bible passages pinpoint God's active attention toward our behavior and the place of testing in our earthly sojourn:

> Moses speaking to the nation of Israel before they entered the Promised Land:
> *Remember how the Lord your God led you all the way in the wilderness these forty years, to humble and test you in order to know what was in your heart, whether or not you would keep his commands.* (Deut 8:2)
>
> *And you, my son Solomon, acknowledge the God of your father, and serve him with wholehearted devotion and with a willing mind, for the Lord searches every heart and understands every desire and every thought. If you seek him, he will be found by you; but if you forsake him, he will reject you forever.* (1 Chr 28:9)

---

49. Oxford Free Online Dictionary, "Probation."

> *The Lord looks down from heaven on all mankind to see if there are any who understand, any who seek God.* (Ps 14:2)

> *I the Lord search the heart and examine the mind, to reward each person according to their conduct, according to what their deeds deserve.* (Jer 17:10)

Jesus speaking to the church at Thyatira regarding the false prophetess Jezebel:
> *I will strike her children dead. Then all the churches will know that I am he who searches hearts and minds, and I will repay each of you according to your deeds.* (Rev 2:23)

God frequently used particular incidents to scrutinize people's hearts. Consider Abraham: "Sometime later God tested Abraham" (Gen 22:1) by asking him to sacrifice his only son Isaac as a burnt offering on a mountain in Moriah. When Abraham had the knife raised the angel of the Lord stopped him, saying, "Now I know that you fear God, because you have not withheld from me your son, your only son" (Gen 22:12). God wanted to see if Abraham was trustworthy enough to receive the blessing he wanted to give him—to multiply his descendants greatly and to bless the nations through him (Gen 22:16–18). In another example, God allowed Job to be tested. Satan asserted that Job served God because God had been good to Job; remove all of his blessings and Job would curse God to his face. So, God gave Satan permission to afflict his family, possessions, and even his body to show Satan how Job would respond. God tested Hezekiah to see what was really in his heart (2 Chr 32:32). God tested the nation of Israel as a whole numerous times to see if they would obey his commands or not: with manna and in the wilderness wanderings (Exod 16:4; Deut 8:2); he tested their love with false gods and prophets (Deut 13:3); he tested their perseverance after Joshua had died (Judg 2:21, 3:4); in general to help his people remove spiritual impurities (Ps 66:10; Jas 1:1–4). Jesus tested Philip's thoughts on Jesus's power by asking him how they were to feed five thousand men (John 6:5). Peter and James counseled their hearers that they should rejoice even though they experience grief and trials, which God uses not to harm or discourage but to encourage perseverance and to test, refine, and mature their faith. This is to result in praise and glory to God when Christ returns (1 Pet 1:6–7, 4:12–13; Jas 1:2–4).

This all shows that God not only wants to know what is in our hearts, he wants to bring about good things from testing those hearts. He wants us to rise to the occasion and respond with trust, love, dependence, and obedience. Before ending we must clarify that it is neither necessary nor desirable that sin should be the cause of testing. Paul squashed the thinking that sin should be used to bring about good (Rom 3:8). However, it seems that fleshly desires, which allow temptation to occur, are elements God has allowed in our being in order to test and perfect us.

WHAT CAN WE CONCLUDE ABOUT THE NATURE OF EVIL DESIRES AND THE FLESH?

Based on our work in this chapter, five general conclusions can be made:

- The Bible affirms humans have evil or fleshly desires. The definition of "flesh" that applies to our discussion resembles definitions 5 and 6 above. Fleshly persons have given themselves up to their own aims in opposition to God's.

- Our survey does not provide conclusive evidence as to the source of fleshly desires. Evidence from chapter 3 affirms the source of human evil is the human heart (the self or "I"), not God, Satan, Adam (original sin), or the world. These desires were present in Adam and Eve and all subsequent humanity. God has allowed humans to have good and evil desires. Desires become fleshly or sinful when they are pursued in an inordinate way.

- Evil desires (the flesh) are powerful. Whether they are coercive or not is not directly stated, however the context suggests they are an influence and not a cause. This is an inference since persons are told by God's representatives to give up their evil desires. The flesh can and does lead to actual sin. Non-Christians are (and Christians can become) slaves to sin. The biblical writers suggest that if evil desires are repeatedly indulged in, they become stronger and harder to resist, leading to spiritual bondage. The effects of sin cannot be overcome by the non-Christian's human will.

- The flesh operates in an incompatibilist or libertarian mode.

- A plausible reason for God allowing the flesh to exist is that it acts as a means of testing and maturing.

SUMMARY AND PLAUSIBLE MODELS FOR SECTION I

We described various historical viewpoints on original sin and sin in chapter 1, which can be grouped into varying categories:

Regarding original sin:

WHAT ARE FLESHLY DESIRES? 169

- No effects from original sin, since Adam and Eve did not exist. (Neo-orthodoxy and other modern theologies)
- Indirect influence, mostly no-guilt views (Judaism, Pelagianism, Semi-Pelagianism, Roman Catholicism, Eastern Orthodoxy, Anabaptist, some Wesleyan-Arminian, Stone-Campbell)
- Direct cause, mostly guilt views (some Wesleyan-Arminian, Reformed Protestantism)

Regarding the definition of sin:

- Sin as a conscious and intentional turning away from God, his will, and law and toward supreme self-gratification (Judaism, Roman Catholicism, Eastern Orthodoxy, Anabaptist, Wesleyan-Arminian Protestantism, Stone-Campbell, Neo-orthodoxy)
- Sin, as above, which flows from a previous cause—original sin (Some Wesleyan-Arminian, Reformed Protestantism)

Chapters 2, 3, and 4 discussed relevant scriptural passages and secondary sources, and each chapter ended with general conclusions, which favor some and disfavor other of these historical viewpoints. However, these favorable conclusions are not a complete analysis. The Introduction provided a series of steps by which we can best spiral toward the truth regarding original sin, the definition of sin, and the meaning and nature of the flesh (these were the first of our questions). Now the combined favorable conclusions need to be systematized into a coherent theology and compared against other credible models using inference to the best explanation (IBE) criteria.

Given the presuppositions discussed in the Introduction, two credible theological models integrate the doctrines discussed in chapters 1–4.

- Model 1 concludes:
  - Original sin is an indirect influence toward actual sin and no guilt attaches to it.
  - Actual sin is an intentional turning away from God, his will, and law and toward supreme self-gratification.
  - All people are influenced by fleshly desires and have allowed these desires to lead them to commit actual sin. Fleshly desires are not the direct result of original sin.
- Model 2 concludes:
  - Original sin, whether followed by actual sin or not, produces moral guilt.

- Original sin is the source of fleshly desires, which are present in all persons.
- Actual sin is a conscious and intentional turning away from God, his will, and law and toward supreme self-gratification, and is caused ultimately by original sin through the intermediary of fleshly desires.

EVALUATION OF MODELS ACCORDING TO IBE CRITERIA[50]

Explanatory Power and Scope

Original sin, the definition of sin, and the definition of the flesh

Model 1 seems to agree better with *tota Scriptura* (see evaluations in chapters 3 and 4) on the topics of original sin, the definition of sin, and the meaning of the flesh. The biblical passages investigated do not support the concept of original sin, define sin in a heart-caused as opposed to an Adam-caused way, and define the flesh as an influence rather than a cause. These are all congruent with Model 1, but not Model 2.

God's Relationality

The Bible portrays God as inherently relational,[51] and this relationality overflows in the way he interacts with his image-bearers and their need for intimate bonds among themselves. God interacted extensively with the people of Israel and responded regularly to their obedience and more frequent disobedience, disciplining and persuading them to follow him faithfully. God became more intimate with humanity through his son, Jesus Christ. Christ taught those who would listen, asking all to be his disciples. Some accepted and were received with joy; most did not, which grieved Jesus's heart. Model 1 presents a more relational, synergistic relationship, one that seems more in line with God's relationality, human relationality, and the conclusions of chapters 3–4. Model 2 describes a more one-sided relationship where a largely impotent party (us) is moved by a sovereign (God) to

---

50. Because a failure in one evaluation criterion has effects on another, there is some overlap of offenses.

51. The term "perichoresis" defines the interpenetration, oneness, fellowship, and intimacy among the members of the Trinity.

fulfill a mysterious plan that involves humans performing both good and evil actions. Humanity is the playing field where God's sovereignty, human fleshly desires, and the impact of original sin act and the outcome is either foreordained or foreknown. Relationality and synergy between the two parties is weaker in this model.

Adam and Eve's Behavior

If fleshly desires result from the fall (Model 2), there is no accounting for Adam and Eve's pre-fall fleshly desires and their ability to sin without these desires. Fleshly desires acting as an influence (Model 1) and as a testing/perfecting tool better account for Adam and Eve's temptation experience in the Garden. Relatedly, if it is denied that Adam and Eve had fleshly desires in the first place, explaining their sin is even more problematic for Model 2.

General Human Experience

Humans generally perceive themselves as being agents and not automatons. They perceive that they make choices based on certain factors—whim, emotional state, deliberation, selfish or altruistic desires, etc., and that these factors were not causes, but influences. They also perceive that when they develop behavior habits that these habits become hard to break and can even form a bondage that cannot be overcome without outside help. Moreover, humans acknowledge the principle of justice and that it is unjust to punish persons who could not avoid doing a wrong (in our case, original sin is in this category). Ability must coexist with responsibility and accountability. These observations coincide with Model 1, while Model 2 has difficulty explaining the accountability without ability idea.

Universal sin

Both models give adequate explanations for universal sin. Model 1 accounts for it using the elements of the indirect influences toward sin (the influence of the flesh, the world, and the devil), which are all elements of universal temptation. The model does not require every person to sin, but describes the reality that everyone has sinned. It is theoretically possible in Model 1 that a person could go his or her whole life without sin, but the model says this has never happened and predicts it never will, considering the potency of the influences. Model 2 necessitates that all have sinned because original sin and the flesh are causative factors—humans can only sin (or as it is sometimes stated—humans are not able not to sin). Therefore, this model guarantees universal sin.

God's Justice and Love

God's justice is described as distributive—it rewards those who do good and punishes those who do evil.[52] Model 2 has difficulty explaining how original sin and causative fleshly desires fit with God's justice. It is unjust to either allow or purposely create irresistible and sin-producing causes and eternal punishments for persons who did not choose those causes, especially in the case of the pre-born, infants, and those mentally incompetent. Some defenders of Model 2 portray God's justice as somehow different or "higher" than what he has revealed to us in Scripture and use verses such as Isaiah 55:8–9 to defend it. However, God never portrays that he has a different concept of justice other than what he has revealed to us. The context of Isaiah 55:8–9 is God summoning all nations to himself and pardoning all who forsake evil and turn to him. To expand the meaning of those verses beyond that context is not defendable. Model 1 explains these factors as influences and does not need to resort to mystery or other techniques to adjust the definition of distributive justice.[53]

Model 2 has further difficulty explaining why original sin and causative fleshly desires exist in the first place. Since they are God-initiated or God-allowed, how do they express God's love? It is difficult to understand their justification and necessity in light of God's love for humans, his desire for all to love him in return, and the goals of his kingdom. On the contrary, Model 1 affirms that God has neither allowed nor created anything that coerces us to sin. He has done everything he could to prevent sin and to make it as rare as possible in his kingdom on earth. It is more congruent with God's character that he allows influential fleshly desires to exist in the human person in order to test and perfect us.

---

52. Feinberg, *No One Like Him*, 347–48.

53. See the argument in Peterson, et al., *Reason and Religious Belief*, 158–59. They argue convincingly that the concept of higher divine morality is meaningless since the defenders of the view do not know what this morality is and therefore cannot know if it supports their position or not.

The Power of God and the Good

Model 1 explains that evil exists because individuals willfully succumb to fleshly or evil influences. They could have availed themselves of God's mercy and power to live holy lives in his kingdom. Evil is not necessary; good can prevent evil. Model 2 affirms that Adam's sin has such power over human decisions that they can only do what is evil. We cannot escape the conclusion, then, that evil has more power than God—somehow it burdened humanity with a sin-ward pull that will ultimately damn countless souls. The forces of evil can compel God's creatures to sin and God can't reciprocate in kind—he can only persuade, or as some believe, he chooses to effectually call only a few to eternal life. Therefore good cannot prevail. Evil cannot be prevented; it can only be remedied after the fact. This is contradicted by the conclusions of chapters 3 and 4 (see especially Jas 1:13–15).

God's Response to Sinners, to include Eternal Judgment

God's response to sin has been one of anger (Deut 32:16), sadness (Ezek 6:9), regret (Gen 6:6), patience (Neh 9:30), pleading (Deut 30:19; Jer 3:12, 4:1; Ezek 33:11; Hos 11:1–9, Matt 11:28), and an expectation of better. Model 1 predicts these responses because sin is against God and his desires. Model 2 has to explain some of these away. For example, it is illogical to be angry with beings who do evil because they must. Pity would be more appropriate. There is no need for God to patiently wait for sinners to repent since waiting will not change the outcome. It is nonsensical to plead with people to change their hearts if they are unable to do so. God should not expect better because there is no possibility of better. Model 2 predicts God should have expected what he did get—continual sin. If he got what he expected, how could he feel regret?

Model 1 best explains the scriptural assertion of human responsibility for sin. Humans are influenced toward sin but not caused, therefore they justly bear the consequences of indulging in it. Model 2 asserts the contradictory and incoherent view of compatibilism. In this view either God or Adam are ultimately responsible for human sin, one because he controls all human desires and therefore the resultant actions, and the other because he is the representative of humanity; his sin is our sin.

The seriousness and finality of eternal judgment more appropriately fits individuals who have chosen evil as an option, as Model 1 affirms. Those who have had their evil choices dictated by an irresistible and inherited sin nature, as in Model 2, are more to be pitied than condemned. In this case the punishment just doesn't fit—it is much too harsh and far-reaching for an involuntary or even compatibilist act.

Logical Consistency

We commented throughout chapters 3 and 4 regarding observed logical errors made by certain scholars. This is the biggest problem for Model 2. Within this model the logical offenses are suppressed evidence (see comments on Gen 6:5, 8–9, 13; Exod 32:9–14; Deut 24:16; Ezek 18; Eccl 7:29; Isa 5:1–7; Jer 2:21), weak analogy (Josh 7), composition (Ps 51:5–6), false premises, missing the point, unsound argument (Schreiner; Moo; Rom 5:12–19), and poorly defined terms (Moo; Dunn; Rom 7:5–25). See the Appendix for more detailed descriptions of these logical fallacies.

As noted above under Explanatory Power and Scope, Model 2 believes human moral choices are caused by an outside agent or previous states (God controlling human desires or preexisting evil desires controlling human action) and also by the human agent—at the same time for the same act. To avoid offending the law of noncontradiction, adherents redefine freedom in a non-standard and meaningless way. This is an unsuccessful *ad hoc* adjustment to rescue the theory. Model 1 does not commit such logical errors and as a consequence it prevails on this factor.

Coherence and *ad hoc* features

Model 1 has good coherence with mutually reinforcing beliefs. Original sin and the flesh acting as influences and sin as a conscious and intentional choice among options cohere with each other. However, Model 1 does not guarantee that all persons will sin, but gives reasons why all do. Under Model 1's inductive argument, it is theoretically possible that someone could go their whole life without sinning, which would contradict the doctrine that all have sinned. If such a person existed, it would contradict the biblical revelation and seriously weaken the model.

Model 2 lacks coherence in several arguments (note discussions of Deut 1:39, 24:16; Ezek 18; Rom 5:12–19; Moo; Cranfield in chapter 3). Further, coherence problems are tied to the connection between Model 2's version of original sin and fleshly desires acting as causes. Humans are held responsible for irresistible desires and may suffer eternally for the act of another (Adam). This does not cohere with the Model 2 adherents' belief in God's justice or their definition of sin. How God is just in this situation is defined as a mystery. There is further incoherence and *ad hoc*-ness when exceptions are made for the pre-born, infants, and the mentally incapable. For many who hold to Model 2, these humans do not suffer the penalty of eternal death even though they possessed Adam's damning sin nature. Only those who commit actual sins are condemned. They must add another *ad hoc* feature to their sin definition (sin as an act *and* a state) to accommodate this incoherence.

Another coherence issue for Model 2 is Adam and Eve themselves. If all acts of sin flow from original sin and sinful fleshly desires, this does not account for Adam and Eve's sin, since they had no such nature. Again, how they could sin without both of these causes is left as a mystery—it does not cohere with their explanation of how actual sin occurs.

Based on this discussion, Model 1 appears the most coherent and least *ad hoc*.

Integration

Evolutionary psychology, previously referred to as sociobiology,[54] is one field of scientific study that addresses human nature and must be interpreted and integrated by our models. Critics sometimes propose that evolutionary psychology (EP) advocates genetic determinism. Adherents respond by clarifying that the evolutionary approach does not propose that biology is our destiny. Human behavior is too complex to be caused solely by genes. There is another factor—the environment (to include culture), which influences how genes are expressed. These two determine behavior, however, how the two produce behavior is not the question EP tries to answer. Rather, it asks *why* certain behaviors occur and assumes the ultimate answer is to maximize an individual's contribution to the human gene pool for the next generation. This is not the immediate or conscious motive behind the many behaviors humans exhibit, but immediate motives ultimately serve the end of survival and propagation.[55] Some theorists see room for libertarian

---

54. Evolutionary psychology applies evolutionary theories to the study of human behavior and interprets human behavior in light of those theories, to include the idea of natural selection.

55. Dunbar, et al., *Evolutionary Psychology*, 4–6, 9. The authors go on to say on p. 9 that evolutionary processes do not have to depend on genes: "*Anything* that causes a correlation between parents and offspring has the capacity to be a Darwinian process. The things that an organism learns in its lifetime and passes on to its offspring can also undergo a process of natural selection. . . . Cultural processes can therefore have very important evolutionary effects and this is especially true of our own evolution. In other words, understanding human behaviour from an evolutionary perspective may not require the involvement of genes at all."

freedom within the synergy of genes and environment.[56] Ted Peters agrees, taking human libertarian freedom as a given, citing the common-sense evidence of our personal experience. We confront situations that require our action, we develop and then mull over alternative courses, and finally pick one of them.[57] However, most modern psychological theorists believe in psychological determinism, which states that human behavior is caused by the strongest motives and desires, which are the direct products of genes and environment. Some of these motives are unknown to us and are therefore unconscious, so that our perception of libertarian freedom is illusory.[58] Our behavior really results from antecedent causes and circumstances. We are free in the sense of being able to respond to our most powerful desires. This view defines compatibilism, and is the dominant view among modern secular philosophers.[59]

Ethically, sociobiologists suggest any good done to others or any apparent self-denial must ultimately benefit our individual survival (and thus the survival of our genetic information) or the survival of offspring and relatives (related genetic material).[60] Richard Dawkins furthered this idea in his book, *The Selfish Gene*, explaining that all human behavior fosters the individual's genetic reproduction. Because he assumes this is the goal of living organisms—to win the battle of natural selection and be the "fittest" organism—he concludes that human behavior is somehow dictated by the genetic data. Similarly, the concept of *kin selection* describes apparently altruistic behavior toward blood (genetic) relatives. However, this is still selfish, since it promotes "inclusive fitness," or the propagation of DNA of close relatives at the risk of harm to one's self. Likewise, the apparently altruistic action of *reciprocal altruism* is bent on giving and receiving mutual aid with those who are not genetically related. This cooperation aids the survival of both parties as they foster each other's well-being and is thus ultimately selfish.[61]

Most of the preceding discussion is on the philosophical and theoretical level. Little empirical evidence is set forth. Peters catches this, noting that EP is a form of speculative genetics; there are no experiments that either confirm or falsify its claims. Some evidence is suggestive, however. For example, a correlation was found between abnormal X chromosomes and violent behavior in eight Dutch male relatives. All were mildly retarded and

---

56. Williams, *Doing without Adam*, 144.
57. Peters, *Playing God*, 18–21, 35–36, 58.
58. An earlier proponent of this view is Wilson, *Sociobiology*.
59. Kane, *Significance of Free Will*, 6, 10, 12.
60. Shaw, "Human Brain," 154.
61. Teo, "Human Altruism," 170–71.

exhibited habitual exhibitionism and voyeurism. They habitually responded with inappropriate anger and aggression (rape, attempted murder, arson) to mild provocations. In a second example, it has been suggested that the XYY male genotype is a cause of criminal behavior (However, later critique rightly faulted the study's methodology and revealed that 96 percent of XYY males never commit serious crimes.). Thirdly, two Harvard researchers postulated there is a "type" of person who is a criminal—a young urban male, mesomorphic (muscular build), having a criminal biological father, lower in intelligence, impulsive and extroverted, with a autonomic nervous system that responds more slowly to stimuli. However, a direct link to genetics was lacking; there were no "born criminals." Some traits were heritable, but these acted along with the environment. The most one could say is that the traits were conducive to criminal behavior.[62] Fourth, neurologists at the University of Wisconsin compared two types of brain scans between a Wisconsin prison's general inmates and those identified as psychopaths (violent criminals who show little remorse for their actions or empathy for their victims). Researchers focused on two areas of the brain, the amygdala, which experiences and manages fear, and the ventromedial prefrontal cortex, which is responsible for empathy, regret, and guilt. Brain scans revealed less substantial connections and less electro-chemical communication between these areas, suggesting a possible cause for psychopathic behavior.[63]

Andy Ridgway has compiled the results of other recent studies that relate empirical research to the seven deadly sins (lust, gluttony, sloth, envy, pride, wrath, and greed). He interviewed Adam Safron, a research consultant at Chicago's Northwestern University, about the latest research. Safron studied lust using MRI scans of persons watching erotic movies, noting that the limbic system, especially the nucleus accumbens, which is involved in experiencing pleasure and cravings, was very active. Safron's study couldn't conclude that we are "hard-wired" for sin, but could see which brain areas were active when humans are stimulated with visual erotica.

The same reward circuits are activated when we eat. Some people's circuits are in overdrive and experience extreme desires to eat, often in excess. What might have been helpful in an environment of food scarcity is not so in today's world of relative food abundance. Ridgway sees the tendency toward gluttony as helpful for self-preservation, but in modern society it is viewed at "sin." He and Safron conclude the same for sloth, since in the evolutionary past, resting saved calories for growth and repair in a harsh environment. Today it would be viewed as being lazy.

62. Peters, *Playing God*, 67–72, 74–76.
63. Motzkin, et al., "Reduced Prefrontal Connectivity," 17348, 17357.

Ridgway talked with other researchers in Japan who were studying envy. Male and female volunteers were presented with three situations involving 1) someone of the same sex who was intelligent, had similar life goals to the volunteers, was attractive, and had a beautiful or handsome beau, 2) someone of the opposite sex, also intelligent and attractive, but with differing life goals, 3) someone of the opposite sex with mediocre intelligence, physical attractiveness, and popularity. In all cases volunteers' brain scans showed increased blood flow and activity in the anterior cingulate cortex, a brain region associated with pain sensation, when reading about person #1. This response was interpreted as envy, the pain of which can lead positively to increased personal performance, neutrally, to a change in strategy (since you decide you don't compare well with the successful), or negatively, to a desire to see the highly successful person harmed.

Pride was the subject of researchers at Montclair (NY) State University. Subjects were found to normally "enhance" self-descriptions; they saw themselves as a little better than they were. When a magnetic coil stimulated the prefrontal cortex, thereby stopping its normal functioning, subjects used much fewer self-flattering words, suggesting this brain portion controls self-perception. Self-deprecation is centered in the same region, which researchers interpreted as pride in disguise. In both cases this suggests to Ridgway that pride is natural.

Wrath, or anger, was the subject of scientists at the University of New South Wales in Australia. Subjects were verbally abused while in a brain scanner in order to illicit anger. The more self-controlled persons activated the moderating effect of the prefrontal cortex more quickly, as in the last study. Safron believes this illustrates the constant conversation between the more primitive and emotional limbic system and the more rational cortex. They are both necessary for normal brain functioning, for when the connection is severed, it is difficult for individuals to regulate behavior. The final "sin," greed, seems to be a more complex behavior and the environment and learning seem to play a larger role.[64]

While Ridgway's article highlighted brain areas that are active during certain mental states, it hardly backs up its claim that humans are hard-wired for sin. Though it is sometimes helpful to describe "parts" or functions of our humanness, such as body, soul, mind, emotions, spirit, etc., we function as a unit. Therefore it would be expected that mental states would be noticeable on scans of certain parts of the brain. This says nothing about the origin of behavior. The earlier studies on criminal behavior provided the most convincing evidence that behavior might be at least strongly influenced by our

---

64. Ridgway, "The Human Brain," Focus Magazine.

physical state. However, even this is inconclusive, since the mechanism of action is not stated or even known. In the end, EP includes a series of *ad hoc* and *post hoc* arguments that are interesting to consider, but have inadequate backing.[65]

Timothy Shaw relates the structures and functions of the human brain to moral and religious behaviors. Shaw describes a theory with substantial explanatory power for human moral behavior called "triune brain theory." This theory explains three basic structural/functional areas of our brain, ordered by their complexity and function. The lowest part of this overlapping neural hierarchy is the "protoreptilian formation," which is located at the base of the human cerebellum and whose structures are common to reptiles, birds, and mammals. This portion is the source of the struggle for power, adherence to routine, imitation, submissive behavior, and deception. The next highest part is the "paleomammalian formation," which includes much of the limbic system (more primitive parts of the cerebral cortex and cerebrum in general), and accounts for nursing/care-giving behavior, vocal communication with offspring, and play. Further, this system is associated with emotional responses to stimuli, physiologic drives, perception of pleasure and emotional pain, and what constitutes rewards and punishments. This area is limited in fish and reptiles and found mostly in mammals. The highest part is the "neomammalian formation," which is found in higher mammals, and is most complex in humans. It is centered in the cerebral cortex (the thin outer layer of the cerebrum). There are several cerebral lobes (parietal, occipital, temporal, frontal) but the most important for controlling human behavior is the frontal, especially the prefrontal cerebral cortex. This area in humans is very large and complex compared to any other mammal. Functions originating here include problem solving, task focusing ability, anticipation and response to unpleasant stimuli, planning and goal setting, motivation to act and act creatively, insight and empathy, self-perception, inhibition of behavior, ability to predict and expect results of actions, all sensory data integration, decision making, assigning priorities to limbic system stimuli, and control of the limbic system's urges and drives. These functions best account for human expression of morality, empathy, religion, altruism, complex language, and aesthetic appreciation/creativity.[66]

Humans, therefore, have a superior ability to assess the consequences of actions and in modifying or denying the urges and desires of the limbic system. However, this ability does not imply there is no struggle to resist these tendencies. It can be reasonably inferred that these urges are akin to

---

65. Peters, *Playing God*, 52.
66. Ibid., 149–54. See also MacLean, *Triune Brain*.

the Apostle Paul's description of the desires of the "flesh" and of our "old" or "natural self." Our biological urges are not sinful in themselves and many are helpful for our survival. However, Christianity affirms that when people disobey the two Great Commandments or give greater importance to fleshly drives than to spiritual goals, this is sinful. Shaw concludes that human higher brain functions can override the natural limbic and protoreptilian tendencies, but asks the question of why they would ever want to.[67] An answer must await the summary discussion of Section II.

So, how does one integrate the above data with our model's views on original sin, sin, and the flesh? Philosophically, secular and Christian compatibilists vary in the mechanism they espouse for determining behavior. The difference is the one selects genetics and environment as the causes, and the other selects God or previous states as the cause.

But to what end does a secular compatibilist think human nature leads? We saw that EP and sociobiology suggest the end is genetic self-interest/survival. Adrian Teo adds that this end dovetails well with several other secular theories. Behaviorism holds that humans are motivated to seek pleasure and avoid pain. Classic psychoanalysis assumes we have innate sexual and aggressive desires that must be expressed. In economics, utility maximization theory suggests that consumers try to get the best value for the least expenditure.[68] These views seem to agree with the idea that humans are naturally selfish. Both Model's 1 and 2 agree that humans are selfish, but Model 2's view on original sin seems to agree more with the deterministic tenets of evolutionary psychology. Model 2 also agrees more with Ridgeway's conclusions, even though his survey of research was descriptive and did not provide empirical evidence supporting a "hard-wiring" for sin.

On the other hand, secular libertarians agree with Christian advocates that genes, the environment, and God (if they believe in one) influence our non-moral and moral behavior but do not cause it. Though none support their contentions with convincing empirical evidence or a proposed mechanism, some theories, such as Shaw's triune brain theory, make a good case for libertarian human nature. His research on non-pathological brains suggests humans can control their baser urges. He and other theorists do not describe physical urges as causes, but as influences. This seems to best agree with Model 1's assertions on the influential nature of fleshly desires as opposed to viewing them as a determinant or cause of sinful behavior.

Contrary theories within EP support one or the other of our models, but since no research could verify a compatibilist or incompatibilist

---

67. Peters, *Playing God*, 156, 160.
68. Teo, "Human Altruism," 175.

viewpoint, this field of study does not definitively support either Model 1 or 2.

Existential Livability

Both Models 1 and 2 propose that fleshly desires beset all humans. However, Model 1 gives Christians more confidence they can successfully overcome fleshly desires and resist the other influences of the world and the devil. There is less mystery and paradox as to how God works and this makes God's ways easier to understand personally and helps Christians explain and defend God's ways to non-Christians apologetically. It allows and encourages Christians to live in a manner consistent with the Bible's holiness commands. Model 2 is livable, but limits the expectation of overcoming original sin and fleshly desires based on the power attributed to each. There is less hope one can make significant progress against the flesh, world, and devil and fulfill the scriptural mandates.

IBE AND A CUMULATIVE CASE

When looking at the conclusions of chapters 2–4 and the above IBE evaluation, we infer that Model 1 presents the best cumulative case and is the superior explanation of the effects of Adam's sin, the definition of sin, and the definition and nature of the flesh.

SECTION II

What Do the Scriptures Say about the Definition and Nature of Holiness, God's Expectations of Us, and Our Ability to Be Holy?

Section II will also follow the plan developed in the Introduction and will discuss holiness in several chapters. Chapter 5 will define key words associated with holiness and what holiness entails. Chapter 6 will identify God's moral expectations of his people and conclude with a summary and evaluation of chapters 5–6.

5

Holiness Defined

JUST AS SIN IS a concept that God is the author of, so it is with holiness. The word "holiness" appears later in the OT than does sin, and like sin, there are several Hebrew and Greek words that are synonyms for it. Unlike sin, holiness describes both God and humans, suggesting our expression of it has some similarity to God's. In fact, God instructed Moses to tell the Israelites that because he is holy they are to be holy (Lev 19:12), a statement reiterated by the apostle Peter (1 Pet 1:16) to his Christian hearers. How fully we can express it is discussed later in the chapter. To begin, however, we will center on the word holiness and other similar words that will give us a better picture of what God means when he tells us to be holy. Relatedly, we will discuss various foundational meanings for the word "righteousness." Following that we will investigate the source of holiness, discover its proper motive, explore what attitudes, thoughts, and actions are associated with it in both testaments, and conclude with a definition and an interaction with historical conceptions.

WORD STUDY

There are a number of Hebrew and Greek words that the biblical writers use to define holiness and each adds to a fuller understanding of it. This summary of each word's meaning will include illustrative scriptural examples.

Hebrew Words

qādôš (adj. 7705), holy, sacred, consecrated, set apart as dedicated to God, by extension pure or innocent; *qādaš* (v. 7727), to be holy, sacred, consecrated; *qōdeš* (n. 7731) holy or sacred thing, person, place.[1] This word group is used over 750 times in the OT, but almost all of the 470 uses of *qōdeš* refer to holy things or places.

The adjective form refers at times to lay Israelites. Although they did not possess a priestly type of holiness through birth or rite, they were expected to achieve an ethical holiness by obedience to God's commands. They were to be holy because he was, therefore they were to stay in line with God's ways and honor him as God. This entailed worshipping God alone (Exod 20:3) and having no idols (Exod 20:4; Josh 24:15). Israel was a separate nation unto God (Lev 20:26). God gave them purity and dietary rules (Lev 11:44–45), moral standards (Exod 20; Lev 19), and prohibitions against foreign religious practices. By keeping the commands they would become a holy people unto the Lord their God (Deut 26:16–19).[2]

The verb form includes the ideas of separateness and consecration. Consecration is a separation unto God and therefore entails a separation from what is not like God, such as the world and its sinful practices. The noun form describes a person, thing, place, or time.[3]

> *"You are to be my holy people. So do not eat the meat of an animal torn by wild beasts; throw it to the dogs.* (Exod 22:31)
>
> *The Lord said to Moses, "Speak to the entire assembly of Israel and say to them: 'Be holy because I, the Lord your God, am holy.'"* (Lev 19:1–2)
>
> God tells Ezekiel of the wickedness of Israel's priests:
> *Her priests do violence to my law and profane my holy things; they do not distinguish between the holy and the common; they teach that there is no difference between the unclean and the clean; and they shut their eyes to the keeping of my Sabbaths, so that I am profaned among them.* (Ezek 22:26)

ṣādaq (v. 7405), to be righteous, innocent, vindicated; *ṣedeq* (n.m. 7406) and *ṣᵉdāqâ* (n.f. 7407), righteousness, justice, rightness, acting according to

---

1. As in chapter 2, the transliterated word names, numbers, and definitions are from Goodrick and Kohlenberger, *Strongest NIV*.
2. VanGemeren, *New International*, vol. 3, 883.
3. Ibid., 879, 885.

God's standard, doing right, being in the right. Altogether these words are used over 520 times in the OT.

The verb describes behavior that is in accord with some assumed or denoted standard. The standard could be the natural law or the covenant. For instance, Noah was righteous (lived rightly, Gen 6:9) and the standard is self-evident to the Genesis author, but it is not denoted. However, in 2 Samuel 22:21–25, David declared himself righteous because he has followed God's ways and obeyed his laws and decrees. In Psalm 15, David (a possible author) describes a blameless and righteous person. Abram's act of faith is righteousness for him (Gen 15:6).[4] The context links being righteous with a denoted standard—God's laws, righteous acts, and an act of faith. The Mosaic Law and covenant provide the most visible standard for how the righteous are to behave.

> *This is the account of Noah and his family. Noah was a righteous man, blameless among the people of his time, and he walked faithfully with God.* (Gen 6:9)

> *Who is wise? Let them realize these things. Who is discerning? Let them understand. The ways of the Lord are right; the righteous walk in them, but the rebellious stumble in them.* (Hos 14:9)

yāšār (adj. 3838), straight (not crooked or twisted), also morally straight, upright, innocent; *yāšar* (v. 3837), to do good, be right, to make straight or smooth; *yōšer* (n. 3841), upright, straight, honest, integrity. Altogether these are used over 150 times in the OT.

As suggested by the definitions, these words can have both physical and moral meanings. Morally, these words allude to what is legally, morally, or religiously right based on a standard, which is God's truth or law. The adjective form refers to the inner attitude of the heart and mind. It is used to describe those who uphold justice, are loyal to God, and who associate themselves with the righteous and shun the company of the wicked. The word implies doing what pleases the Lord and following him only. This form also characterizes the positive reigns of Israel's good kings—they "did what was right in the eyes of the Lord." This meant they took action through various reforms to make certain the people followed the law and covenant. The noun form indicates an integrity of heart by which the upright walk.

---

4. Ibid., 748, 750–51, 753.

The upright therefore walk a "straight" path, which morally accords with God's wishes.[5]

> Asa did what was right *in the eyes of the Lord, as his father David had done.* (1 Kgs 15:11)

> *This only have I found: God created mankind* upright, *but they have gone in search of many schemes.* (Eccl 7:29)

> *In the land of Uz there lived a man whose name was Job. This man was blameless and* upright; *he feared God and shunned evil.* (Job 1:1)

tam (adj. 9447), blameless, flawless, perfect; *tōm* (n. 9448), blamelessness, integrity, innocence; *tāmîm* (adj. 9459), without defect, blameless, perfect; *tāmam* (v. 9462), to complete, finish, perfect. These forms are used over 130 times in the OT.

The NIV translates these Hebrew words most often as "blameless" or "integrity" when referring to human moral conduct. "Flawless" is reserved almost always for God's word and "perfect" describes God and his ways. *Tāmîm* refers to sacrifices that are "without blemish" in just over half of its ninety-one uses with a third of the other references describing blameless moral character. One who is "*tāmîm*" is pious and upright before the Lord (Ps 19:13).[6] In Psalm 19:20–26, David describes himself as righteous, clean, not guilty, blameless, and kept from sin. He adds the words "faithful" and "pure" to describe the person who God responds positively toward.

The translation "integrity" implies being "complete, blameless, just, honest, perfect, [and] peaceful."[7] *Tōm* is regularly used with a verb meaning "to walk" and refers to blameless or innocent conduct, which is the result of an inner desire to obey God and love people.[8] A variant is used frequently in Job and "describes the character and quality of a life that is guided by the fear of the Lord and by the ethical principles of uprightness, honesty, and loyalty; namely integrity . . . the results of which are perfection, peace, and ultimate happiness."[9]

---

5. VanGemeren, *New International*, vol. 2, 565–67.
6. VanGemeren, *New International*, vol. 4, 307.
7. Ibid., 306.
8. Ibid., 308.
9. Ibid.

HOLINESS DEFINED

> *He said to Aaron, "Take a bull calf for your sin offering and a ram for your burnt offering, both* without defect, *and present them before the Lord." (Lev 9:2)*

> *"Surely God does not reject one who is* blameless *or strengthen the hands of evildoers." (Job 8:20)*

> *Vindicate me, Lord, for I have led a* blameless *life; I have trusted in the Lord and have not faltered. (Ps 26:1)*

> *I put in charge of Jerusalem my brother Hanani, along with Hananiah the commander of the citadel, because he was a man* of integrity *and feared God more than most people do. (Neh 7:2)*

Greek Words

Several Greek words are very close synonyms for the above Hebrew ones and illustrate that these concepts are unified across the Testaments. The following three words approximate the Hebrew concept of blameless:

anenklētos (adj. 441), blameless, free from accusation. This word is used by Paul to define character traits of acceptable deacons and elders in the church (2 Tim 1:6–9; cf. 1 Tim 3:1–12). These candidates must be above reproach spiritually as well as in ordinary standards of decency. It also describes the state in which we will be presented to Christ at his Second Coming (1 Cor 1:8). It is used five times in the NT.

> *An elder must be* blameless, *faithful to his wife, a man whose children believe and are not open to the charge of being wild and disobedient. Since an overseer manages God's household, he must be* blameless—*not overbearing, not quick-tempered, not given to drunkenness, not violent, not pursuing dishonest gain. (Titus 1:6–7)*

amōmos (adj. 320), unblemished, blameless. This word, used eight times, is used mainly to describe the condition of Christians as they are presented to God at glorification.

> *Do everything without grumbling or arguing, so that you may become* blameless *and pure, "children of God without fault in a warped and crooked generation." Then you will shine among them like stars in the sky. (Phil 2:14–15)*

amiantos (adj. 299), pure, faultless. James uses this word to depict a pure form of religion (Jas 1:27). It is used four times in the NT.

> Religion that God our Father accepts as pure and faultless *is this: to look after orphans and widows in their distress and to keep oneself from being polluted by the world.* (Jas 1:27)

hagios (adj. 41), holy, consecrated; *hagiazō* (v. 39), to sanctify, set apart, make holy. Cognate nouns (n. 40, 42, 43) mean holiness. These words are similar in meaning to the Hebrew *qādôš* and are used over 275 times in the NT.

As with *anenklētos*, holiness is the condition of those who Christ gathers at his Second Coming (Col 1:12; Heb 12:14). But, believers are holy before that great event. For Paul, the holy are those who have made themselves slaves of righteousness and not of sin (Rom 6:19–22; 1 Thess 4:3–7). They have offered themselves up as spiritual sacrifices (Rom 12:1). Believers strive after it (Heb 12:14). The holy are obedient and do not conform to their previous evil desires (1 Pet 1:14–16). Contrary to evil desires and falsehoods, Christ has sanctified them in the truth (John 17:17–19).[10]

dikaios (adj. 1465), right, righteous, upright; *dikaiosynē* (n. 1466), righteousness, justice, what is right, right act (according to God's standards), being in right relation to God; *dikaioō* (v. 1467), justify, vindicate, declare righteous, to put in right relationship legally or morally, as God with humans; *dikaiōs* (adv. 1469), justly, rightly, righteously. These words parallel the meaning of the Hebrew *sādaq* and its cognates, and are used over 210 times in the NT.

Most occurrences of these words are in the gospel of Matthew and in Paul's letters. Matthew records Jesus teaching his disciples that their righteousness must exceed that of the scribes and Pharisees (Matt 5:20), whose external righteousness was from an unclean heart (Matt 23:25) and was therefore no righteousness at all. Jesus centered on clean hearts (Matt 23:26) and the heart motive behind actions, thereby intensifying OT commands (Matt 5:21–48) and highlighting humility by doing righteous deeds regardless of who might see them (Matt 6:1–18).[11]

Paul, and to a lesser extent John, uses this word group the most and gives it its widest range of meaning.[12] These words have several connota-

---

10. Brown, *New International*, vol. 2, 230–32.
11. Brown, *New International*, vol. 3, 360.
12. See also the discussion of Blameless, Perfect, Righteous, and Sinless below.

tions—relational, forensic, and ethical—which will be discussed in more detail below.

> *Because Joseph her husband was* faithful to the law [righteous in NASB], *and yet did not want to expose her to public disgrace, he had in mind to divorce her quietly.* (Matt 1:19)

> *Then the* righteous *will answer him, "Lord, when did we see you hungry and feed you, or thirsty and give you something to drink?"* (Matt 25:37)

> *For in the gospel the* righteousness *of God is revealed—a* righteousness *that is by faith from first to last, just as it is written: "The* righteous *will live by faith."* (Rom 1:17)

> *Dear children, do not let anyone lead you astray. The one who does what is* right *is* righteous, *just as he is* righteous. (1 John 3:7)

teleios (adj. 5455), perfect, mature, finished; *teleioō* (v. 5457), to perfect, complete, finish; *teleiotēs* (n. 5456), maturity, perfection. Used over forty times in the NT.

Paul's use of the adjective form is several times translated as "mature" and refers to those who are spiritually mature in the faith (1 Cor 2:6; Phil 3:15; Col 1:28) and who manifest the fullness of Christ's character (Eph 4:13). James states that spiritual maturity is a result of perseverance (Jas 1:4).[13]

At other times the adjective is rendered "perfect." Jesus linked being "perfect" or "whole" with loving not only friends, but enemies (Matt 5:48) and with wholehearted devotion and following of him (Matt 19:21). Christ also came that his followers may be perfect in unity (John 17:23). James says that perfect persons control whatever words come from their mouths (Jas 3:2). John uses the verb form and declares that when we love one another, God's love is perfected or completed in us (1 John 4:12, 17). Further, this complete love casts out fear of punishment (1 John 4:18).[14]

> *He is the one we proclaim, admonishing and teaching everyone with all wisdom, so that we may present everyone* fully mature *in Christ.* (Col 1:28)

---

13. Brown, *New International*, vol. 3, 61–62.
14. Ibid., 63–64.

For by one sacrifice he has made perfect *forever those who are being made holy.* (Heb 10:14)

Let perseverance finish its work so that you may be mature and complete, *not lacking anything.* (Jas 1:4)

Blameless, Perfect, Righteous, and Sinless

A question can arise when thinking about the meaning of these words—does being holy mean we are sinless, in the sense of incapable of sinning? Several words, especially those translated as blameless or perfect, seem to connote this. Let us look at verses that contain these ideas more closely.

Blameless

As we have seen, the Hebrew *tam* and the Greek *anenklētos, amiantos,* and *amōmos* are frequently translated as blameless. Several persons are described as blameless. To begin, Noah was blameless (Gen 6:9). Hamilton suggests Noah is not being described as sinless but as "wholesome" or "sound."[15] Wenham adds the word "completeness" and believes the "blemish-free" meaning of *tam* applies to Noah's character. The blameless abstain from iniquity (Ezek 28:15) and walk in God's law (Ps 119:1).[16] Job also was blameless (Job 1:1, 8). Tremper Longman III translates *tam* in these verses as "innocent."[17] David Clines believes "blameless" is best, and suggests the contrast is between the "righteous" and the "wicked." The question is whether Job is a "sinner" or not, which he clearly is not.[18] Goldingay interprets *tam* here as "integrity," noticing that this is lacking in both Satan and Job's wife (Job 2:3, 9). In Job's integrity he realizes he is not God and that he must accept bad and good things at his hand. Integrity and reverence go together here.[19] In another passage, David describes himself as blameless, not overlooking his grievous sin against Uriah and Bathsheba (2 Sam 22:26). To be judged accurate, "blameless" assumes David's actions were not characteristic.[20] David is taking the tack that since God has delivered him,

---

15. Hamilton, *Book of Genesis*, 277.
16. Wenham, *Genesis 1–15*, 170.
17. Longman, *Job*, 79.
18. Clines, *Job 1–20*, 12.
19. Goldingay, *Old Testament*, 267.
20. Bergen, *1, 2 Samuel*, 456.

he is vindicated and accepted in God's sight.[21] In the NT, Zechariah and Elizabeth are blameless (Luke 1:6) because they faithfully obeyed God and the full range of his commandments. They were spiritual exemplars.[22] The final group of "blameless" people considered is Paul and his co-workers. They acted blamelessly in front of the Thessalonians. Gene Green affirms that this moniker was frequently used in ancient funerary epigraphs and heralded a person who had unfailingly fulfilled their obligations to God's law. It has the same meaning for Paul's referents.[23]

Perfect

As we saw above, perfect, mature, and complete encompass most of the translations of the Greek *teleios* and cognates. Jesus uses the word when he describes the kind of love his followers are to have for each other, the world, and our enemies—they must be perfect as their heavenly Father is perfect (Matt 5:48). In the previous five verses Jesus has, as he has just done with several other OT sayings and commands, countered or augmented them. In verses 46–47, we see that even sinners love their friends and those who love them in return. However, Christ's disciples are to love *enemies* and do them *good*.[24] God himself does this when he showers down rain on all, irrespective of their character. It is likely that perfect here suggests completeness in the sense of obeying all Jesus's commands and adhering to all his teachings.[25] Donald Hagner agrees that loving our enemies is the gist of Jesus's use of perfection here, adding that the verb here is emphatic—"you are to be perfect." This unrestricting love reflects God's love and encompasses the core of ethical perfection.[26]

John also uses *teleios* to explain love. He describes Christ's followers as those who obey God's commands and in whom the love of God is perfected or made complete (1 John 2:5). "Love of God" is difficult to translate. It can mean "God's love for us," "our love for God," or "God's kind of love." Daniel Akin believes "our love for God" (as it is in the NIV) fits John's point that when we keep Christ's word our love for God reaches completion,

21. Arnold, B., *1 & 2 Samuel*, 631.
22. Bock, *Luke 1:1—9:50*, 77–78.
23. Green, *Letters to the Thessalonians*, 133.
24. There is no OT command to "hate your enemies" (Matt 5:43). It may have been an ethical principle followed by some Jews. Jesus is zeroing in on the love command and not on this added element.
25. Osborne, *Matthew*, 214.
26. Hagner, *Matthew*, 135.

perfection, or the ultimate goal.²⁷ In other words, we can't do any better than that. This does not imply we are not empowered by God's love for us (vv. 16 and 19 make that clear), but it is not the point John is making here. Later, in 1 John 4:12 and 17 the point comes up again. When we love one another, God's love finds its fullest possible earthly expression (v. 12).²⁸ Love is made complete, and when we act in the world like Jesus acted (v. 17), we can have assurance on the Day of Judgment. This is how the NIV translates it. Some commentators think it may be God the Father who is the referent, since the Greek says "just as the one is present, so are we in this world. If God the Father is implied, then the verse says that our love is made complete when the God of love abides with his people.²⁹ Both interpretations acknowledge that our love can only be complete when God is our source.

Does John in his first epistle suggest this "completion," "perfection," or "fullness" in love includes sinlessness? It seems not, since earlier he affirmed that those who claim to have never sinned are deceived, liars, and Christ's truth is not in them. John doesn't want anyone to sin, but *if* they do, they have an advocate with the Father who can atone for their sins (1 John 1:8—2:1). Loving completely doesn't imply the necessity of sinning, but it also doesn't assume sin will never occur in those people either.

James 1:2-4 uses the same word, referring to the result of perseverance under trial:

> 2Consider it pure joy, my brothers and sisters, whenever you face trials of many kinds, 3because you know that the testing of your faith produces perseverance. 4Let perseverance finish its work so that you may be mature and complete, not lacking anything.

James avers that trials test our faith and develop perseverance. Dan McCartney, using Greek moral literature as a guide, defines the word perseverance (or endurance) as continuing on our course and not letting any distress change our convictions, thinking, or lifestyle. James exhorts his hearers to not give up prematurely, but to let this kind of endurance finish its work. God's testing and desire for long-term obedience has a good end in mind—our maturing, completing, and equipping. Becoming full-grown and filled with integrity prevents the double-mindedness that James later laments and is a preliminary to the ultimate "perfecting" when we receive the crown of life (Jas 1:12).³⁰

27. Akin, *1, 2, 3 John*, 93.
28. Yarbrough, *1–3 John*, 245.
29. Ibid., 259.
30. McCartney, *James*, 87–88.

Paul believes the process of maturity and perfecting is aided by good leaders:

> 11 So Christ himself gave the apostles, the prophets, the evangelists, the pastors and teachers, 12 to equip his people for works of service, so that the body of Christ may be built up 13 until we all reach unity in the faith and in the knowledge of the Son of God and become mature, *attaining to the whole measure of the fullness of Christ.*
>
> 14 Then we will no longer be infants, tossed back and forth by the waves, and blown here and there by every wind of teaching and by the cunning and craftiness of people in their deceitful scheming. 15 Instead, speaking the truth in love, we will grow to become in every respect the mature *body of him who is the head, that is, Christ.* (Eph 4:11–15)

Leaders equip fellow believers so they can serve each other and the world. Leaders also bless the church itself; the body of Christ's development is compared to the growth, strengthening, and completion of a building. There are three aspects to this building up. Andrew Lincoln suggests the first one— "until we all reach unity in the faith and in the knowledge of the Son of God"—has an emphasis more on the content of faith than the exercise of faith. Paul's mention of false teaching (v. 14) belies his concern that believers need to hold onto truth and avoid error. "Knowledge of the Son of God" likely involves all the knowledge that is involved in salvation and in Christ, in whom all the treasures of wisdom and knowledge are hid (Col 2:2–3). The "until" that begins this phrase implies that this unity and knowledge has begun but it still remains to be fully attained, a process completed only at Christ's return for his bride.[31]

The second and third aspects are to "become mature, attaining to the whole measure of the fullness of Christ." The church is the dwelling place of Christ's attributes and powers on this earth and it must seek to more and more reflect that glory. Leaders are to push forward that whole process, which will help immature believers grow up and not be led astray by crafty deceivers (v. 14).[32] The goal is the "whole measure," stature or "size" of Christ, which means we reflect his virtues and likeness in their mature form.[33] The goal is not to just get by. Contrary to these cunning schemers the church is to speak the truth in a loving way. Christ's body, just like

---

31. Lincoln, *Ephesians*, 255–56.
32. Ibid., 257, 259.
33. Arnold, C. *Ephesians*, 266.

Christ, must bring truth and love simultaneously. We can then become like Christ "in every way," and his body will then look like it belongs to its head.

Hebrews 5:14 also suggests the idea of spiritual maturity, since the believers are ones "who by constant use have trained themselves to distinguish good from evil." They have exercised their faculties through repeated experience and have thus developed the ability to discern what is good from what is not.

Righteous

A third word that might be associated with sinlessness is righteous. We have already described the righteousness of Noah. Job, already portrayed as blameless, was also called upright (Job 1:1, 8). This means Job did what he knew to be morally correct; he obeyed God.[34] The verses themselves elaborate, "he feared God and shunned evil." Other synonyms are "righteous" and "good" and these are relational terms, implying right relations with and behavior toward others.[35] Job's conscience was clear of wrongdoing (Job 27:6) and his behavior towards others was exemplary (He was a friend to the poor, the needy, the blind, lame, dying, and oppressed. See Job 29:11–17).[36]

In the NT, John address righteousness and sin in his first epistle:

> 6No one who lives in him keeps on sinning. No one who continues to sin has either seen him or known him.
>
> 7Dear children, do not let anyone lead you astray. The one who does what is right is righteous, just as he is righteous. 8The one who does what is sinful is of the devil, because the devil has been sinning from the beginning. The reason the Son of God appeared was to destroy the devil's work. 9No one who is born of God will continue to sin, because God's seed remains in them; they cannot go on sinning, because they have been born of God. (1 John 3:6–9; cf. 1 John 5:18)

Yarbrough suggests the sinning in verses 6 and 9 is not the continuance in sin as translated in the NIV and as held by many commentators, but "aberrant doctrine, ethics, or devotion that have recently marred the community's integrity."[37] However, it seems more likely the sinning described is as a way of life, a pervasive habit or lifestyle. Christians will sin on occasion and

---

34. Longman, *Job*, 79.
35. Clines, *Job 1–20*, 12.
36. VanGemeren, *New International*, 755–56.
37. Yarbrough, *1–3 John*, 183.

will need forgiveness and cleansing (1 John 2:1), but their pervasive lifestyle is righteous, as stated in verse 7. Again, it is not occasional righteousness, but a habitual practice of righteousness that is meant. Those who live the opposite, habitual sinners, have neither seen, perceived, nor known Christ experientially; they belong to another family—the devil's. Verse 9 restates verse 6, emphasizing it is those born of God who have his "seed"; they abide in him and do not sin. They cannot sin in this continual way because they are new in Christ and his life enables and motivates them to live righteously.[38] These interpretations strongly suggest an ability to be righteous and do what God commands. This habitual righteousness does not deny the occasional sin, and therefore suggests sinless perfection is not John's meaning here.

We must conclude that the biblical authors do not directly address the ideas of sinlessness when using the word "blameless," "perfect/mature," or "righteous." We can only make conclusions by looking at the whole of the referent's life. For example, David had obvious sins, but was considered blameless. Our other examples sinned too. Jesus implied that perfection/completeness involves loving to the uttermost—even our enemies. Paul never claimed to be sinless, stating he was not "perfect," but "mature" (Phil 3:12–15). Hebrews and James agree with "maturity" being the important meaning of *teleios*. John, in his first epistle, sees righteousness as necessarily a habitual lifestyle and a defined character. It is the habitual pattern of the righteous that marks them. The righteous can and sometimes do sin and must confess, repent, receive forgiveness, and strive to not sin again. Likewise, the meaning of our three words seems to center on this habitual and long-term obedience—if a person was faithful toward God and his law/faith requirements, and repented of known sins, then it was appropriate to call him or her blameless, mature, or righteous. These words, then, do not connote being sinless.

TYPES OF RIGHTEOUSNESS

The NT writers infer several types of righteousness—relational, forensic, and ethical. Each is distinct yet complementary to the others. An analogy is a rubber ball having three different-colored sections, each one representing an aspect of righteousness. The ball always includes all three sections or it would not be a ball. One can rotate the ball and look at (investigate) one aspect if one wishes, all the while realizing it is part of a whole.[39]

---

38. Akin, *1, 2, 3 John*, 142–48.

39. The grouping of relational, ethical, and forensic aspects of righteousness is from Diehl, "Meaning of Righteousness."

Relational Righteousness

For the God of the Bible, holiness and righteousness imply a relationship between him and his people. This relationship always took the form of a covenant—an agreement between God and those in his image. God pledged to be faithful to his promises. Most of the time a human response was necessary. Even if God upheld his end, if humans didn't the agreement would come to naught. When humans were faithful or loyal to God and his covenants, they were deemed righteous.[40] This meaning is especially implied by the Greek verb for righteous, *dikaioō*.[41]

Forensic or Judicial Righteousness

This type of righteousness involves a "declaring" of a state of righteousness and is also frequently described using the same Greek verb, *dikaioō*. This is what happens when a Christian is born again—Paul uses a law court term to describe one aspect of the Christian's new condition—she is now "not guilty" or "acquitted." God, as judge, has found in her favor, forgiven her sins, acquitted her of all charges, and has pronounced her "just" or "justified."[42] This is the type of righteousness Paul seems to be getting at in Romans 3–4. Paul concludes his argument then, saying, "Therefore, since we have been justified through faith, we have peace with God through our Lord Jesus Christ." (Rom 5:1). This happens in a moment and continues until one is glorified.

Colin Brown suggests that the Jews were trying to be justified by the works of the law (perfect obedience to it), or, in other words, their ethical righteousness (discussed below). Paul agreed that this is how justification by the law works (Rom 2:13), but also affirms no one was obeying it perfectly (Rom 9:31–32). Contrarily, God's "declared" righteousness is by faith (and always has been) and through Christ (Rom 10:3–4).[43] This "declared righteous" state implies the existence of relational righteousness and allows one to proceed to the ethical righteousness described below.

---

40. Rad, *Old Testament*, 371, 373.

41. Ziesler, *Meaning of Righteousness*, 1–14, 212.

42. Wright, N., *Justification*, 90–91.

43. Brown, *New International*, vol. 3, 363. See Brown's whole discussion for further detail on this topic, pp. 360–73.

Ethical Righteousness

Relational righteousness is expressed is attitudes, thoughts, and actions—toward God, others, and the creation; this is ethical righteousness. Rad agrees, stating that righteousness "is the standard not only for man's relationship with God, but also his relationship with his fellows. . . . it is even the standard for man's relationship to the animals and to his natural environment."[44] This ethical righteousness is therefore never impersonal. This was true from the beginning—Adam and Eve were put in a right relationship with God, each other, and the creation. Until they sinned they were righteous.

In the OT ethical righteousness frequently refers to obedience to the law, "And if we are careful to obey all this law before the Lord our God, as he has commanded us, that will be our righteousness" (Deut 6:25). Relatedly, personal and social ethics were the constant demand of the OT prophets. They spurred Israel to be faithful and obedient to the law, to show mercy and generosity to the needy, and to worship God alone. This was much better than hypocritical sacrifices (Isa 1:11–17).

The NT also interprets righteousness as right conduct, implying loving the brethren (Matt 25:37, 46; 1 John 3:7, 10–17), compassionate acts (Matt 6:1), and godly behavior (Rom 6:13, 16, 20; and Romans 6 and 8 generally). The righteousness of faith is one of righteous deeds (Rom 2:6–10, 13, 16).[45]

In this case a believer is said to be "made" righteous. This is the same as transformation of character, becoming Christ-like, growing in holiness, or "becoming" righteous.[46] This follows and flows from justification (being declared righteous), is a result of the new life the Spirit works in the regenerated believer, is a life-long and progressive process, is never finished on this earth, and culminates in glorification. Stephen Westerholm sums up that this ethical righteousness is the ordinary meaning in the Scriptures, and it refers to right conduct in God's eyes. It is the righteousness described in Romans 6 and is the lifestyle of those who live "according to the Spirit" (Rom 8:4).[47] This is the same type that was defined by many of our Hebrew words, by the Greek adjective *dikaios* and noun *dikaiosynē*,[48] and the above discussion of the word righteous.[49]

---

44. Rad, *Old Testament*, 370.
45. Diehl, "Meaning of Righteousness," 5.
46. Wright, N., *Justification*, 90–91.
47. Westerholm, "Righteousness of the Law," 254, 264.
48. Ziesler, *Meaning of Righteousness*, 1–14, 212.

49. There has been great debate through the centuries about the proper interpretation of the righteous word group. Catholic, Protestant, and now "New Perspective" interpreters of Paul disagree especially over when Paul means "declared" righteous,

In conclusion, these three types of righteousness form a dynamic whole, like our original three-sectioned ball.[50] When we begin our walk with God we are "declared" righteous; we are now in right standing with God. This new right relationship with God can continue until we are glorified. This forensic and relational righteousness produces ethical righteousness, which is a fruit of relationship and the indwelling Holy Spirit. It is produced with our cooperation and is encouraged by the community of faith. It is this "made" righteousness that is of greatest interest when considering holiness.

THE NATURE OF HOLINESS, RIGHTEOUSNESS, AND SPIRITUAL MATURITY

The foregoing definitions of holiness-related words, the descriptions of three types of righteousness, and the meaning of blameless, perfect, and righteous are well-and-good as far as they go, but they are very broad concepts that need augmenting. What is the source of holiness? What motivates a holy person? What does such a person believe, say, think, and do? How detailed are the Scriptures in their guidance? Let us investigate answers to these questions.

What is the Source of Holiness?

In chapter 2 we discussed the source of sin as the human heart. This is appropriate, since God is not a source of sin and Satan and his demons can only influence us—they cannot force us to sin. Chapter 3 concluded that Adam and Eve are indirect sources for our sin, but as in chapter 2, we are

---

when he refers to "ethical" righteousness, and what each entails. Catholics traditionally espouse justification as occurring at baptism and the beginning of a "real" or ethical righteousness. Thus, justification and sanctification (ethical righteousness) progress together through the Christian life and one is finally pronounced "justified" at the final Judgment. Protestants assert that at the new birth a believer is "declared" righteous by God, and Christ's "real" righteousness is imputed to their account, and in that sense they possess his righteousness as theirs. They have no real righteousness of their own yet, but his perfectly meets God's demands through the atonement. Ziesler is astute to note that neither side negates the necessity of both aspects. See Ziesler, *Meaning of Righteousness*, 2–7. For a good summary of Ziesler's conclusions, see chapter 9. New Perspective proponents stress that it is not that Christ's real righteousness is imputed to Christians, but that now the Christian is in right relational standing with God within the New Covenant. Each is now vindicated, acquitted, in the right, and forgiven. See Wright, N., *Justification*, 66, 90–92.

50. Diehl, "Meaning of Righteousness," 6.

the final determiner of our moral conduct. We mentioned that the heart was also the source of goodness, and this was suggested by Proverbs 4:23 and Matthew 12:33–35. However, God is the ultimate source of all goodness and we need to coordinate these two ideas to come to a full-orbed and consistent doctrine.

God is good and from that goodness flows many acts of love (Ps 107). Every good gift comes from him (Jas 1:17). Goodness is a broad word and difficult to define, but certainly includes all those moral traits that are a part of his character (love, holiness, kindness, mercy, justice, longsuffering). Further, since we are creatures made in God's image, God sees it as desirable to command us to be like him in his moral attributes. We are commanded to be holy (1 Pet 1:15), to love (John 13:34), and to do good (Gal 6:10). The power to be like him comes from him, and in God's economy belongs only to those who are his children. This is evident in John's words in his first epistle; he reminds believers that "love comes from God" (1 John 4:7). Love is manifested not that we loved God, but that he loved us. Now we can (1 John 4:19) and ought to love one another (1 John 4:10–11).

Paul makes clear that the ability to be holy and overcome sin comes from the Holy Spirit, who now resides in believers. The Spirit indwells them and gives them life, and when they cooperate with God, he frees them from the law of sin and death. We now live according to the Spirit (Rom 8:1–4). As further evidence, the Holy Spirit produces wonderful moral fruit (Gal 5:22–23).

Love—The Motive for Holiness

Motive is important in determining the ultimate goodness of any human act. Discussing motive also answers our earlier concern for detail when understanding the nature of holiness. God and the biblical writers expand on the implications of the Hebrew and Greek words defined above and address the topic of motive. There is a hint in Scriptures we have already quoted from—Lev 19:2 and 1 Pet 1:16—regarding why we should be holy, and that is *because God is holy*. Everything about God's character is good and God commands us to be like him in all the ways we are able. Morally, this involves becoming like him in our motives.

The shortest and most overarching description of what God is like is given by the apostle John—"God is love" (1 John 4:8, 16); love is his nature, just as holiness is. Coming from this, the broadest guidance God the Father gave to the people of Israel (the Shema of Deut 6:4–5) is echoed by Jesus himself. When queried about the *greatest* commandment in the Mosaic law, he replied, "'Love the Lord your God with all your heart and with all your soul and with all your mind.' This is the first and greatest commandment. And the second is like it: 'Love your neighbor as yourself.' All the Law and the Prophets hang on these two commandments" (Matt 22:38–40). Love toward God is the motive for holiness.

Similarly, days before his death Jesus speaks his final words to his disciples and he gives them a horizontal and "new" command—to love each other *as he has loved them* (John 13:34, 15:12). This is a self-sacrificial love, a love which gives itself up for friends (John 15:13). Jesus has lived with his disciples for three years now, giving them a living love model. Now, the disciples will truly be his friends if they do as he has commanded them and love in this sacrificial way (John 15:14). This obedience to Jesus's command is so central that Jesus repeats it four times in a short span—he who loves me will obey my commands (John 14:15, 21, 24, 15:10).

Our conclusion is that love and a desire to be like God are behind holiness and obedience. What does love look like? Again, we will investigate the more detailed meaning of Hebrew and Greek words to answer this question.

Hebrew and Greek Words

The root word for love in Hebrew is *'hb*. A major form is *'āhab* (v. 170), to love, like, be a friend. This love can refer to friendship, familial, romantic, or a covenant-loyalty love. The noun forms (171, 172, 173) can mean love, thing loved, lover, or the same as the verb definition. These forms are used over 250 times in the OT.

Versions of *'hb* describe God's love toward humans or human love toward God. For our purposes we are centering on our human love response toward God. This love implies several co-actions: reverential fear of God (Deut 10:12, 13:3–4), walking in his ways (Deut 11:22, 19:9), and honoring him as the true God (no idols) (Exod 20:2–6, 23:32–33, Deut 4:19–24). Love is commanded to the Israelites and this command can only be fulfilled by those who have the inner spiritual power that God grants his followers. God circumcised their hearts so they could love him totally (Deut 30:6). This total love means love must be from the whole heart (Deut 4:29, 10:12, 30:6); it is a dynamic and total cleaving to God. "Total self-entrusting and faithful love to God, then, is at the heart of what the OT regards as genuine piety and a love that necessarily includes an attitude of gratitude, . . . trust, . . . and consistent solidarity (*hesed*)."[51] The prophets continually emphasized the need for this inner genuineness, demanding covenant loyalty (*hesed*) and holi-

---

51. VanGemeren, *New International*, vol. 1, 286.

ness, true conversion of heart, and keeping of the commandments. Since love is "commanded," the idea conveyed by love is more appropriately one of *relationship* and a *behavior pattern* commensurate with covenant-keeping. The idea of love as a *feeling* is an indirect and secondary one, though feelings can certainly accompany this love.[52]

Love toward fellow humans is also commanded using versions of *'hb*, but the instances are few (e.g., Lev 19:18, 34; Deut 10:18–19). Their use refers to love toward fellow Israelites or sojourning foreigners (Exod 22:21–22), even when an act or feeling of revenge and hatred would seem more appropriate. Unlike the NT command to love one's neighbor, implying everyone, love to neighbor here did not seem to refer to others outside of the national border.[53]

> Love *the Lord your God with all your heart and with all your soul and with all your strength.* (Deut 6:5)

> *"'Do not seek revenge or bear a grudge against anyone among your people, but* love *your neighbor as yourself. I am the Lord.* (Lev 19:18)

hesed (n. 2876), unfailing love, loyal love, devotion, kindness, often based on a prior, usually covenant, relationship. Used over 240 times.

This noun is frequently used when referring to God's attitude and actions toward humans, since the context is usually of a superior helping an inferior, or someone with means helping a needy dependent. However the word has an inherent sense of presumed mutuality, hence it is also used for humans expressing love, loyalty, and kindness toward God (2 Sam 22:26; Hos 6:6; Mic 6:8; Prov 19:22).[54]

> *"To the* faithful *you show yourself* faithful,
> *to the blameless you show yourself blameless . . ."* (2 Sam 22:26)

agapaō (v. 26), Greek for to love, in the NT, God the Father's love for his Son and his people and his people's love for God, others, and even enemies. *agapē* (n. 27), the same meaning as the verb form. Used over 250 times in the NT.[55]

---

52. Ibid., 286–87, 289.

53. Ibid., 290.

54. VanGemeren, *New International*, vol. 2, 216.

55. Sometimes the Greek verb *phileō* is used similarly as *agapaō*. It tends to be more limited, however. It is used for love of friends (Jesus and Lazarus, John 11:36), fellow believers (2 Pet 1:7), or relatives, signifying it is between those who are closely connected. Peter uses *phileō* in his response to Jesus when Jesus asks Peter if he loves

The Gospels rarely refer to the motive behind love. Rather, it is frequently described using its attributes, such as mercy or compassion; examples (parables) are also common. For example, love frequently chooses to suffer, as Jesus's crucifixion and the ill treatment experienced by the disciples and that first and second-century Christ-followers attest. Relatedly, love involves self-sacrifice (e.g., God' love, John 3:16, 15:12–13; 1 John 3:16) and self-denial (losing one's life, Matt 10:35–37; taking up one's cross, Matt 16:24). A new aspect for Jewish minds was loving one's enemies (Matt 4:44–48; the parable of the Good Samaritan, Luke 10:25–37).[56]

Paul certainly speaks of what love is like. First Corinthians 13 is Paul's great depiction of what *agapē* love acts like. He encourages the saints in all his letters to love each other through service, forgiveness, a humble attitude, patience, mutual encouragement and prayer, and providing physical needs.

John emphasizes loving God (*agapaō*) through keeping his commandments and living as Jesus did (1 John 2:3, 5, 6). Love manifests itself in dying to sin (1 John 3:4–6, 9), loving fellow believers, meeting their physical needs, and sacrificing for them, even to the point of death (1 John 3:10–11, 16, 17, 4:12, 20–21).

> Jesus speaks to the Pharisee who invited him to dinner, referring to the sinful woman at his feet:
> *You did not put oil on my head, but she has poured perfume on my feet. 47 Therefore, I tell you, her many sins have been forgiven—as her great* love *has shown. But whoever has been forgiven little* loves *little."* (Luke 7:46–47)
>
> Love *must be sincere. Hate what is evil; cling to what is good.* (Rom 12:9)
>
> *In this same way, husbands ought to* love *their wives as their own bodies. He who* loves *his wife* loves *himself.* (Eph 5:28)
>
> *God is* love. *Whoever lives in* love *lives in God, and God in them.* (1 John 4:16b)

Love certainly seems to be the engine behind the holy lives of God's followers. But sometimes it is hard to know how love and holiness manifest themselves, especially for new Christians who may have spent a lifetime rejecting God's overtures and have few if any love models to follow. For those people and even growing Christians, it can be hard to know how God

---

(*agapaō*) him. Some commentators believe the two forms show Peter expressing a lesser form of love, but it is generally believed that John has just used a variant, as he does in other situations. VanGemeren, *New International*, vol. 2, 542–43.

56. VanGemeren, *New International*, vol. 2, 543–44.

wants us to live in our specific circumstances. The next section gives us some guidance.

How Does a Holy Person Behave?

We have seen that the "law of love" is the distillation of the duty of Christ's followers. Our source of love and holiness is God himself and his workings in our heart. However, what does love and holiness look like? We have been given some help already, but does God give us more detail?[57] This question was answered well by G. F. Moore as he observed the general commands God gave Israel (such as the two Great Commandments or the Ten Commandments):

> Such condensations of the essentials of the moral law into a dozen great precepts or into one comprehensive rule are of interest to us as exhibiting a sound estimate of religious and moral values, and for the intrinsic unity of fundamental principle. They were never meant to be taken for sufficient regulatives of conduct, for which, indeed, they are wholly inadequate, and the broader and more elevated they are, the less they are adapted to any such end. . . . For the actual conduct of life, and above all for the practical morals of a community or a people in any age, explicit rules, defining cases and prescribing what is to be done in concrete instances, are indispensable. . . . The Jews possessed such a legislation in the form and with the authority of divine revelation, and on it the ethics of Judaism were founded . . .[1]

---

1. It is needless to enlarge on the fact that the Christian church from the beginning did the same thing.

---

57. This is akin to the popularity in the 1990s (and beyond) of the expression "What would Jesus do?" As an outgrowth youth and adults began wearing bracelets labeled WWJD to remind them how they should behave in everyday situations. This phrase had its source in an 1896 novel by Charles Sheldon, *In His Steps*, in which this question helped the characters act out how Jesus might respond to the social and spiritual needs around them. Although this phrase is helpful in centering our minds, it seems we humans need more detailed help, for we also have books like Garry Wills's—*What Jesus Meant*! We, like those who want to answer WWJD, or the disciples who couldn't understand Jesus's parables, need help figuring out what God is saying and what his expectations are.

Old Testament Attitudes and Behavior

God saw fit to give Israel such detail in its laws, decrees, and statutes.[58] Though some are not valid for Christians today, many principles and some specifics still apply. To give us a bigger picture, John Gammie aptly notes that God's call to holiness was responded to in three different but complementary ways by the priests, prophets, and sages in Israel.

The priests understood holiness to be separation or purification from what is unclean.[59] These are examples of such separation:

1. Abstaining from daily work on the Sabbath in order to honor God.
2. Worshipping only one God and not the gods of their neighbors.
3. Not intermarrying with neighboring peoples.
4. Establishing national boundaries.
5. Not eating blood or any unclean animal.
6. Obeying special dietary and sanitary restrictions that were different from their neighbors.
7. Observing many cleansing rituals to address physical and spiritual contamination.
8. Following specific religious rites, sacrifices, feasts, and modes of worship dedicated solely to Yahweh.
9. Following specific ethical principles, laws, and punishments when interacting among themselves, with foreign individuals, and with other nations. Topics included general morality, sex, finances, charity, fairness, interacting with the poor and the foreigner, and judicial propriety (see Lev 17–26, frequently called the "Holiness Code").

The ethical component of the priestly activities was not lost on the priests. They knew that the religious and ethical aspects were inseparable and complementary, and were part of what it meant to be holy unto the Lord. One illustration is the priests' involvement with the various sin offerings (burnt, sin, guilt) and the Day of Atonement. They helped Israel as individuals and

---

58. God gave Israel a series of laws, statues, and decrees so they could live as he intended and be a witness to the surrounding nations. For one, there were instructions on how to properly build and set up the Tabernacle (Exod 25–40). God further delineated five main offerings (Lev 1–7), the priests' duties (Lev 8–10, 21–22), dietary rules for clean and unclean animals, purifications, and cleansings (Lev 11–15), the Day of Atonement actions (Lev 16), the annual festivals (Lev 23), miscellaneous rules (Lev 24–25), and rules for holy living in the land (Exod 20–23; Lev 17–20).

59. Gammie, *Holiness in Israel*, 2, 9.

as a nation to purge and cleanse themselves from sin. This is because God expected purity among his people ritually and ethically, just as he instructed Abram to walk before him and be blameless (Gen 17:1).[60]

This leads seamlessly to the prophetic understanding of holiness, since the prophets were heirs to the priestly understanding. They didn't add anything new to Israel's moral code, but in their mission they called Israel back to God and to following his laws and ways. However, they emphasized the moral more than the ritual aspect of holiness. For example, in Ezekiel 18, the priest-prophet commended many of the same moral acts as we see in Job 31 (sexual purity, fairness to servants, generosity to widows/orphans/the poor, trust in God and not wealth, no gloating over enemies' misfortune, being transparent about personal sins), the Ten Commandments, and Psalm 15 (the holy are truthful, do not slander, despise evil and honor the good, honor promises, eschew usury, and reject bribes).[61] Isaiah commanded the people to stop bringing meaningless offerings and sacrifices because their hearts were unclean (Isa 1:13–16) and put the spotlight on Israel's failure to provide social and legal justice for the powerless and poor (Isa 1:16–17, 27). This meant integrity was especially needed in the king and other rulers, but such qualities were sadly lacking (Isa 1:23, 11:3–4, 32:5–7).[62]

The theme of social justice was significant since Israel's power brokers sometimes took advantage of the poor or weak. Amos and Micah address this. Amos calls for justice in the courts for all, fair taxes for the poor, no bribe taking, and a destruction of idols or God's judgment would fall (Amos 5). Micah decries the robbery and fraud of wealthy landowners, false prophets, unjust leaders, cheating grain dealers, judges who take bribes, and disloyal family members (Mic 2–3). To these specific ills Micah concludes:

> *He has shown you, O mortal, what is good. And what does the Lord require of you? To act justly and to love mercy and to walk humbly with your God.* (Mic 6:8)

Israel's sages and wisdom literature also promoted purity and holiness, especially on the individual level. Two examples have already been cited. Job testifies to the good things he has consistently done in his life that equate with the holiness God desires in his people (Job 31). David, in Psalm 15, described the behavior of one who can dwell in God's sacred tent and live on

---

60. Ibid., 34, 39, 43–44.
61. Ibid., 51.
62. Ibid., 71–72, 83.

his holy mountain. He even testified to his own pattern of following God's ways, obedience, and reliance on his faithfulness (Ps 26).[63]

Jo Bailey Wells highlights the importance of the law and Israel's obedience to it in God's overall plan for humanity. By being holy they would become a blessing to the nations.

> The law provides a means of response of Israel to God and to what he has done. This elicited response points to the fact that God has chosen not to do everything in this world by himself. However much the story keeps God at the centre as the agent of Israel's redemption, the law insists that there are important human initiatives and responsibilities to be undertaken. These are understood to be the implications of Israel's new identity as a priestly kingdom and a holy nation. They include not only worshipping God in an appropriate manner . . . but also furthering the cause of justice within and outside of Israel . . . and more generally conforming the world to God's will. This is not accomplished fully by God's salvific acts. Israel, too, is given a role in promoting and enhancing the purposes of God for creation, in building upon the foundations that God has established. Israel, in turn, becomes a part of these foundations from which God achieves his purposes for the whole earth.[64]

For Israel, being holy is also a response to God's holy character. God's command to be holy is to "be what you already are" and what he is. This is to be understood dynamically and not statically. They are to act out in practice (the law) what God has already made them (a holy people); they are to live out their identity. By doing this they truly represent him.[65]

Wells thinks that Exodus 19:1–8 is a very good summary of what Israel is to be all about. The nation had exited Egypt and was now camped at the foot of Mt. Sinai. Moses went up to God and God called to him from the mountain:

> *3 This is what you are to say to the descendants of Jacob and what you are to tell the people of Israel: 4 "You yourselves have seen what I did to Egypt, and how I carried you on eagles' wings and brought you to myself. 5 Now if you obey me fully and keep my covenant, then out of all nations you will be my treasured possession. Although the whole earth is mine, 6 you will be for me a kingdom of priests and a holy nation." 7 So Moses went back and summoned*

---

63. Ibid., 149.
64. Wells, *God's Holy People*, 60.
65. Ibid., 62, 69.

the elders of the people and set before them all the words the Lord had commanded him to speak. 8The people all responded together, "We will do everything the Lord has said." So Moses brought their answer back to the Lord. (Exod 19:3b–8)

If there is a summary of the whole Pentateuch, this is it. We can see that this business of being holy was part of the identity of Israel and of God's purpose for the whole world. When Israel veered sideways morally (which was often), then God had to bring them back on course, something that was always painful. As a result the world as a whole missed the witness Israel was meant to be.

Holiness Then and Now

We have seen that God did give Israel much more detail so they could understand how holiness was to be lived out. Some of this illuminates how God wants us to live *today*. Exceptions to this are the sacrifices and priestly duties, which were supplanted by Christ and his once-for-all atonement (see Hebrews), and Israel's dietary laws, feasts, rituals, and national identity rules. The Gospels and the apostle Paul note that many of the forms of the Old Covenant have been replaced by the New.[66] However, some laws and principles in the Mosaic covenant are perpetually good since God's character had not changed and our human design and purpose is still to be like God. For example, the Ten Commandments are good and the Christian will naturally fulfill them as she follows Christ. From the list of nine Israelite distinctives listed above, number 2, adaptations of 1 and 3, and parts of number 9 are still good for Christians to follow. Further, God would no doubt be very pleased if Christians acted like Job 31 or Psalm 15 out of love for him.

New Testament Attitudes and Behavior

The OT frequently described holiness by what a person did or didn't do. This trend continued in the Gospels and to a lesser extent the Epistles. Jesus's Sermon on the Mount details modifications he made to the acts/attitudes proscribed by the Ten Commandments (Jesus emphasized the proper heart attitude that should be behind any outward obeying of God's commands

---

66. See Matt 5, 9, 11, 12, 15, 19; Rom 2–4, 7–11, 13; 1 Cor 8, 10–11; 2 Cor 3; Gal 3–5; Eph 1–3; Phil 3; Col 2; 1 Tim 1; and Hebrews for discussions of aspects of the New replacing the Old.

and made some commands more strict for his followers.). He then tells his disciples how to give, pray, fast, think (don't worry, don't judge), and pray again (ask, seek, knock). Much of his teaching was done through parables, which frequently emphasized themes known to the Hebrews (love, humility, mercy, forgiveness, commitment, sacrifice). Craig Blomberg sees them as "weapons of warfare" in which Jesus drew "people into a seemingly innocuous story only to confront them with the demands of discipleship in ways that subvert conventional religious tradition and expectation" (e.g., a Jew would be shocked to hear a story with a Samaritan hero).[67] There has been debate throughout Christian history as to the applicability of the Sermon to present-day Christians. Blomberg aptly summarizes the options and appropriately concludes that the "kingdom theology" approach is most warranted. This holds that the Sermon is meant for believers now. Blomberg suggests Jesus's teaching is only partially realizable in the present age and is the ideal for which we continually strive. Such holiness is a "fruit befitting repentance" mode rather than a "works-righteousness" one.[68] However, Blomberg does not denote which parts are beyond us and which parts are not. Contra Blomberg, it seems Jesus meant all of his words to be followed by his hearers then as well as now, and didn't suggest any parts were beyond us.

The non-Gospel NT writers take a somewhat different tack, frequently employing lists of virtues and/or vices to detail what a holy person is like; the writer encourages his hearers to possess the virtues and to shun the vices. Love is the unifier of the virtues and Paul makes this clear in Colossians 3:12–14:

> 12 *Therefore, as God's chosen people, holy and dearly loved, clothe yourselves with compassion, kindness, humility, gentleness and patience. 13 Bear with each other and forgive one another if any of you has a grievance against someone. Forgive as the Lord forgave you. 14 And over all these virtues put on love, which binds them all together in perfect unity.*

This idea is expanded in 1 Corinthians 13 where Paul declares that all virtues are worthless without love behind them—prophesying, having faith, being generous, or suffering in the body are of no gain without love (vv. 1–3). Furthermore, if one loves, then he also performs the other virtues, such as patience, kindness, contentment, humility, selflessness, forgiveness, the giving of due honor, self-control, hope, trust, and perseverance (vv. 4–7).

---

67. Blomberg, *Jesus and the Gospels*, 300.
68. Ibid., 286–87.

There are several so-called "virtue lists" in the NT (2 Cor 6:6–10; Gal 5:22–24; Eph 4:2–3; Eph 4:25—5:2, 9, 15, 20; Eph 6:1–3, 13–18; Col 3:12–17; 1 Tim 3:2–3; Titus 1:7–8, 3:1–2; Jas 3:17–18; 2 Pet 1:5–7). A survey of these texts provides the following list of virtues and their descending frequency:

Gentleness: 6
Kindness/consideration: 6
Love: 6
Peaceableness/unity-making: 6
Purity/righteousness: 6
Goodness: 5
Self-control/being temperate: 5
Faith/faithfulness: 4
Longsuffering/forbearance/patience: 4
Compassion/mercy: 3
Humility: 3
Admonition/encouragement: 2
Forgiveness: 2
Joy: 2
Obedience: 2
Thankfulness: 2
Wisdom: 2
Family leadership: 1
Generosity: 1
Hospitality: 1
Impartiality: 1
Industriousness: 1
Perseverance: 1 (+5 in other passages—Rom 5:3; 2 Thess 1:4; Heb 12:1; Jas 1:3; Rev 2:2, 19)
Prayerfulness: 1
Sincerity: 1

It appears the writers were not attempting to be comprehensive, but were endeavoring to highlight the most important virtues and the most applicable ones for their hearers' contexts (Each group likely had its own situation, specific sins, and weaknesses that the virtue would address and strengthen). For example, Paul targets the virtues of hospitality, family leadership, and temperateness when addressing the qualifications of elders and overseers. James, who addresses Diaspora believers in a way suggesting intimate acquaintance with their lives, emphasizes taming the tongue and overcoming selfish quarrels. Hence, he underscores being considerate, peaceable, obedient, impartial, and sincere.

The presence of vices reveals one is not love-motivated (see vice lists in Gal 5:19–21, 26; Eph 4:31, 5:3–7; Col 3:5–9; Titus 3:3). They were obviously discouraged.

The idea behind holiness in the NT is godly action and virtue. The authors describe the behaviors and virtues that please God, emulate his character, and thus make us holy. This detail is of great help for the Christian who wants to live a holy life.

CONCLUSION

This chapter looked at what it means to be holy. We have surveyed definitions of related words and discovered that holiness and righteousness include several concepts. One concept is *separateness from the sinful world and its ways and union with God*—we are set apart for God's use. A second concept is *purity of heart and conduct*; the second flows from the first. Purity implies a right relationship with God and the right attitudes and actions that follow. Purity also implies singleness of vision and integrity; a holy person loves God and the neighbor as oneself. Thirdly, holiness implies *maturity of character and action* such that we reflect Christ much more than not. This means we are not sinless, but are habitually righteous.

As suggested above, the motive of holiness is love; love is behind all the expressions of holiness. This love is not self-generated but is from God. God loves us and enables us to love him and all others in return; we even love enemies and those who do not love us back. The greatest expression of God's love was in the sending of his son to atone, forgive, redeem, and reconcile us to himself. Moreover, the New Covenant gives us special blessings of enabling, status, and power to fulfill what God asks of us. God declares us judicially righteous at our conversion and empowers us to live ethically and righteously throughout the remainder of our Christian lives. Becoming ethically righteous is a process of reflecting more and more of God's character. Because he has given us what we need to be like him, we are both commanded and expected to be Christ-like in our actions and in displaying godly virtues. Whether the fleshy desires *decrease* as the virtues increase is not directly stated in Scripture; the Bible states that walking in the Spirit overcomes the desires of the flesh (Gal 5:16), the flesh can be crucified (Gal 5:24), and our transformation is from glory to glory (2 Cor 3:18). The experience and testimony of Christians throughout history indicates that the flesh's effects can be reduced; as sanctification increases the temptations of sin become less. What is not indulged loses its strength. A relationship with God and holy habits replace unholy relationships and habits.

The OT commands, the example and parables of Jesus, the models of the biblical saints, and the virtues listed in the NT help us understand what holiness looks like when it is lived out. God has not left us in the dark but has shone his light upon our minds to instruct us.

6

God's Expectations of His People
What Are They and Can They Be Fulfilled?

DOES GOD COMMAND AND THEREFORE EXPECT HIS PEOPLE TO BE HOLY?

WE LOGICALLY BEGIN OUR discussion of God's expectations with the special revelation he gives us in his Word. He communicates expectations and commands to his people and frequently offers rewards and punishments to emphasize the seriousness of the commands. He models the traits he desires and empowers his followers to attain them (God will circumcise their hearts so they can love him, Deut 30:6, 11–14; the Spirit sets them free from the law of sin and death, Rom 8:1–4). This expectation pattern began with Adam and Eve (do not eat from the tree in the middle of the Garden or you will die, Gen 2:17) and continued with Abraham in his testing with Isaac (Gen 22), Moses and the Sinaitic Covenant (blessings and curses, Deut 28; love the Lord and keep his commands, Deut 30:15–20), and the New Covenant (blessings for putting Jesus's words into practice, Matt 7:21–27; Jesus's instruction to deny self and take up your cross and God's reward for good deeds, Matt 16:24–27; parable of the talents and parable of the sheep and goats, which were separated based on ministry to the least of these, Matt 25). To better understand the detail of what God's expectations are, we will survey God's commands from both Testaments.

Old Testament Expectations and Commands to be Holy

The first recorded command by God to be holy was given to Abram:

> *When Abram was ninety-nine years old, the Lord appeared to him and said, "I am God Almighty; walk before me faithfully and be blameless.* (Gen 17:1)

We have already discussed the word blameless and that it communicates the idea of blemish-free and completely faithful. This seems to be God's wish for Abram here—he is to emulate Noah's moral purity.[1] Abram has been commanded to take his family and move to the land God will show him. God promised to make him into a great and numberless nation and that all people would be blessed through him. God will soon ask him to keep the covenant of circumcision (Gen 17:10–14) and will test him by asking him to sacrifice the heir of the covenant, Isaac (Gen 22). "Walking" blamelessly connotes being obedient to all God's commands and to walking in integrity.[2]

The Mosaic Covenant is especially replete with commands to love, obey, and be holy. The Israelites agreed to obey, and God accepted their declarations. He knew their hearts were divided, but he did not step in and tell them they were promising more than they *could* deliver. He commanded and expected them to obey:

> *Love the Lord your God with all your heart and with all your soul and with all your strength.* (Deut 6:5)

> *The Lord said to Moses, "Speak to the entire assembly of Israel and say to them: 'Be holy because I, the Lord your God, am holy.'"* (Lev 19:1–2; cf. Lev 20:26)

> *"Do not seek revenge or bear a grudge against anyone among your people, but love your neighbor as yourself. I am the Lord."* (Lev 19:18)

> *The Lord your God commands you this day to follow these decrees and laws; carefully observe them with all your heart and with all your soul. You have declared this day that the Lord is your God and that you will walk in obedience to him, that you will keep his decrees, commands and laws—that you will listen to him. And the Lord has declared this day that you are his people, his treasured*

---

1. Wenhan, *Genesis 1–15*, 20.
2. Arnold, B., *Genesis*, 169.

> *possession as he promised, and that you are to keep all his commands. He has declared that he will set you in praise, fame and honor high above all the nations he has made and that you will be a people holy to the Lord your God, as he promised.* (Deut 26:16–19)

Jo Bailey Wells summarizes the relation of Israel's holiness to obedience:

> In every instance of the description of Israel as holy, it is accompanied by a concern for obedience to God's covenantal laws. Because they have been declared holy, so they must live in a particular way, by the careful keeping of the Torah. Holiness affects the lifestyle of every individual in Israel; and the Torah touches on every aspect of life. Holiness is demonstrated most especially in those who are made holy as priests.[3]

Holiness was Israel's identity and self-understanding. Their holiness unto the Lord permeated their religious (feasts, worship, sacrifices, public prayer), social (nation-to-nation and tribe-to-tribe relations, family, friends, foreigners) and individual lives (private prayers, personal attitudes and conduct).

New Testament Expectations and Commands to be Holy

The expectations of godly living continue in the NT and begin with Jesus. One of his most profound teachings on the ethics of the kingdom of God is his Sermon on the Mount in Matthew 5–7. "Entrance into the kingdom is at the heart of the Sermon, for it is all about the kingdom ethics demanded of God's people in the new community."[4] For example, in Matthew 5:17–18, Jesus taught that he came not to abolish the Law and Prophets, but to fulfill them (give them their full meaning).[5] They will continue (as they are fulfilled and interpreted by Jesus) until the end of heaven and earth.

Matthew 5:19–20; Matthew 7:21

He continues in Matthew 5:19–20:

---

3. Wells, *God's Holy People*, 70.
4. Osborne, *Matthew*, 273.
5. Ibid., 182–83. Osborne suggests three ways that Jesus fulfilled the OT law: 1) Jesus realized the law completely in his deeds and teachings. 2) Jesus gave the law its highest meaning by his interpretation of it, and enabled his followers to live out the law more completely. 3) He completed the law as a covenant-promise by bringing about a new redemptive relationship with God.

> 19 Therefore anyone who sets aside one of the least of these commands and teaches others accordingly will be called least in the kingdom of heaven, but whoever practices and teaches these commands will be called great in the kingdom of heaven. 20 For I tell you that unless your righteousness surpasses that of the Pharisees and the teachers of the law, you will certainly not enter the kingdom of heaven. (Matt 5:19–20)

Verse 20 identifies righteousness as living according to God's will (ethical righteousness). This righteousness must surpass the external-only and hypocritical motivations of the Pharisees (Matt 23). Their hearts were impure, therefore they neglected love and mercy. Jesus called them "whitewashed tombs" (Matt 23:27). God's righteousness is of the heart as well as external. Without this kind of righteousness one cannot enter God's kingdom.[6] Hagner adds other details. The commands in verse 19 are the commands of the law *given their full meaning in Jesus's interpretation*, some of which are explained here in the Sermon on the Mount. The "least" commands are likely the easiest to fulfill, not the least important. The "great" in God's kingdom follow the easiest, all the other commands, and teach others to do the same.[7]

Likewise, Matthew 7:21 affirms that only those who do the Father's will can enter the kingdom of heaven:

> 21 "Not everyone who says to me, 'Lord, Lord,' will enter the kingdom of heaven, but only the one who does the will of my Father who is in heaven. (Matt 7:21)

Professing the very reverential name "Lord, Lord" (similar to "revered teacher") is not sufficient. The people making this pseudo-profession could have been false teachers or prophets mentioned in 7:15, who use eloquent greetings and boast of deeds done for God (v. 23). The main point is that profession must be accompanied by obedient action and a changed life.

John 13:34–35; John 15:12–17

During the week of his Passion, Christ gave his disciples a specific and *new* command:

> 34 "A new command I give you: Love one another. As I have loved you, so you must love one another. 35 By this everyone will know that you are my disciples, if you love one another." (John 13:34–35)

---

6. Ibid., 185.
7. Hagner, *Matthew*, 108–9.

> 12My command is this: Love each other as I have loved you. 13Greater love has no one than this: to lay down one's life for one's friends. 14You are my friends if you do what I command. 15I no longer call you servants, because a servant does not know his master's business. Instead, I have called you friends, for everything that I learned from my Father I have made known to you. 16You did not choose me, but I chose you and appointed you so that you might go and bear fruit—fruit that will last—and so that whatever you ask in my name the Father will give you. 17This is my command: Love each other. (John 15:12-17)

Jesus is expecting his disciples to follow his words here—he has "chosen" and "appointed" them to love. The command to love is not new—Israelites and now Christians were both commanded to love God supremely and their neighbor as themselves. The new aspect, as we saw earlier, is "as I have loved you." Jesus commands us to imitate him in his self-sacrifice, even to the point of physical death for our fellow believers (the love of fellow brothers and sisters is central here). When the world sees that, they will have no doubt who we belong to.[8] Michaels also perceives the newness of this command, and notes that it doesn't replace the two Great Commandments, but adds to and goes alongside them. This new command accents love's mutuality within the body of Christ and that the source of this love is God—the Father's love for his Son and Jesus's love for his disciples.[9]

The key verse for our purposes in the next passage is John 15:16, regarding fruit bearing. There are several proposals as to what the fruit is since Jesus is not specific here. It could be, looking at what Jesus is mainly talking about here, that the fruit is love for one another (fellow believers). Other ideas include Christian character in general, disciple making, or all these things together. Regardless, all of these naturally develop as we "remain" or "abide" with Christ (15:4). The point is that bearing any of these fruits is commanded, expected, and do-able. God empowers us as we remain connected to him, the true source and vine.

1 Peter 1:14-16

We have already seen that Peter reiterates the reason a Christian is to be holy is that God is holy:

---

8. Keener, *Gospel of John*, 924-26.
9. Michaels, *Gospel of John*, 759.

GOD'S EXPECTATIONS OF HIS PEOPLE 219

> *14As obedient children, do not conform to the evil desires you had when you lived in ignorance. 15But just as he who called you is holy, so be holy in all you do; 16for it is written: "Be holy, because I am holy." (1 Pet 1:14–16)*

Peter's call to holiness centers on conforming to God himself and not to their former evil desires. Whether they were Jew or Gentile to begin with, they are now newly born (1 Pet 1:3). Further, God's character has not changed between covenants, he is always holy and so should his followers be. Both covenants had the goal of creating people conformed to God's character. Both covenants also set believers apart from the surrounding culture—they were both a chosen people, a royal priesthood, and a holy nation that declares God's praises (1 Pet 2:9). One difference is that Peter does not proscribe the specifics of the Levitical code for Christians. Christians live post-resurrection and the curtain of the Temple has been torn in two. The rituals, sacrifices, and other codes of the Old Covenant no longer apply.[10]

Hebrews 2:14

Similarly, the writer of Hebrews exhorts:

> *14Make every effort to live in peace with everyone and to be holy; without holiness no one will see the Lord. (Heb 12:14)*

Although some see the holiness described here as more "declared" than "ethical,"[11] it is hard to envision pursuing what one has already been granted. Holiness, then, is more likely to have its common ethical meaning here and is something that Christians should earnestly pursue. The writer's use of "make every effort" stresses this.

James 1:22–25

James commands Jewish believers to be doers of the word and not hearers only:

> *22Do not merely listen to the word, and so deceive yourselves. Do what it says. 23Anyone who listens to the word but does not do what it says is like someone who looks at his face in a mirror 24and, after looking at himself, goes away and immediately forgets what he looks like. 25But whoever looks intently into the perfect*

---

10. Jobes, *1 Peter*, 113–14.
11. Lane, *Hebrews 1–8*, 450.

> law that gives freedom, and continues in it—not forgetting what they have heard, but doing it—they will be blessed in what they do. (Jas 1:22–25)

James uses a present tense imperative form of the verb "be" here, emphasizing both the current and repetitive nature of the action he commands. Listening is a necessary preliminary, but it is the doing that must follow. James uses a hyperbolic example to make his point since no one looks in a mirror and then immediately forgets his own image; it is likewise absurd to look intently at God's law and then neglect to do it.[12] McCartney adds that forgetting is not merely a failure to remember, but neglect, inattention, or disregard.[13] The "perfect law that gives freedom" or perfect law of liberty is probably the gospel message which is now written on believers' hearts; it brings true freedom, as Galatians 5:13 and John 8:32–36 attest. This law must also be persevered in and following it naturally results in God's blessing.[14]

1 Corinthians 3:1–3; Hebrews 5:11–14

> Brothers and sisters, I could not address you as people who live by the Spirit but as people who are still worldly—mere infants in Christ. 2I gave you milk, not solid food, for you were not yet ready for it. Indeed, you are still not ready. 3You are still worldly. For since there is jealousy and quarreling among you, are you not worldly? Are you not acting like mere humans? (1 Cor 3:1–3)

> 11 We have much to say about this, but it is hard to make it clear to you because you no longer try to understand. 12In fact, though by this time you ought to be teachers, you need someone to teach you the elementary truths of God's word all over again. You need milk, not solid food! 13Anyone who lives on milk, being still an infant, is not acquainted with the teaching about righteousness. 14But solid food is for the mature, who by constant use have trained themselves to distinguish good from evil. (Heb 5:11–14)

The Apostle Paul also commands and expects love, holiness, and maturity from the church. The Corinthian church struggled with spiritual maturity

---

12. McCartney finds other examples of where hearing is insufficient and doing is commended: Ezek 33:31–32; Matt 7:24–27; and Rom 2:13–16. McCartney, *James*, 120.
13. McCartney, *James*, 121.
14. Blomberg and Kamell, *James*, 89–92.

and Paul exhorts them to grow up. He uses the metaphor of milk, reproaching them because they should have been able to handle solid spiritual food by now. But, since they act like spiritual infants, all they can handle is milk (1 Cor 3:1–3). Similarly, the writer of Hebrews has stern words for Jewish believers, who ought to be teachers but are still students. They don't try to understand and consequently can only perceive elementary doctrines; the mature doctrines of righteousness are beyond them. They need to grow up so they can handle solid food (Heb 5:11–14).

Ephesians 5:1–2

Echoing Jesus's command to love in John 13 and 15, Paul encourages believers to walk in love:

> 1Follow God's example, therefore, as dearly loved children 2and walk in the way of love, just as Christ loved us and gave himself up for us as a fragrant offering and sacrifice to God. (Eph 5:1–2)

"Follow God's example" is sometimes translated as "be imitators of God," (ESV, NRSV, NASB) and is the only case where this expression is used in Scripture. We imitate God, as the previous verse implies (4:32), as we forgive and love each other because God was kind, compassionate, and forgiving toward us in Christ. The imperative verb used here implies that our action should be ongoing and developing. The source of this love is not ourselves, but the love the Holy Spirit has poured into us (Rom 5:5).[15] Similarly, Paul says in Ephesians 1:4, "For he chose us in him before the creation of the world to be holy and blameless in his sight [in love]." God destined us to run on the fuel of his love, and from that flows what one would expect—holiness and blamelessness since we are acting as he would act.

Galatians 5:13–25

Paul writes extensively on the idea of sin and the new power believers have to overcome it. He encourages the church to put off the old self and put on the new. This is attained "in Christ" or "by the Spirit." We will consider two larger passages, Galatians 5:13–25 and Romans 6, realizing that Paul repeatedly stresses this topic in his general epistles.[16]

---

15. Arnold, *Ephesians*, 309–10.
16. Similar exhortations are found in Eph 4:1—6:20 and Col 3:1—4:6.

Paul uses the terms "freedom," "love," and "by the Spirit" as a way of expressing this expectation to live in a holy manner. He exhorts the Galatian believers:

> 13 You, my brothers and sisters, were called to be free. But do not use your freedom to indulge the flesh; rather, serve one another humbly in love. 14 For the entire law is fulfilled in keeping this one command: "Love your neighbor as yourself. 15 If you bite and devour each other, watch out or you will be destroyed by each other.
>
> 16 So I say, walk by the Spirit, and you will not gratify the desires of the flesh. 17 For the flesh desires what is contrary to the Spirit, and the Spirit what is contrary to the flesh. They are in conflict with each other, so that you are not to do whatever you want. 18 But if you are led by the Spirit, you are not under the law.
>
> 19 The acts of the flesh are obvious: sexual immorality, impurity and debauchery; 20 idolatry and witchcraft; hatred, discord, jealousy, fits of rage, selfish ambition, dissensions, factions 21 and envy; drunkenness, orgies, and the like. I warn you, as I did before, that those who live like this will not inherit the kingdom of God.
>
> 22 But the fruit of the Spirit is love, joy, peace, forbearance, kindness, goodness, faithfulness, 23 gentleness and self-control. Against such things there is no law. 24 Those who belong to Christ Jesus have crucified the flesh with its passions and desires. 25 Since we live by the Spirit, let us keep in step with the Spirit. (Gal 5:13–25)

Paul is here writing to a church that was having theological problems—they were being influenced by certain false teachers who taught that they still needed to be circumcised and obey the Law of Moses. There is also a hint they were struggling with libertinism, or the tendency to use their freedom from the law to commit sin. Paul reminds them of two things: 1) They are indeed called to be free, but God's freedom is not to do whatever they like, but to love him and others humbly. They are now free to be "love slaves" of one another. 2) They are to live "in the Spirit" and not in the flesh.[17] The love Paul enjoins fulfills the "love thy neighbor" command God gave in the beginning of the Old Covenant. We can even love in the sacrificial way of Christ because of the new life we have in the Spirit. If we "walk" and continue walking[18] by the Spirit by conducting ourselves as the Spirit directs, then we will not live sinful fleshly lives. Moo notes that there is a "conflict between God's Spirit and the impulse to sin, an impulse that no

---

17. Longenecker, *Galatians*, 238.

18. The verb form strongly suggests continuous action—they should continue to walk by the Spirit. See Longenecker, *Galatians*, 245; and Moo, *Galatians*, 353.

longer rules the believer but still exerts influence that must be resisted. . . . The crucifixion of the flesh does not mean that it is totally destroyed but that it is definitely judged and its power decisively broken."[19]

The works of the flesh and Spirit that Paul enumerates next make it clear what the flesh and Spirit produce (vv. 19–23). The lists are not exhaustive and are likely tailored to the temptations the Galatians were facing. The point is that now the Galatians are "free" to live out the wonderful fruit of the Spirit. Longenecker notes that not only has the Spirit given them life, but has sensitized them to what is fleshly, instilled an intrinsic standard of what is good, and enabled them to be good, which always benefits others. The law does not have to command these things, the Spirit produces them. They are not of human origin, but neither are we passive in their expression. Believers must actively express what the Spirit inspires—we must "walk" continuously (v. 16) and "keep in step with the Spirit" (v. 25).[20] Surely it appears God has given us all we need to love, fulfill his will, and walk in his ways.

Romans 6:1–23

This is one of the most extensive passages on this topic:

> 1 What shall we say, then? Shall we go on sinning so that grace may increase? 2 By no means! We are those who have died to sin; how can we live in it any longer? 3 Or don't you know that all of us who were baptized into Christ Jesus were baptized into his death? 4 We were therefore buried with him through baptism into death in order that, just as Christ was raised from the dead through the glory of the Father, we too may live a new life.
>
> 5 For if we have been united with him in a death like his, we will certainly also be united with him in a resurrection like his. 6 For we know that our old self was crucified with him so that the body ruled by sin might be done away with, that we should no longer be slaves to sin—7 because anyone who has died has been set free from sin.
>
> 8 Now if we died with Christ, we believe that we will also live with him. 9 For we know that since Christ was raised from the dead, he cannot die again; death no longer has mastery over him. 10 The death he died, he died to sin once for all; but the life he lives, he lives to God.
>
> 11 In the same way, count yourselves dead to sin but alive to God in Christ Jesus. 12 Therefore do not let sin reign in your mortal

---

19. Moo, *Galatians*, 354, 368.
20. Longenecker, *Galatians*, 247, 259, 265.

> *body so that you obey its evil desires. 13Do not offer any part of yourself to sin as an instrument of wickedness, but rather offer yourselves to God as those who have been brought from death to life; and offer every part of yourself to him as an instrument of righteousness. 14For sin shall no longer be your master, because you are not under the law, but under grace.*
>
> *15What then? Shall we sin because we are not under the law but under grace? By no means! 16Don't you know that when you offer yourselves to someone as obedient slaves, you are slaves of the one you obey—whether you are slaves to sin, which leads to death, or to obedience, which leads to righteousness? 17But thanks be to God that, though you used to be slaves to sin, you have come to obey from your heart the pattern of teaching that has now claimed your allegiance. 18You have been set free from sin and have become slaves to righteousness.*
>
> *19I am using an example from everyday life because of your human limitations. Just as you used to offer yourselves as slaves to impurity and to ever-increasing wickedness, so now offer yourselves as slaves to righteousness leading to holiness. 20When you were slaves to sin, you were free from the control of righteousness. 21What benefit did you reap at that time from the things you are now ashamed of? Those things result in death! 22But now that you have been set free from sin and have become slaves of God, the benefit you reap leads to holiness, and the result is eternal life. 23For the wages of sin is death, but the gift of God is eternal life in Christ Jesus our Lord.* (Rom 6:1–23)

In Romans 5 Paul emphasized that Christ conquered the realm of sin and death; we are now justified by Christ's shed blood. God's grace has increased all the more as sin increased. It is possible that some of Paul's hearers developed the mistaken impression that since Christians are under such overflowing grace that it doesn't matter if or how much they sin—grace will cover it! Paul strongly negates this thinking by declaring in chapter 6 that we are victors over sin in Christ; sin is defeated and we now have a new master. Paul uses several images to make his point—death/life, slaves/masters, freedom—and thus discusses the inseparable companion to justification, which is ethical righteousness or holiness.[21]

Chapter 6 can be divided into two sections, the first describes the negative side—the believer's death to sin (vv. 1–14) and the second highlights the positive side—our dedication to God and righteousness (vv. 15–23). In the first section Paul begins by making clear that Christians are now dead to sin

---

21. Moo, *Epistle to the Romans*, 350.

and ought not to live in it any longer (v. 2). There is a definite break or separation from sin that goes beyond the penalty of sin to the power of sin. Paul's discussion of baptism implies this death occurred at conversion. In fact, baptism seems to signify conversion in general here. Separation means the believer cannot live in sin as a lifestyle or habit, not that he or she will never sin again.[22] Moo directs us to the purpose of our being baptized into Christ's death—that we may then live a new life. The verb meaning and tenses suggest the action of walking in a new lifestyle—a beginning and a continuing in. This new life is empowered by Christ's resurrection and God's Spirit (v. 4; Rom 7:6). Paul's verb tenses here and in the rest of chapter 6 also highlight the "indicative" side of salvation, since we are already dead to sin and alive to Christ. The "imperative" side emphasizes that we must continue to *live out* our Christian lives.[23] This is another way of expressing a theme noticed before—we must live out who we already are. This dying and rising theme is repeated in verses 5–10. Our "old self was crucified with him" so we might "live with him." This "old self" is likely not a part of us or some nature, but an orientation. Our nature hasn't changed, but our orientation to God and our relationship with him has.[24] Colin Kruse notes that this freedom from sin is a freedom not to sin, though the possibility of sinning is still real. This freedom is also not automatic, we must choose righteousness in its place.[25]

Therefore, Paul states in verse 11 that because you are like Christ, who died to sin and is alive to God, then *count yourselves* as having done the same. Verses 12 and 13 elaborate on what this "counting" looks like. We are not to let sin reign in our "mortal bodies." Some scholars consider this body the physical body, but others think Paul is referring to our whole person as it relates to the sinful world around us.[26] The body is not evil in itself, but is the stage where evil desires play out. Evil desires, then, are not limited to

---

22. Moo, *Epistle to the Romans*, 357–58.

23. Ibid., 366–67.

24. Moo avers there are not two natures warring in the Christian, but those in Christ exist as the "new self." Col 3:9–11 says that the old self has been taken off and the new put on. However, in Eph 4:22–24, Paul says the old self must be put off and the new put on. So, is this putting off past or present? Moo suggests it is both—we now belong to the new age but must still resist the powers of the old, hence the imperative of Ephesians 4. See Moo, *Epistle to the Romans*, 373–75. Kruse agrees, citing that the image of taking off and discarding clothing refers to throwing away one's old way of life prior to conversion, that way of life we lived in solidarity with Adam. He believes the "body ruled by sin" is synonymous with the "flesh," which is our human nature under sin's sway. Kruse, *Paul's Letter to the Romans*, 263.

25. Kruse, *Paul's Letter to the Romans*, 264.

26. Ibid., 268. Kruse favors an interpretation that mortal body refers to our physical body.

physical passions and appetites, but include "mental" ones as well—selfishness, greed, power seeking, etc. Our "parts" or members need not be limited to our limbs or other body parts, but could include all our natural capacities. All of us, our bodies and every other capacity, should be offered to God for righteous use. Our offering up ourselves is an action representative of themes mentioned earlier—slavery and mastery. Paul has already hinted at these in verses 8 and 12–13. Consequently in verse 14, Paul declares sin will no longer be your *master*—now or ever—since we are done with the old realm (the law) and are now a part of the new (under grace).[27]

Paul continues with the slave and master imagery in the second section, verses 15–23. The synergy of our union with Christ is evident—we are slaves to whomever we offer ourselves to. He implies that the Romans have already changed their allegiance and are freed from sin, having now offered themselves to Christ as slaves of righteousness. Further, Paul describes no middle ground, where one can be partly enslaved to sin and partly enslaved to God and righteousness. They had to choose between the two and they have made their choice. Paul further stresses the way they are to pursue God; they are to "offer themselves as slaves to righteousness" (v. 19, similarly, v. 13). Moo expresses the intensity of this phrase: "[Paul] thus makes clear that Christians should serve righteousness with all the single-minded dedication that characterized their pre-Christian service of such 'idols' as self, money, lust, pleasure, and power. Would that we would pursue holiness with the zeal that so many of us pursued these other, incomparably less worthy goals!"[28] The outcome of this pursuit is "holiness," sometimes translated "sanctification" (vv. 19, 22). Paul's connotation seems most plausibly to be the process of becoming holy;[29] we become like God when we denounce what God denounces and love what he loves. Becoming holy is not the final result; the final result is eternal life, God's gift to us in his son, Christ Jesus (vv. 22–23).

Romans 6, then, paints a picture of new life and new headship. Paul affirms to the Romans that they were once dead in sin, have now died to sin, and are alive in Christ. They have changed allegiances—they were once slaves to sin but have now offered themselves wholeheartedly to God and his righteousness. They are holy and are becoming more so, culminating in

---

27. Moo, *Epistle to the Romans*, 381–89. Cranfield refers to this freedom with a less definitive sense of victory. The freedom we have in Christ is freedom "to resist sin's usurped power with new strength and boldness." The possibility of victory is not discussed. Cranfield, *Epistle to the Romans*, 320.

28. Moo, *Epistle to the Romans*, 404.

29. Ibid., 405. Some see it as both a process and a "state" to which yielding to righteousness leads. See also Kruse, *Paul's Letter to the Romans*, 284.

our final experience of eternal life. There is no hint that Christians must live in a habit of sin, on the contrary Paul portrays our life as generally one of victory over sin and of dedication to God.

CAN WE BE HOLY?

The foregoing OT and NT passages that illustrate God's expectations and commands regarding holiness strongly imply we can fulfill God's expectations. However, there are voices in the Christian world that say that we cannot possibly live up to God's laws and standards, even under the New Covenant. No one can obey the two Great Commandments or any of the more detailed ones God gave; the Israelites couldn't and the Christian can only feebly do so. All Christians' attitudes and acts are tainted by sin, our motives are never totally pure, and any completeness whatsoever in our Christian lives will have to wait until the new heavens and earth. The author has personally heard these views from the mouths of evangelical pastors and seminary professors.

Other voices come from Christians in general. Barna Research Group surveyed 1003 persons in January 2006 on the subject of holiness. Their report is titled, "The Concept of Holiness Baffles Most Americans."[30] The survey included American adults, and participants were categorized by beliefs, age group, and ethnicity.[31] Five questions are applicable to our topic and the answers are noted in the following two tables:

---

30. Barna Group, "The Concept of Holiness," www.barna.org. Several items of data for Table 2 had to be obtained by personal communication with Pam Jacob, Senior Research Director at the Barna Group.

31. *National average* includes all persons surveyed, regardless of belief status.

Born-agains say they have made a personal commitment to Jesus Christ that is important in their life. They believe they will go to heaven when they die because they have confessed their sins and accepted Christ as their Savior.

Evangelicals meet the born-again criteria plus seven other conditions. They believe: 1) Their faith is important in their life. 2) They have a personal responsibility to share their Christian beliefs with non-Christians. 3) Satan exists. 4) Eternal salvation is possible only through grace. 5) Jesus Christ lived a sinless life on earth. 6) The Bible is accurate in all it teaches. 7) God is an all-knowing, all-powerful, perfect deity who created the universe and rules it today.

Revolutionaries: 1) Had a clear sense their life has meaning and purpose. 2) Describe their relationship with and faith in God as the top priority in their life. 3) Consider themselves to be Christian. 4) Read the Bible regularly. 5) Pray regularly. 6) Deem their faith to be an important part of their life. 7) Contend that the main objective in their life is to love God with all their heart, mind, soul, and strength. 8) Describe God as the all-knowing, all-powerful being who created the universe and still rules it today. 9) Have made a personal commitment to Jesus Christ that is important in their life today. 10) Believe that

TABLE 1: AMERICANS DEFINE HOLINESS

What does it mean to be holy?	
1. I don't know	21%
2. Being Christlike	19%
3. Making faith the top priority	18%
4. Living a pure or sinless lifestyle	12%
5. Having a good attitude about people/life	10%
6. To focus completely on God	9%
7. Being guided by the Holy Spirit	9%
8. Being born-again	8%
9. Reflecting God's character	7%
10. Exhibiting a moral lifestyle	5%
11. Practicing biblical truth	5%

---

when they die they will go to heaven because they have confessed their sins and accepted Christ as Savior. 11) Say their faith in Christ has "greatly transformed" their life.

TABLE 2: AMERICAN RESPONSES TO BARNA HOLINESS SURVEY

	Strongly agree—God expects me to become holy.	Yes response—Do you think it is possible for any person to become a holy?	Yes response—Do you personally know someone you describe as holy.	Self-describe as holy.
National average	35%	73%	50%	21%
Born-agains	46%	76%	55%	29%
Evangelicals	59%	69%	55%	32%
Revolutionaries	54%	71%	55%	38%

Table 1 suggests that there is a substantial agreement about what holiness entails in America's general public.[32] Seven of the eleven answers (2–4, 6, 9–11) seem to fit reasonably well into a biblical definition of holiness. Since the survey was of Americans and not just Christians, the "I don't know" answer is understandable.

Table 2 is interesting due to the responses of those who consider themselves either evangelical or revolutionary. If any groups would be expected to believe what the Bible teaches, these groups would be included. Though we have seen that the Scriptures are clear about God's holiness expectations, only 54% of revolutionaries strongly agree with the scriptural mandate. Only 71% of revolutionaries think holiness is even possible and only 38% consider themselves holy! This is disconcerting, considering that all revolutionaries affirm that they read the Bible regularly, their main goal is to love God with all their being, and their faith in Christ has "greatly transformed" their life. Apparently, regular Bible reading, desiring to love God, and being "greatly transformed" does not equate significantly with either expecting to be holy (54%) or considering themselves holy (38%)! There is a better correlation with considering it as even possible (71%). The percentages for evangelicals are ± 6 percentage points from these values.

---

32. The percentages total over 100, so people were allowed to give more than one answer, thus making it impossible to tell the absolute percentages for each answer.

We are Able

However, the above assertions and Christian opinions are not congruent with scriptural expectations and commands. In the following passages, we see that both God and his representatives directly affirm or strongly imply our *ability* to do what he commands.

Deuteronomy 30:11–14

Beginning with the OT, Moses reiterates that God has given a law that can be obeyed:

> 11Now what I am commanding you today is not too difficult for you or beyond your reach. 12It is not up in heaven, so that you have to ask, "Who will ascend into heaven to get it and proclaim it to us so we may obey it?" 13Nor is it beyond the sea, so that you have to ask, "Who will cross the sea to get it and proclaim it to us so we may obey it?" 14No, the word is very near you; it is in your mouth and in your heart so you may obey it. (Deut 30:11–14)

God's law was not overly idealistic or impracticable. Any theology that espouses that God intentionally made his law too hard to follow unnecessarily exalts the gospel by disparaging the law. Moses further declares that the law is attainable with two metaphors (up in heaven and beyond the sea). The law is simple to understand but difficult to obey—it requires whole-heartedness. It is also something that is to be internalized (see Ps 1, 19, 119); it is not just external. It is near us, just like God is (Deut 4:7). In fact, it is do-able because it is as near as our mouths and hearts.[33]

John 8:34–36

Jesus, in the NT, declares that we are able to not sin:

> 34Jesus replied, "Very truly I tell you, everyone who sins is a slave to sin. 35Now a slave has no permanent place in the family, but a son belongs to it forever. 36So if the Son sets you free, you will be free indeed. (John 8:34–36)

---

33. Wright, C., *Deuteronomy*, 290–91. Israel responded to the giving of the law with promises to obey it all (Exod 19:8, 24:3, 7). God never told them they were promising more than they could deliver. God responded to Moses that all that the people had said and promised was "good." He wished their hearts would always be so inclined (Deut 5:28–29).

Jesus says if you sin you are a slave to sin, and just like the slave in a household, you do not receive the inheritance, as a son would. If you are a son, then you are a part of the family and enjoy the benefits—in this case freedom from sin and eternal life. The slave experiences neither of these. J. Michael Ramsey agrees, stating that the issue is not only slavery and freedom, but eternal life and eternal death. The last sentence, however, concludes with the emphasis on being really free from sin ("free indeed"). When the disciples know the truth as it is in Jesus, and know Jesus himself, they are free from sin's power.[34]

1 Corinthians 10:13

The ability to overcome sin is evident also in Paul. He tells the Corinthians:

> 13No temptation has overtaken you except what is common to mankind. And God is faithful; he will not let you be tempted beyond what you can bear. But when you are tempted, he will also provide a way out so that you can endure it. (1 Cor 10:13)

Preceding this, he has warned them about idolatry by looking at the history of Israel. From verse 6 onward, he warned them about Israel's idolatry, sexual immorality, their testing of God, and their grumbling. These, and other temptations "common to mankind" are ones God will enable us to endure. This doesn't eliminate the possibility that he will remove it, but the emphasis is on bearing up under it.[35] Ciampa and Rosner add that God always provides a way out or an exit path, similar to the Israelites exodus through the Red Sea. This is a testimony to his ever-present faithfulness to his people. Further, like the Lord's Prayer affirms, God will not lead us toward temptation, but with it will deliver us from evil (or the evil one).[36]

2 Corinthians 3:18

Paul, in his second letter to the Corinthians, compares the greater glory of the New Covenant compared to the Old. In the Old, the glory that radiated from Moses's face as he spoke with God eventually faded; he veiled it to conceal its fading from his fellow Israelites (Exod 34:29–35). Paul now declares

---

34. Michaels, *Gospel of John*, 506–7.
35. Garland, *1 Corinthians*, 468.
36. Ciampa and Rosner, *First Letter to the Corinthians*, 468.

the unveiled glory that lasts and is manifest in the spiritual changes that are currently taking place in Christ's followers:

> 18And we all, who with unveiled faces contemplate the Lord's glory, are being transformed into his image with ever-increasing glory, which comes from the Lord, who is the Spirit. (2 Cor 3:18)

The glory that we contemplate, or as some translations put it—"behold or see reflected as in a mirror" (NASB, NRSV), is God's glory in Christ and his gospel. As a result, Paul's readers (and we) are transformed into that same image. The transformations at present are not likely to be our physical bodies, which are wasting away (2 Cor 4:16), but our inner selves, the aspect that is a "new creation" (2 Cor 5:17).[37] Paul emphasizes our transformation is currently taking place by using the present tense verbs of "contemplate/behold" and "are being transformed."[38] Our transformation by beholding Christ is mainly visible to others by our Christ-like behavior. "Ever-increasing glory" notes the progressive nature of our change—our progressive sanctification. As we are daily renewed in God's Spirit we polish our marred and tarnished image and reflect Christ's glory more and more (This was God's plan all along—Rom 8:29). This process is consummated when we finally receive our new "spiritual" and glorious bodies like that of the risen Christ.[39]

2 Peter 1:3–11

Peter also echoes this ability to be godly:

> 3His divine power has given us everything we need for a godly life through our knowledge of him who called us by his own glory and goodness. 4Through these he has given us his very great and precious promises, so that through them you may participate in the divine nature, having escaped the corruption in the world caused by evil desires.
>
> 5For this very reason, make every effort to add to your faith goodness; and to goodness, knowledge; 6and to knowledge, self-control; and to self-control, perseverance; and to perseverance, godliness; 7and to godliness, mutual affection; and to mutual affection, love. 8For if you possess these qualities in increasing measure, they will keep you from being ineffective and unproductive in your knowledge of our Lord Jesus Christ. 9But whoever does not

---

37. Harris, *Second Epistle to the Corinthians*, 314–15.
38. Barnett, *Second Epistle to the Corinthians*, 207.
39. Harris, *Second Epistle to the Corinthians*, 316–19.

have them is nearsighted and blind, forgetting that they have been cleansed from their past sins.

10Therefore, my brothers and sisters, make every effort to confirm your calling and election. For if you do these things, you will never stumble, 11and you will receive a rich welcome into the eternal kingdom of our Lord and Savior Jesus Christ. (2 Pet 1:3–11)

Peter affirms that God has faithfully given Christians ample provision to life godly lives.[40] His divine power can work in us because we now have personal knowledge of Christ. Our calling is not of our own doing, but as a result of God's goodness and glory. Because of God's goodness, he has given us promises. Richard Baukham believes these promises likely refer to his promises of future glory in heaven (cf. 2 Pet 3:8–9, 13, 1:11) and therefore our participation in the "divine nature" is not on this earth, but in the new heavens and earth. There are no evil desires in heaven that lead to corruption and no physical body that suffers decay. "Divine nature" then suggests we will be *like* God in reflecting his immortality and incorruptibility.[41] Gene Green sees the divine nature as more akin to our acquiring God's moral character now, examples of which Peter gives in verses 5–7. Peter uses a similar phrase in 2 Peter 2:20, where believers escape the moral corruption of the world by knowing Christ. Escaping them doesn't mean we have left the world.[42] Bauckham suggests that the moral virtues (vv. 5–7) are qualifications for attaining that future destiny. Green affirms that these virtues are our necessary earthly response to the divine nature God has bestowed on us. Green's interpretations seems most likely since Paul is talking more of his hearers' present actions; he is asking them to do these things now.

Peter next avers that we need to "make every effort" to develop the eight virtues he lists. The list probably has faith in first position because it is the most basic of our Christian life.[43] Love is last and is the motive behind all the others and sums them all up. The virtues in the middle seem to be in no particular order. Number two is "goodness" or virtue and is probably

---

40. Commentators note that Peter uses many Greek words that are characteristically Hellenistic, likely fitting in with the audience he is writing to (e.g., "divine power," "godly," "self-control"). In such cases he adapts them for a Christian context so there is no misunderstanding as to his intent. Similar words are used in other works contemporary with 2 Peter, such as the Shepherd of Hermas and 1, 2 Clement. See Green, *Jude and 2 Peter*; and Bauckham, *Jude, 2 Peter*, for further discussion.

41. Bauckham, *Jude, 2 Peter*, 181–82.

42. Green, *Jude and 2 Peter*, 187–88.

43. Green believes the better word would be "faithfulness," since this is a list of moral virtues. This loyalty toward God and his people allows the other virtues to develop. See Green, *Jude and 2 Peter*, 192.

a general word depicting moral excellence. "Knowledge" could refer to the practical gift of wisdom and discernment, both vitally necessary for Christian growth. "Self-control" or self-discipline is needed to combat inordinate physical and mental desires. "Perseverance" or steadfastness signals a courageousness to endure times of testing, suffering, or evil, knowing that these are temporary and our blessed life in heaven is eternal. "Mutual affection" is the familial love between brothers and sisters in Christ, a love between those who are one in Christ. As stated above, "love" is the crowning virtue and is behind all the other virtues.[44] Peter says if these traits are present and increasing we will be effective servants of Christ and our calling will be confirmed; we will avoid stumbling over spiritual hazards and be finally welcomed into our Savior's kingdom.

This passage denotes that God has given us everything we need to live like Christ and that God looks for us to *live* like who we *are*—those who have partaken of his very nature and who seek to confirm our final destination, a joyous eternity in God's presence.

These examples show that God's expectations, seen in both Testaments, are not empty. God has given his children adequate abilities and helps to obey all his commands. He has graced them with the gift of moral choice, the indwelling Holy Spirit, the help of fellow believers, the ministration of angels, and his own presence, encouragement, and unction.

Scriptures Suggesting Inability to be Holy

Some biblical texts describe the universality of sin or the imperfection of human righteousness and these verses are commonly used to defend the idea that Christians cannot please God or refrain from sinning. It is suggested that even righteous acts are tainted with evil.

Psalm 14

> 1 *The fool says in his heart, "There is no God." They are corrupt, their deeds are vile; there is no one who does good. 2 The Lord looks down from heaven on all mankind to see if there are any who understand, any who seek God. 3 All have turned away, all have become corrupt; there is no one who does good, not even one.*
>
> *4 Do all these evildoers know nothing? They devour my people as though eating bread; they never call on the Lord. 5 But there*

---

44. Bauckham, *Jude, 2 Peter*, 185–87.

> they are, overwhelmed with dread, for God is present in the company of the righteous. 6You evildoers frustrate the plans of the poor, but the Lord is their refuge.
>
> 7Oh, that salvation for Israel would come out of Zion! When the Lord restores his people, let Jacob rejoice and Israel be glad!

Psalm 14 is a wisdom lament, significantly duplicated by Psalm 53 and partially copied by Paul in Romans 3:10–12. It is less reflective than many wisdom passages and instead has the tone of a lament, ending with the hope of deliverance.[45] The nature of a "fool" is described in verses 1–3; a fool does not acknowledge God and his corruptness produces vile deeds that lack any goodness. If taken alone, this section could describe universal sinfulness, but verses 4–6 denote that this group is specific, which is fools. They are the ones who oppress God's people and make life difficult for the poor and weak. The "all" of verses 2–3 might suggest the whole of humanity, but verse 4 implies it refers to evildoers. Verses 4–6 describe "my people," "the righteous," and "the poor" as counterparts to the "all" and "evildoers," suggesting the term is not all-inclusive of humanity. God's description of the pervasive corruption that surrounded the righteous in the time of Noah (Gen 6:11–12) is similar.[46] The psalmist closes by praying that God would restore and save his people in the midst of the evil around them (v. 7).

As Goldingay notes, the commonness of deep corruption surrounded Israel. Though Israel had its own share of corruption many times, this is not the topic of the psalmist. There are still righteous persons in Israel (v. 5). This passage does not suggest Israel cannot obey God's commands, only that fools and evildoers do not do so.

Romans 3:9–18

Romans 3:9–18 quotes Psalm 14:1–3 and will be considered next. Throughout the book of Romans, Paul confirms that both Jews and Gentiles are sinners. In Romans 1:18–32, the target is Gentiles and in Romans 2:1—3:8 it is Jews. Paul now summarizes that though Jews have certain advantages, when it comes to sin all people are in the same boat:

> 9What shall we conclude then? Do we have any advantage? Not at all! For we have already made the charge that Jews and Gentiles alike are all under the power of sin. 10As it is written:

---

45. Craigie, *Psalms 1–50*, 146.
46. Goldingay, *Psalms 1–41*, 212–14.

> "There is no one righteous, not even one; 11there is no one who understands; there is no one who seeks God. 12All have turned away, they have together become worthless; there is no one who does good, not even one." 13"Their throats are open graves; their tongues practice deceit."
>
> "The poison of vipers is on their lips." 14"Their mouths are full of cursing and bitterness."
>
> 15"Their feet are swift to shed blood; 16ruin and misery mark their ways, 17and the way of peace they do not know." 18"There is no fear of God before their eyes." (Rom 3:9–18)

Paul amasses several passages from the Psalms, Ecclesiastes, and Isaiah to make his point. Commentators decipher three groupings in the text: 1) verses 11–12 depict the ubiquitous nature of sin, 2) verses 13–14 illustrate sins of speech, and 3) verses 15–17 concentrate on violent sins against others. Though many of the passages describe the sins of Israel, Paul's intent here is to show all are under sin's power.[47] Verse 18 is perhaps a summary of all these evils, noting that in all cases there is no fear of God in these people.

Paul's point is clear, all Jews and Gentiles are under sin's power. He reiterates this in two other places—Romans 3:23 and Romans 5:12. Sin is universal, but this does not mean that there are literally none who are righteous. The OT is full of references to specific righteous individuals and Paul himself discusses the righteousness that comes by faith in the rest of Romans 3. He even extols the righteousness of Abraham in Romans 4, the victory of Christ's gift over Adam's trespass in Romans 5, and the life and righteousness available to Christ-followers in Romans 6.

Isaiah 64:4–7

> 4Since ancient times no one has heard, no ear has perceived, no eye has seen any God besides you, who acts on behalf of those who wait for him. 5You come to the help of those who gladly do right, who remember your ways. But when we continued to sin against them, you were angry. How then can we be saved? 6All of us have become like one who is unclean, and all our righteous acts are like filthy rags; we all shrivel up like a leaf, and like the wind our sins sweep us away. 7No one calls on your name or strives to lay hold of you; for you have hidden your face from us and have given us over to our sins. (Isa 64:4–7)

---

47. Moo, *Epistle to the Romans*, 202, 204; and Cranfield, *Epistle to the Romans*, 194.

Isaiah 40–66 is commonly divided from the earlier chapters into a second section. In Isaiah's day Israel had already been judged by God and had fallen to the Assyrian empire; only Judah was left. Isaiah prophesied the future defeat of Judah by the Babylonians and foresees Judah's exile under them (ch. 39). Also prophesied is Babylon's fall (ch. 46–47). Our passage is contained in the looking-forward-to-God's-restoration section. Isaiah is praying for God's intervention, either on behalf of the future exiles to be released or on behalf of his people before the end-time judgment. Chapter 64 seems to be describing the pervasive sinfulness that typified Judah before God judged them and sent them into exile. The focus for our purposes is verses 5–7, especially the reference to "all our righteousness are like filthy rags" (v. 6).

Isaiah laments Judah's persistent sin and describes her as unclean and compares what appears to be her righteous deeds to filthy menstrual rags. Further, Judah is a dead shriveled leaf on a tree—their sins are like a wind that has blown them away from their branch.[48] On the other hand, good healthy trees flourish near water and their branches and leaves receive continual nourishment as they abide in God (cf. Ps 1 and John 15). Unfortunately, this has not been Judah's course. Our passage's references to uncleanness, filthy rags righteousness, and dead leaves testifies to the iniquity of the generation that is in exile or may even refer to God's OT people as a whole and what they have become over the centuries. It is not likely a referral to universal human sinfulness or an insinuation that any righteous person's good deeds are always spoiled by sin.[49] This conclusion seems reasonable since it is only Judah who is the topic of Isaiah's lament and not the whole of humanity. He is decrying her sinfulness that has led God to take away her nationhood and allow the holy city Jerusalem and its temple to be destroyed (Isa 64:10–11).

Philippians 3:11–15

> 11I want to know Christ—yes, to know the power of his resurrection and participation in his sufferings, becoming like him in his death, and so, somehow, attaining to the resurrection from the dead.
>
> 12Not that I have already obtained all this, or have already arrived at my goal, but I press on to take hold of that for which Christ Jesus took hold of me. 13Brothers and sisters, I do not consider myself yet to have taken hold of it. But one thing I do: Forgetting what is behind and straining toward what is ahead, 14I

---

48. Smith, *Isaiah 40–66*, 690–91.
49. Goldingay, *Old Testament*, 263–64.

> *press on toward the goal to win the prize for which God has called me heavenward in Christ Jesus.*
> *15All of us, then, who are mature should take such a view of things. And if on some point you think differently, that too God will make clear to you.* (Phil 3:11–15)

In these verses Paul is describing the benefits he has received in Christ. He has just stated that whatever advantages he had in life are considered loss or garbage because of the surpassing value of knowing Christ and having righteousness through faith in him (v. 8–9). Verse 12 speaks of Paul's *telos* or "goal," a word that has been variously interpreted. The most plausible meaning is to what he has been referencing in the previous verses—the complete knowing and gaining of Christ. Paul asserts he hasn't yet obtained or taken hold of this (see both vv. 12 and 13); he has approached this goal in his life of love, sufferings, and service to Christ. He has yet "to be perfected / reach his goal." Many commentators believe this could be a reference to the Gnostic idea of attaining perfect knowledge of God in this lifetime. Gordon Fee adds that Paul is also not arguing against some sort of moral perfectionism.[50] Paul, in these types of ideas, is affirming he has not reached this goal, since this "perfection" or "goal" awaits him at Christ's Second Coming.[51] Until that occurs, Paul in the present presses on and strains toward that goal, an image that many commentators believe represents the efforts of a runner to achieve a coveted wreath (v. 14). The "call" seems to suggest the call to salvation and the "prize" in our context is the complete knowledge and fellowship with Christ, the attainment of everlasting life at the eschaton.[52]

Paul uses *teleioi* again in verse 15 in an apparently different sense.[53] In this case the word is best translated as "mature"—those who are spiritually mature are urged to pursue "perfection," (complete knowledge of Christ in glory) as Paul does. He encourages, but doesn't assume, that all the Philippian Christians will also act in this mature manner. Fee adds that the pursuit of a full knowledge of God at the eschaton is Paul's emphasis, since he reminds them in verses 20–21 that their citizenship is in heaven and that they are to eagerly expect Christ's return, when their bodies will be transformed into the likeness of his. God's purposes will not be complete until their salvation is consummated in this way. Paul wants the Philippians

---

50. Fee, *Paul's Letter to the Philippians*, 344.
51. O'Brien, *Epistle to the Philippians*, 420–25.
52. Ibid., 432–36.
53. It was a common literary technique to use a different sense of a word in the same context. Paul uses *teleioi* in other epistles to mean "mature" (1 Cor 2:6, 14:20; Eph 4:13; Col 1:28, 4:12). See O'Brien, *Epistle to the Philippians*, 435–36.

to not look on their earthly circumstances, but to keep their gaze steady on Christ and their future with him.[54]

So, this passage stresses that we are not "perfect" because we haven't joined Christ at his Second Coming. It is not likely it refers to moral righteousness in our present experience. This idea has been suggested by some who say we can never be perfect in this life—just look at Paul—if he can't, then we surely can't! But this misses Paul's contextual intent here.

James 3:2

> 2 We all stumble in many ways. Anyone who is never at fault in what they say is perfect, able to keep their whole body in check. (Jas 3:2)

James, here writing to scattered Jewish believers, has preceded our verse with talk about the importance of combining faith and deeds and in taming the tongue. In James 3:1, he acknowledges that because even Christian leaders can have difficulty with appropriate speech, he warns teachers that they will be judged the more strictly because of the weight of their ministry. In verse 2, he admits that we all "stumble." He may be inferring here that these sins are more unintentional or minor with this verb[55] as many errors in speech are considered "slips of the tongue," or mind, to be more exact! James also says we stumble "in many ways" with our speech. McCartney seems to reasonably conclude that when a person can control their tongue, they have become grown-up or spiritually mature. This requires self-discipline and those who master the tongue are few. Because of the maturity this requires, such a person will be able to take captive all other sins ("able to keep their whole body in check").[56] It seems likely James is still referring to teachers in this verse, but it is possible he includes all Christians in the temptation of ill-speaking.[57]

---

54. Fee, *Paul's Letter to the Philippians*, 347, 350–51.

55. Blomberg and Kamell, *James*, 152.

56. McCartney, *James*, 180. Others see the "body" as referring to the "body of Christ," or the church. See McKnight, *James*, 272. This seems possible but less likely based on the context. Moo concurs (see Moo, *Letter of James*, 151–52).

57. Sometimes we harm others in ignorance and therefore unintentionally. John Oswalt gives an example: "Suppose something has happened in your past that has left you especially sensitive in some area of your life. I know nothing of this and make some remark that touches that area and hurts you deeply. I did not intend to hurt you, but I did. I have not willfully transgressed God's known law. But I have sinned unintentionally. My insensitive actions have hurt you, and if you tell me so, I need to ask your

James further states that "no human being can tame the tongue. It is a restless evil, full of deadly poison" (Jas 3:8). The context of verses 2–12 zeroes in on our speech and how easily it can become sinful. We need constant vigilance to monitor what comes out of our mouths. Consequently, must the Christian be relegated to a no-win struggle with sinful speech? James suggests not in the rest of the chapter. He expects his rhetorical questions in verses 11–12 (fresh vs. salty water and olive vs. fig trees) to be answered with "no"—one cannot come from the other, just like praise to God *should not* come from the same mouth that curses others (v. 10). The solution is to make one's speech "fresh" and good. The solution is also to become wise, since the wise reveal themselves by a good life and humble deeds (3:13). This wisdom is not of our own making, but is from "heaven" and results in a "harvest of righteousness" (3:17–18).

1 John 1:6–10

> *6If we claim to have fellowship with him and yet walk in the darkness, we lie and do not live out the truth. 7But if we walk in the light, as he is in the light, we have fellowship with one another, and the blood of Jesus, his Son, purifies us from all sin. 8If we claim to be without sin, we deceive ourselves and the truth is not in us. 9If we confess our sins, he is faithful and just and will forgive us our sins and purify us from all unrighteousness. 10If we claim we have not sinned, we make him out to be a liar and his word is not in us.*
> (1 John 1:6–10)

Commentator Colin Kruse believes that there is a specific audience John has in mind with his comments in this chapter and that their opinion is that they have not sinned since they came to know God.[58] Karen Jobes tends to agree with this, noting that in verse 10, John uses the perfect tense "have

---

forgiveness and God's. If I do so, then there is never a break in my fellowship with God. And if you do not tell me what has happened, the blood of Christ cleanses me in my ignorance and permits me to continue walking in his light. If this is what those who stand in the Reformed tradition are talking about when they speak of sinning 'daily in thought, word, and deed' and thereby needing the atoning blood of Christ to be applied constantly, I agree with them most heartily. . . . But if this statement is meant to say that Christians regularly and helplessly commit sins 'with a high hand,' sins of willful transgression, then I must disagree on the strength of the entire New Testament, but especially Romans 6 and 1 John 1–3." Oswalt, *Called to be Holy*, 175. Whether one needs to ask God for forgiveness for this type of offense is not specified in Scripture (cf. Paul before Ananias, Acts 23:1–5).

58. Kruse, *Letters of John*, 66.

sinned," suggesting persistent sinning in the past and up the present (not an isolated event). She hypothesizes that some of John's readers may be minimizing the seriousness of sin and the need for atonement and replacing that with an emphasis on Jesus's moral teachings and example.[59] It is likely these persons are trying to lead John's hearers, who are "in the light," astray into darkness (2:19, 26). John appears to describe these false teachers several times as he rephrases his description of them. For example, "If we claim to have fellowship with him and yet walk in the darkness" (1:6) is paralleled by "If we claim to be without sin," (1:8) *but are sinning nonetheless*, and by "If we claim we have not sinned," (1:10) *even though we surely have*. These false teachers are also suggested by John in 2:3, "Whoever says, 'I know him,' but does not do what he commands is a liar," and by "Anyone who claims to be in the light but hates a brother or sister" (2:9). John's direct audience, however, is the ones who are "in the light." He addresses them as "My dear children/friends" (2:1, 7, 12–14, 18, 28 . . .).

Some Christians claim that our passage defends the idea that any Christian who affirms there is no current sin blocking his or her fellowship with God is lying. However, this conclusion does not fit the context of John's audience. John is correcting wrong thinking that certain deceivers have about themselves. On the contrary, he believes Christians are to live above a sinful lifestyle. In chapters 2 and 3 he tells them he does not want them to sin (2:1); he wants them to deeply know God and others, to keep God's commands, obey his word, live like Jesus did (2:1–6), not sin, do what is right, and love each other (3:7–10).

These passages do not significantly alter the idea that Christians can live out a significant holiness. They either describe those outside the faith, a subgroup inside the faith who have faltered, or erroneous thinking about the Christian life.

The Experience and Example of Past Believers

There is experiential testimony that holiness is achievable. Numerous people are described as holy or righteous in the Bible. In the OT, Noah and his family, Abraham, Moses, Joshua, Job, David, Solomon (in the beginning), the psalmists, and the prophets[60] are righteous. Christopher J. H. Wright expounds:

---

59. Jobes, *1, 2, 3 John*, 72.

60. Even though a prophet like Isaiah considered himself "a man of unclean lips" when he beheld God's glory, God cleansed him (Isa 6:5–8) and used him as a trustworthy servant (Isa 20:2). Zechariah, John the Baptist's father, prophesied about the *holy*

> The frequent claims by various psalmists to have lived according to God's law are neither exaggerated nor exceptional. They arise from the natural assumption that ordinary people can indeed live in a way that is broadly pleasing to God and faithful to God's law, and that they can do so as a matter of joy and delight. This is neither self-righteousness nor a claim to sinless perfection, for the same psalmists are equally quick to confess their sin and failings, fully realizing that only the grace that could forgive and cleanse them would likewise enable them to live again in covenant obedience. Obedience to the law in the OT, as has been stressed repeatedly, was not the means of achieving salvation but the response to a salvation that was already experienced.[61]

In the NT, the disciples (minus Judas), Paul and his associates (Luke, Mark, and all his helpers mentioned in his letters), disciples mentioned in the text of Acts and all the Epistles, the hall of faith in Hebrews 11, those noted in Revelation—the 144,000 from Israel, the multitude in white robes (Rev 7), and all those in the book of life (Rev 20) are righteous. Moreover, there is the example of all God's saints from creation to the present day—millions no doubt! We may have personally read the story of some faithful Christian in a biography or read personal stories of overcoming faith in Christian history books. We each likely have people of our own acquaintance that we revere as models of holiness. So, there is ample testimony that God considers many people righteous.

Some may counter that there are also examples of Christians who have been poor examples—they have acted unrighteously. God's followers have sometimes acted like the world or have done things in the name of God that later believers look on with shame. This is true. But the attempt to say that all followers of God and Christ can never achieve a significant holiness is unfounded. God has offered his law (written on stone and on human hearts), enabling, grace, and Holy Spirit to all believers. Whether individual believers reach out and avail themselves of God's grace is another matter.

What is "New" about the New Covenant that Relates to our Ability to be Holy?

There are several biblical statements affirming the superiority of the New Covenant over the Old and these certainly apply to the Christian and holiness. David Peterson reminds us that Israel, as a whole, failed to offer itself

---

prophets of the OT (Luke 1:70).

61. Wright, C., *Deuteronomy*, 290.

as a meaningful self-sacrifice so that God could fulfill his purposes through them. He states that part of the "newness" and power of the New Covenant is revealed in the book of Hebrews.

Forgiveness, Cleansing, Perfecting

The writer of Hebrews declares that Christ, in his bodily life, offered himself as a perfect sacrifice and as one who was perfectly obedient. He acted as a high priest who was tempted in every way we are but remained sinless (Heb 4:15). He was a holy blameless offering given once for all for the people (7:26–27). His blood offering obtained "eternal redemption" (9:12), ransomed us so we could be set free from sins (9:15), and cleansed our consciences from sin so we can serve God (9:14). Christ came to "do away with sin" (9:26) or "take away the sins of many" (9:28).

Under the Old Covenant, purification rites cleansed the worshippers from ceremonial uncleanness so they could worship in the community again. The gifts and sacrifices, however, could not cleanse the conscience (9:9, 13), make perfect (10:1), or remove guilt (10:3). Now our hearts are sprinkled with the blood of the unblemished Christ, which cleanses our guilty conscience (9:14, 10:22) and allows us to serve him rightly. His death made possible a type of consecration that couldn't occur under the Old Covenant:

> 10... we have been made holy through the sacrifice of the body of Jesus Christ once for all.
>
> 14For by the one sacrifice he has made perfect forever those who are being made holy.
>
> (Heb 10:10b, 14)

In these verses the writer equates this act with the prophecy of Jeremiah 31 in which God promised to put his laws in his followers hearts, write them on their minds, and remember their sin no more (10:16–18).[62] How Christ's sacrifice makes us holy (10:10, 14) is not explained. One suggestion is that "making holy" is the same "cleansing from sin" and "cleansing of the conscience" described already.[63] This the OT sacrifices couldn't do (9:13); they could only provide a sort of outer physical cleansing. Hebrews 10:10 states that we *have been made* holy, and verse 14 that we *are being made* holy. This suggests both the "declared" and "made" elements of righteousness discussed previously. Cockerill believes the writer calls for continual participa-

---

62. Peterson, *Possessed by God*, 34–37.
63. Cockerill, *Epistle to the Hebrews*, 443.

tion from God's "holy ones." Christ's sanctifying work was once for all but is also continuous, and must be continuously received so we are enabled to live in faithful obedience.[64] Christ, our High Priest, saves us completely and lives to make intercession for us (7:25).

The Indwelling Holy Spirit

The Holy Spirit had definite interaction with God's people under the Old Covenant. He came upon certain individuals for certain tasks. He came upon the temple artisans so they would have skill to build well (Exod 31:2–5). He came upon Israel's kings so they could serve (Saul, 1 Sam 10:10–13; David, 1 Sam 16:13). However, this filling was not universal or permanent. He was promised to be the baptizer of God's people in the New Covenant (Matt 3:11; Acts 1:5; Acts 11:16) and the One who would be "in" them forever (John 14:16–17). Before his death, Jesus reiterated the Spirit's new role (John 15:26, 16:8–15). Paul mentions this indwelling several times (Rom 8:9; 1 Cor 3:16).

The Holy Spirit has several roles under the New Covenant that are related to holiness. He gives his followers new life (John 3:3–8; Titus 3:5) and keeps us (Eph 4:30). He sets us apart (sanctifies us) as one of his own (2 Thess 2:13). He baptizes believers into one body (1 Cor 12:12–14). He helps us pray (Rom 8:26–27). He empowers believers for service. This is apparent from Acts 1:8 and the stories of the Spirit's working in Christ's followers in the rest of the book of Acts. A complementary way to aid this process is to convict sinners of their sin and its consequences (John 16:7–11). Another complement comes in the gifts the Spirit gives, which are diverse (Rom 12:5–18; 1 Cor 12:4–11; Eph 4:7–16). Further, Jesus said the Spirit will be a teacher of the saints (John 14:26, 16:13–15; 1 Cor 2:11–16).

More pertinent to our topic is his work in helping the believer overcome sin and live a life pleasing to God. We are set free from the "law" of sin and death and empowered by the "law of the Spirit" and living "according to the Spirit" (Rom 8:1–4). The Spirit works the fruit of spiritual virtues in us (Gal 5:22–25). As this occurs we are progressively transformed into the image of Christ, which comes from the Spirit (2 Cor 3:18).

---

64. Ibid., 452.

Suffering, Discipline, and Holiness

God frequently uses suffering and discipline to perfect his followers. Though our current topic is the NT, suffering and persecution were by no means limited to it. The Israelites suffered throughout their history at the hands of evil rulers (from other nations and their own). Individuals suffered as a result of other people's sins. Moving forward, we see that even Jesus himself "learned obedience through what he suffered" (Heb 5:8). Peterson makes a good case that suffering and discipline are necessary ingredients in a NT view of holiness. For one thing, discipline works as encouragement—we see the example of Christ's endurance during suffering and are heartened (Heb 12:5–6). In the next few verses the writer reminds us that God disciplines his children, not only to correct them, but to shape them spiritually.

> 9Moreover, we have all had human fathers who disciplined us and we respected them for it. How much more should we submit to the Father of spirits and live! 10They disciplined us for a little while as they thought best; but God disciplines us for our good, in order that we may share in his holiness. 11No discipline seems pleasant at the time, but painful. Later on, however, it produces a harvest of righteousness and peace for those who have been trained by it. (Heb 12:9–11)

Similarly, other NT authors use the word "trial" as a necessary ingredient in developing godly character, a process that produces joy as we contemplate the result. Paul affirms that sufferings produce perseverance, which leads to character and lastly to hope, which doesn't disappoint us (Rom 5:4–5). James agrees, stating that trials and testings produce perseverance, which produces maturity and wholeness (Jas 1:2–4). Peter contends that those who suffer in the body, as Christ did, are done with sin; they live for the will of God instead of evil human desires (1 Pet 3:18–19, 4:1–2). Peter, in another passage, declares that griefs and trials prove the genuineness of our faith and result in glory and praise to God when Christ returns (1 Pet 1:6–9). The result of allowing God to train and mold us in this way is a life of holiness, righteousness, maturity, and sanctification.[65] This does not imply that others need to sin (producing trials and suffering) so we can become more holy. Paul affirmed in Romans 6:1–2 that we personally shouldn't sin so that grace would abound toward us. It seems just as likely that God would not require others to disobey him so we could become more obedient or holy! Paul's response of "God forbid!" seems just as appropriate here. This also does not mean that our own sin, or sin against us, can't be redeemed by

---

65. Ibid., 71–72.

God. "In all things God works for the good . . ." (Rom 8:28). Whether from sin, the natural struggles of life, or God himself, God uses suffering for our benefit and holiness.[66]

Can the Flesh be Overcome, and if so, How?

Chapter 4 concluded that the flesh was a potent influence toward sin. Can this push toward sinful indulgence be habitually overcome in this lifetime? This chapter has provided ample evidence that it can—Jesus, Paul, Peter, James, and the writer of Hebrews say as much.

From where does this overcoming power come? Jesus said it came from abiding in his love. We can bear no spiritual fruit without abiding in Christ and his love, just like a branch must stay attached to the vine to bear grapes (John 15:4–5). Love was central to Jesus's teaching, the total of which equaled truth. If his disciples held to his teachings they would be truly free from slavery of sin (John 8:31–36). Jesus also declared that his disciples must deny themselves and take up their crosses if they ever hoped to be followers of him. They must die to or "lose" their earthly-centered lives (Matt 16:24–25). This cross-centered theme was taken up by Paul, who said that he had died to the law in order that he might live for God—in essence he was crucified with Christ; he no longer lived, but Christ lived in him (Gal 2:20). Romans 8:1–13 amplifies this connection between freedom, death to the law, and flesh, life, and the Holy Spirit. It is the Spirit who gives life (8:2). Christians are "in the Spirit" and their minds are centered on the Spirit's desires (8:5). They are not obligated to the flesh, but are to live in the Spirit (8:12). This implies that Christians can be affected or influenced by fleshly desires, but they are empowered by the Spirit to overcome them (8:2). In similar metaphors, Colossians 2:11–13 says that our whole fleshly self was circumcised by Christ and buried with him in baptism. Now we

---

66. Bruce Demarest believes that good can come to Christians who experience "painful disorientation" in their lives—sufferings, persecutions, or the "dark night of the soul." See Demarest, *Seasons of the Soul*. See also C. S. Lewis, *A Grief Observed*, as he deals with the pain of his wife's death. Ajith Fernando affirms Christians are called to both joy and pain and that we need to embrace suffering. See Fernando, *The Call to Joy and Pain*. Michael Card encourages Christians to reach out to God with the lost language of lament when we face difficulty and suffering. See Card, *A Sacred Sorrow*. *Foxe's Book of Martyrs*, edited by William Byron Forbush, details the trials and persecutions of Christian martyrs through the centuries and how they endured and triumphed in their sufferings. These are several examples. There are many stories of suffering and courage depicted in the accounts of God's servants throughout history and how God used suffering for good in their lives and in the church at large. The respective Protestant, Roman Catholic, and Eastern Orthodox histories have their own treasury of examples.

have Christ's new life inside us and it is this life that empowers us to overcome. In all of this there is the participation from Christ-followers to abide, love, deny, deliver themselves for crucifixion, and to receive and live life in the Spirit.

CONCLUSION

The overwhelming evidence of this chapter suggests we certainly can be holy. God has commanded and therefore expected this of his followers in both Testaments, has told us through his servants that we are able to please him, has given us personal examples in the Bible, Christian history, and in our own experience of holiness, and has empowered us with the blessings and enablings of the New Covenant. What remains is for us to walk in the power and status he has given us and be a shining light of witness to our needy world.[67]

INTERACTION WITH HISTORICAL CONCEPTS OF HOLINESS, EXPECTATIONS, AND ACHIEVABILITY

There are degrees of agreement when the historical Christian perspectives are compared with our results in chapters 5 and 6. Eastern Orthodoxy uses different terms, but follows very closely the concepts elucidated above. We participate in God's "energies" of love and spiritual fruit as we are united more and more with God. We now share God's life and immortality and partake of a life-long growth in spiritual maturity. Likewise, Roman Catholic doctrine values holiness. As believers walk toward the "beatific vision" expressed in the Sermon on the Mount, they develop virtues, acquired by their own effort, which is elevated by God's gift of grace. The help of the sacraments and our cooperation with the Holy Spirit enable God to infuse

---

67. The author purposely limited the scope of the discussion of holiness to the question of whether it can be attained or not. The details of the nature of our pursuit, what methods or practices might help us, how holiness might manifest itself in various practical scenarios, etc., are covered well by other books. Each Christian tradition—Eastern Orthodox, Roman Catholic, and Protestant—have their able scholars and divines that give excellent guidance. The author has recently read several such attempts, *The Hole in our Holiness* by Reformed pastor Kevin DeYoung, chapters 8 and 9 of *The Divine Conspiracy* by Dallas Willard, and *Free to Live: The Utter Relief of Holiness* by John Eldredge. Books that discuss spiritual formation and the spiritual disciplines are also very helpful in this regard. Sometimes biographies of respected saints can motivate and instruct us. The reader is encouraged to seek out these and similar books that give practical insight into this pursuit.

virtue into our soul with love the dominant virtue. Again, there is a process of becoming more and more Christlike, of maturing in Christian character, love, and virtue. The Protestant Reformed tradition sometimes deemphasizes the degree of holiness Christians can achieve in this life. Some believe in a progressive but modest growth in spiritual maturity and sanctification. There is a continual struggle with the sinful nature and the old self, but the Scriptures goad us on toward holiness (since our natures are against it) and give us God's pattern (the law and the spiritual truths the Holy Spirit reveals). Our hope is to deny ourselves, receive the virtues God gives us, and to be content with the partial attainment of Christlikeness we can experience in this life. Wesleyans, Pentecostals, and Anabaptists generally agree with the progressive increase in holiness throughout the Christian life. Wesleyans are convinced they can achieve a degree of love for God that gives them a rest and repose in their experience of him. They need not strain to obey as they once did. The Christian life can be a struggle, but there is victory over sin such that it is not necessary to commit it. The Stone-Campbell movement's views paralleled our chapter conclusions closely. Holiness involves a purity of heart, which was begun by a work of the Holy Spirit. They accentuate a progressive increase in holiness and a synergistic relationship between God and us in its expression. There can be significant spiritual maturing and conformity of our will to God's in this life.

SUMMARY AND PLAUSIBLE MODELS FOR SECTION II

The Introduction provided a series of steps by which we can best spiral toward the truth regarding the definition of holiness and righteousness, the types of righteousness, the nature of holiness, the behavior of holy persons, the commands and expectations of God regarding holiness, and our ability to obey God's character-related commands. Chapters 5 and 6 discussed relevant passages and secondary sources and each chapter ended with a general conclusion. The evidence and scholarly opinions produced a general consensus regarding the:

- Definition of holiness and righteousness
- Types of righteousness that exist
- Nature of holiness—its source, motives, and common behaviors
- Holiness expectations and commands

There was disagreement on the degree to which Christians can be holy.

Now the conclusions need to be systematized into a theology and compared against other plausible models using inference to the best explanation

(IBE) criteria. Given the presuppositions discussed in the Introduction, two plausible theological models integrate the doctrines discussed in chapters 5 and 6.

- Model 3 concludes:
  - The consensus noted in the conclusions of chapters 5 and 6 is true.
  - The Christian, with the provisions of the New Covenant, is able to obey all God's commands and meet God's expectations. This means Christians can: 1) be holy or righteous, 2) overcome the flesh, abstain from the vices, and exhibit the Christian virtues in an increasing fashion, and 3) love God and others (obey the two Great Commandments). There will always be temptations to sin with varying degrees of desire to engage in it (always resistible). These desires will tend to lessen as they are habitually resisted. Enabling involves the active and devoted participation of the Christian, the empowering of the indwelling Holy Spirit, and the encouragement of fellow believers. This implies that the Christian need not sin, but may, and in such cases repentance, God's cleansing, and the Holy Spirit's power can lead to restoration and increasing sanctification. There can be significant maturing of one's relationship with God, resulting in spiritual maturity and Christlike character.
- Model 4 concludes:
  - The consensus noted in the conclusions of chapters 5 and 6 is true.
  - The Christian, with the provisions of the New Covenant, is able to partially obey all God's commands and meet God's expectations. The means Christians can: 1) make some progress toward holiness, 2) battle with the flesh, abstain from the vices, and exhibit the Christian virtues in a moderate fashion, and 3) love God and others (obey the two Great Commandments), but frequently with mixed motives. There will always be temptations to sin and resisting them will be a constant struggle. Fleshly desires and the effects of original sin will be with us in a significant way while we are on this earth and will only be removed once we are glorified. Enabling involves the active and devoted participation of the Christian, the empowering of the indwelling Holy Spirit, and the encouragement of fellow believers. Though enabled, the Christian does sin on a regular basis, and in such cases

repentance, God's cleansing, and the Holy Spirit's power can lead to restoration and increasing sanctification. There can be a modest maturing of one's relationship with God, resulting in a degree of spiritual maturity and Christlike character.

EVALUATION OF MODELS ACCORDING TO IBE CRITERIA

Explanatory Power/Scope

Model 3 best accounts for God's pervasive expectations and commands to be holy as expressed in the conclusion of chapter 6. Model 4 acknowledges these expectations and commands but limits how often and how well they can be achieved and obeyed.

Model 3 can also better account for the biblical and historical accounts of deeply devoted and consistent followers of Christ. However, the Bible also describes many persons and nations (especially Israel) who were not very holy and whom God expected to do better. Jesus concluded that "wide is the gate and broad is the road that leads to destruction, and many enter through it. But small is the gate and narrow the road that leads to life, and only a few find it" (Matt 7:13–14). He merely explained the facts of the matter and did not explain why. In a similar way, he also had more "against" the seven Asian churches in Revelation 2–3 than he had to commend them on. The NT epistle writers echo this, chiding their hearers on their spiritual lapses and less frequently praising their love and steadfastness. Religious and general history also seem to follow the same pattern, frequently noting the errors of the church and its leaders.[68] Our recent Barna survey also displayed a lack of "holiness confidence" among American Christians. Therefore, Model 4 seems to best account for the deepness and extensiveness of sinful behavior, for it ensures the results Jesus, the epistle writers, and history describe. Model 3 does affirm direct, indirect, and personal results of sin, but the many variables affecting moral behavior and the difficulty

---

68. This finding can be misleading considering the "newsworthiness" of sinful as opposed to good acts. Modern media (TV, radio, movies, phone, internet, books) seldom report on the many good, loving, and sacrificial acts of Christian leaders or laypersons but are keen to proclaim the larger sins of Christian leaders or failures of organized Christianity. Before the advent of media it is likely the talk of the day or even local gossip did not center on how helpful or kind one's neighbor was but instead on what a professing Christian might have imbibed at the local pub, said in anger at the market, or done with a lady of the evening.

in measuring them make it difficult to evaluate if this model sufficiently accounts for sin's extensiveness.

Both models have explanatory strengths and weaknesses. However, since: 1) Scripture has priority over the adjunct of personal experience in our methodological model, 2) Model 3 affirms God's expectations as the most important variable, and 3) Model 3 agrees most closely with the expressions of God, his spokespersons, and Jesus regarding the spiritual character Christ-followers can and should possess, preference is given to Model 3.

Logical Consistency

Both models display general logical consistency, with the exception of a few Model 4 examples. The Protestant Reformed section of chapter 2, which essentially agrees with and tries to explain Model 4, resorts to several definition changes that muddy the waters of our understanding. Adherents of this view use words like "synergism" and "agent" in ways that change the definition of each, much like the case with the word "free." Synergism "holds that God and the human together accomplish what must be done in order for the human to be saved."[69] However, we saw that Reformed theologians redefine it as God-determined. An agent is a person who controls his or her desires and actions; they are first causes. Again, this term is redefined by the Reformed such that an agent is caused by God (through his control of our desires) to do as God wishes.

> In evangelical Protestant spiritual experience, the wills of Christians are renewed, but they are not on a par with God's will. Arminian synergism acknowledges our need for the Spirit's enablement in general, but seems to place human ability on a par with the Spirit's by making the Spirit's love and ministries conditional: they will be exercised only to the extent that humans cooperate. Some place the Spirit under the control of human power, holding that the Spirit cannot work until the human will, like a light switch, turns the Spirit's operations on, or off. The merciful or gracious work of the sovereign Spirit in sanctification is not conditioned on the human "cooperation" but stimulates it. . . . [I]n this divinely initiated synergism, God works all things together for the good of actively yielded agents who work them out, not in the flesh, but motivated by a loving response to the Spirit.[70]

---

69. Erickson, *Christian Theology*, 924.
70. Lewis and Demarest, *Integrative Theology*, vol. 3, 214.

This selection also muddies the water of what "cooperate" and "actively yielded" mean—cooperate normally means "to act or work with another or others, to act together."[71] This is the gist in the Arminian usage, but here the meaning of it and "actively yielded" is unclear; the authors do not define them. They likely follow a compatibilist meaning, which is that God determines our desires, which then control our decisions. We are passive in the process, regardless of the word "actively." This, then, is a variation of the fallacy of *equivocation* or *ambiguous language*. The authors have intentionally redefined terms and their new definitions are either not given or are so hazy that it is difficult to decipher a meaning.

As a result humans act as mere instrumental or intermediate causes and do not initiate independent action, therefore holiness becomes meaningless. We become holy because God works through us and in us, much like electricity passing through the conduit of a copper wire. If God is behind the Christian's desires (and therefore decisions), it is hard to fathom why we are not all more holy than we are.

A second issue for Model 4 is that it rests its case too heavily on less numerous, more descriptive vs. prescriptive, and less didactic Bible passages (e.g., Romans 7 vs. Romans 6, 8 and many other OT and NT commands and expectations), thus exhibiting the fallacy of a *hasty generalization*.

Model 3 seems to lack logical issues and has an advantage on this factor.

Coherence and *ad hoc* features

Model 3's affirmations seem to be internally consistent and to mutually reinforce each other. Model 4 does not coherently explain the biblical injunction and expectation to be holy. It gives too much power to fleshly desires and the old nature such that it denies the power of God's promises and the Holy Spirit to enable Christians to be holy. Though God and the biblical authors say, "Yes, you can. Go and be godly," Model 4 proponents say, "Well, I can make a little progress. I have to endure fleshly desires and a weak body and my motives are always mixed." Therefore God's expectations and Model 4 results do not "stick" together.

---

71. *Webster's Ninth*, "cooperate."

Integration

The existence of apparently "holy" behavior on the part of human beings has not gone without notice in the scientific community. This is reflected in the scientific study of altruism, which in humans is also called the "Golden Rule."[72]

As noted at the end of chapter 4, sociobiologists suggest any good done to others or any self-denial must ultimately benefit our individual survival (and thus the survival of our genetic information) or the survival of offspring and relatives (related genetic material). This frequently means obeying the desires of our "lower" brain parts and any higher parts that improve our fitness to survive (This is usually an unconscious decision.). Apparently unselfish behavior must then follow four conditions: 1) The denial of desires will protect us from danger or achieve a greater reward in the near future. Altruism is only apparent; it is at root selfish. 2) Self-denial will improve the survival chances of our offspring or relatives. This is *kin altruism*. 3) Self-denial benefiting non-relatives will likely produce reciprocal self-denial, defined as *reciprocal altruism*. 4) Self-denial is observed by the social group and will appear to be altruistic. This will improve one's reputation in the group and improve the chances of receiving future self-denying behavior from others in a trustworthy back-and-forth relationship (*cooperative altruism*).[73]

Gantt and Reber question the meaning of altruism in this genetically determined model. They conclude this version is ultimately meaningless since it is reduced to genetic causality. Meaning requires possibility and agency such that the possibility of altruism could have been otherwise. The sociobiology model has neither. These authors affirm there are other, intellectually viable alternative models in the phenomenological thought of Maurice Merleau-Ponty and Emmanuel Levinas. These two affirm that possibility, meaning, and altruism typify human behavior. Our embodied and face-to-face interaction with each other, coupled with the moral and other-centered relational nature of humans, allow altruistic behavior to truly be expressed.[74]

---

72. Scientists define altruism differently. Some define it as doing good to others. Others add that the doing of good is done in order to have good done in return; this is a selfish altruism. Others define it as doing good to others regardless if there is any probability of the good being returned, with some extending that to including self-sacrifice. An author's particular definition will be given if it is known.

73. Shaw, "Human Brain," 156. See also Johnson, "Inadequacies," 94–97.

74. Gantt and Reber, "Sociobiological and Social Constructionist," 14.

The unselfish altruism Gantt and Reber advocate is described by other researchers. A rare type, *extended altruism*, is an unselfish altruism not done for any perceived genetic or other benefit. In the animal kingdom this anomaly harms survival potential and is rooted out by natural selection.[75] C. Daniel Batson has done extensive research on the power of empathy-induced altruistic behavior in humans. He concentrates on motivation and defines altruism as a motivational state whose ultimate goal is the increase of another's welfare regardless of self-benefits. The results of over thirty experiments show that the empathy-altruism hypothesis holds true, which means lack of support for the competing egoistic alternatives. Batson speculates that empathic concern evolved from the parenting instinct. This human instinct is the basis for "cognitive generalization" beyond one's group or family such that a person adopts others. However, Batson believes there are other unselfish motivations besides empathy for the explanation of altruism. Collectivism (the goal is the welfare of the group) and principlism (the goal of upholding a universal and impartial moral principle, such as justice) are two. Contrarily, Batson admits there is *some* evidence that egoistic motives, such as maintaining a positive self-concept and avoiding guilt, are the ultimate motives behind some altruistic behavior. Empathy itself can sometimes be a merely instrumental or intermediary factor. Further, enlightened self-interest and the desire to "appear" moral are possible alternatives to collectivism and principlism. However, the best evidence suggests extended altruism exists.[76]

All forms of altruism seem to diminish when animals and humans are put under stress and when groups are very large. Whether it is rats, monkeys, or humans; physical or emotional stress produces less socially helpful and more self-serving, aggressive, and violent responses. However, humans also exhibit extended altruism under high-level stress (e.g., natural disasters, wars), something not seen among other mammals.[77]

The frequency of extended altruism in humans, with its negative role in genetic fitness and survival, is not well accounted for by evolutionary theories (they predict the opposite), but *is* predicted by several world religions, including Christianity. In Christianity, the command to "love one's neighbors as one's self" fits this model.[78] Christianity, and Christian dualism (spirit vs. flesh), is a viable option when trying to resist the forces of genetic self-interest, but it is a non-Darwinian agency and has no place in a

---

75. Johnson, "Inadequacies," 97.
76. Batson, "Empathy-Induced Altruistic Motivation," 3, 9, 11, 15, 18, 19.
77. Johnson, "Inadequacies," 99–100.
78. Ibid., 102–3.

biological theory. This means when biologists try to categorize self-sacrifice and altruism and morality in general, they must reduce it to the purpose of perpetuating the genome. This is accomplished by social cohesiveness and stability, which controls harmful individual behavior and therefore improves human genetic survival. However, it could be that moral or "holy" behavior also promotes non-biological individual health and stability, something we appear to be designed for and which is also affirmed by Christian doctrine.[79] Shaw reaches similar conclusions. He claims there is no adequate biological explanation for, 1) unselfish avoidance of limbic system (fleshly, in St. Paul's words) rewards, 2) unselfish religious altruism in spite of a reduction in genetic fitness, 3) the feeling of guilt, the need for redemption, and the need for divine approval among many humans, and 4) the time and energy spent by many to pursue a supernatural God. The answer appears to lay in a "spiritual side" of humanity, a concept which better addresses these aspects of human reality.[80]

Does this biological and social research give any clue as to how altruistic we can be? It appears not. It is difficult for empirical research to evaluate altruism because altruism deals with internal "motives" that are not amenable to observation. Motives must be determined by subsequent behavior or self-reports, neither of which are guaranteed to be accurate. Consequently, empirical research into altruism cannot be conclusive. The results of studies so far can be used to support either Model 3 or 4. Because researchers describe the closest thing to biblical holiness (extended altruism) as rare, an edge is given to Model 4, which predicts the same. Theoretically, Model 3 seems to have an edge. It can also more adequately explain the expressions of selfless altruism.

Existential Livability

Both models can muster evidence that they can be lived out. The question is which *should* be lived out. Both models can look to past Christian experience and find examples of Christ-followers who were representative of their theory. Model 3 looks to the many examples of mature spiritual experience in Christian history all the way to the present. Model 4 looks to those same examples, but augments them with the more common examples of mediocre Christian experience and the vast prevalence of non-Christians. Modern surveys by Gallup and Barna would support the tenuous nature of at least modern *American* Christian experience.

---

79. Schloss, "Sociobiological Explanations," 130.
80. Shaw, "Human Brain," 162.

Both models aim at being Christlike, but Model 3 and some adherents to Model 1 believe significant progress can be made in sanctification. Model 3 tends to hold to the expectations of the Sermon on the Mount and chapters 6 and 8 of Romans. Christians can deeply mature in their relationship with Christ, abide in Christ (John 15), and can regularly exhibit the Christian virtues. Model 4 tends toward a Romans 7 Christian experience and a mitigated sanctification; less spiritual progress is expected and more stock is placed on the hindrances of the flesh. This mitigation was hinted at in some of the answers given in the Westminster Larger Catechism (see ch. 1, Protestantism).

Livability also entails the ability of Christians to cope with their total environment, deal with life's challenges, and live the life God has directed. These aspects of livability are best accomplished by Model 3. It enables and encourages believers to live out God's expectations. It empowers Christians to more successfully deal with life's challenges, temptations, and sufferings. Model 4 offers less coping and holiness expectations and less encouragement that life's challenges can be successfully dealt with by the Christian.

IBE AND A CUMULATIVE CASE

Which Model is the best explanation of the data in chapters 5 and 6? Based on scriptural interpretation, Model 3 best agrees with the commands and expectations God has given in the Scriptures. Model 4 seems to best explain the history of Christian spiritual experience as a whole—there is more evidence for lesser degrees of holiness than for greater. Because the biblical revelation has greater weight than experience in our methodology, Model 3 is favored as the best explanation.

7

Conclusions and Implications for Individuals and the Church

LET US LOOK AT where we have come in our discussion. Our method used the biblical revelation with the adjuncts of reason, tradition, and experience helping in the interpretive process. Each chapter came to certain conclusions about original sin, sin itself, holiness, and God's expectations of us. How we interpret these ideas has significant ramifications for our Christian life. They affect how we think, act, and feel towards God, others, and our own selves. Four models were put forth and Models 1 and 3 were the inferences to the best explanation; they presented the best cumulative case. What do Models 1 and 3's conclusions mean for our daily Christian lives?

MODELS 1 AND 3'S IMPLICATIONS FOR THE INDIVIDUAL

There are significant implications for believing the conclusions of our study for our personal lives and our interactions with those around us.

Implications for our Personal Vision, Self-image, and Expectations

A beginning implication is that we are not under the weight of believing in original sin. This improves our personal view of God's character since we know that God has not saddled us, or allowed us to be saddled, with a compulsion that is diametrically opposed to all his purposes and by possessing it we are inexorably led to sin. What a weight is lifted when we see God has not set us up to fail, but to succeed! We do not have to hold in "tension" or as a "mystery" God's love and an understanding of it that allows such a dichotomy to exist.

Omitting original sin further affects our own moral life. Sin is not a state we are born into or a legacy we have inherited. It is an act of thought, word, or deed done against what is known of God's desires and commands. If we are doing our best to become aware of and fulfill God's expectations, we need not worry that we are continually committing unintentional sins. If we find one, we confess, repent, and move one. Consequently, because of sin's nature there is no "must" regarding it, even though we discovered all persons do sin. God's expectations in these models can be met and his expectations are not burdensome. He does not expect us to display the full glory of his own character since we are finite image-bearers. He expects us to be godly, not God. There is no disconnect between expectations and fulfillment; we can truly succeed no matter our circumstances.

Therefore, there can be an expectation of making significant progress in holiness in this lifetime. We can develop a deep relationship with God, become Christlike, mature in the fruit of the Spirit and the Christian virtues, and therefore engage in sin less and less frequently.

Another implication involves our image. God has created us in his image and even though others before us have failed to reflect that image, we still retain its basic functionality. Nonetheless, we live in a world filled with tarnished image-bearers and this certainly pushes us to follow suit. The world, the flesh, and the devil are still alive. This is countered by the drawings of the Holy Spirit, God's "speech" in creation (Ps 19:1–6, Rom 1:19–20), and the testimony and witness of believers. We are not left alone to face our enemies.

Disbelieving original sin also gives us no excuse for sinning. We cannot blame Adam for our actual sins any more than Adam can blame Eve or Eve can blame the serpent. Adam has not gotten us into our personal messes, we have.

God and Perfection

C. S. Lewis's *Mere Christianity* describes what God is up to regarding the Christian life in Book IV, chapters 8–10, and depicts Models 1 and 3's thinking. He describes Christianity as both hard and easy. It is hard because Christ wants all our heart. He has not come to torment our natural "self" with all its desires, but to kill it. He wants to give us a new self; he wants to give us himself. Living this way is much easier than trying to keep our own selves and our own happiness and then trying to be "good." Christ warned that this is not possible—thistles can't produce figs. So, the hard way is easier and is the only effective way. Then, as we are drawn to Christ, we become little "christs" and draw others to become the same. This is the sole purpose God created us for.

For Lewis, God's goal for believers is perfection. We may want something less, but he will give us nothing less. We must count the cost—what do we really want? Though God presses us to perfection he is pleased with our best efforts to serve him. A father smiles and is pleased with his one-year-old's stumbling attempts to walk. When this child is mature he would likewise be pleased with a firm brisk stride—but nothing less. In like manner God is easy to please, but hard to satisfy. To shrink back from God's plan is not humility, it is laziness and cowardice. To submit is mere obedience. As we follow in obedience we must not be surprised if we are in for a rough time. God is not trying to tidy up our "old" house—he is doing a total renovation. While we might be satisfied with a cottage, God is trying to build us into a palace in which he himself lives.

Careful with Comparisons

Lewis concludes that it is not good to start comparing the progress of our "building project" with that of others, or even that of well-behaved non-Christians. The wrong question is to ask how Christian A compares to Christian B on some virtue or to ask why non-Christian C is more generous than Christian A. Due to natural temperaments and upbringing, we all start at different points in our attitudes and behavior. The right question is how generous would Christian A be if he wasn't a Christian and how generous would non-Christian C be if she became one. Another danger of comparing is our lack of knowledge and insight: "What can you ever really know of other people's souls—of their temptations, their opportunities, their struggles? One soul in the whole creation you do know: and it is the only one whose fate is placed in your hands."[1]

In conclusion, Lewis's insights imply that Christians can be both content where they are in their Christian journey and yet not satisfied with the end result. This is the proper balance. This reiterates that God's final goal is not forgiveness, as important as that is, but to make us into his likeness. These ideas express well the implications of Models 1 and 3.

---

1. Lewis, *Mere Christianity*, 184.

Our Identity and Strength in Christ

The NT gives Christians great help in defining who they are. Christians no longer live for themselves, by themselves, or in their own power. They are identified by who they are and whose they are. Paul identifies his Christian readers as saints, not sinners, when he writes his letters.[2] They are not identified with Adam, but with Christ. Believers are referred to as who they are *in Christ*—the salt and light of the world (Matt 5:13–14), adopted sons and daughters (John 1:12–13), slaves of righteousness (Rom 6:18), branches of the true vine (John 15:1–8), friends of Christ (John 15:15), spiritual fruit-bearers (John 15:16), a temple of the Holy Spirit (1 Cor 6:19), the aroma of Christ (2 Cor 2:15), new creatures (2 Cor 5:17), crucified with Christ (Gal 2:20), God's workmanship, created for good works (Eph 2:10), the bride of Christ (Eph 5:25–27), new selves (Col 3:9–10), possessing the spirit of power, love, and self-control (2 Tim 1:7), a chosen race, royal priesthood, holy nation, God's own people (1 Pet 2:9), partakers of the divine nature (2 Pet 1:4), forgiven (1 John 1:9), and overcomers (1 John 5:4). Other accurate words are children of God, redeemed, reconciled, being transformed. These are again expressions of God asking us to live out who we already are.

This does not mean believers cannot sin, for they surely can and do. However, our focus many times determines what goal we reach. Reformed scholar Michael Kruger sees the importance of focus and identity, which is why he thinks Paul emphasizes the new self as opposed to the old and addresses believers as "saints" or "holy ones" instead of "sinners."

> Paul is not naïve about the fact that Christians still sin, and sin in major ways (indeed, his letters are often about their sins!). But, he wants Christians to think of themselves in regard to their new natures, not their old. They are saints who sometimes sin, not sinners who sometimes do right.
>
> And when our true identities are understood rightly, it actually affects the way we view (and respond to) our sins. We might think that the best way to appreciate the depth of our sin is to think of ourselves primarily in the category of "sinners." But, this can actually have the opposite effect. If we think of ourselves only as sinners then our sins are seen as something rather ordinary and inevitable. They are just the result of who we are. Sure, we wish we didn't sin. But, that's just what "sinners" do.

---

2. Paul does refer to himself as the worst of sinners (1 Tim 1:15), however, verse 16 implies this was in his past, since he *was* shown mercy *then*. Romans 7 has already been interpreted as best referencing Paul's (and all other converted Jews') past life.

CONCLUSIONS AND IMPLICATIONS FOR INDIVIDUALS AND THE CHURCH

> If we instead view ourselves as "saints," then we will begin to see our sin in a whole new light. If we really are "holy ones" then whatever sins we commit are a deeper, more profound, and more serious departure from God's calling than we ever realized. Our sin, in a sense, is even more heinous because it is being done by those who now have new natures and a new identity.
>
> And it is this "cognitive dissonance" between our identities as saints and our sinful actions that leads us to repentance. We repent because these sins are *not* ordinary or expected. They are fundamentally contrary to who God has made us to be. It is this tension between our identities and our actions that is lost when we cease to think of ourselves as saints.[3]

Peter likewise reminds his hearers that they need to look to God's power and promises that allow them to partake of the riches of his character (his divine nature), and that if they do not possess these attributes in increasing measure they are short-sighted and blind (2 Pet 1:3–11). Models 1 and 3 imply these types of conclusions.

Like Kruger, Reformed scholar Anthony Hoekema sees the importance of a biblical identity and self-image as especially important for his own community, whom he believes thinks of itself much more negatively than the Scriptures warrant. This self-image has naturally led to a less-than-positive lifestyle. It has emphasized continuing sinfulness and self-abasement more than newness in Christ. This is apparent in formal ways, such as in baptism, where persons are "admonished to loathe themselves" and in the Lord's Supper they are told to "abhor ourselves" for sins committed.[4] Hoekema agrees we should abhor our sins but is not certain we must loathe *ourselves*. Likewise, the attitude is present in the informal "culture" that sees itself through the purple-colored glasses of total depravity. We proclaim we are full of sin in capital letters in the main text and then at the bottom of the page in an obscure footnote admit we are also new in Christ. This, he is convinced, is the New Testament read upside down.[5]

This upside-down attitude has also been fostered by reading passages like Romans 7:14–25 as Christian experience. Hoekema has changed his mind on this passage and now believes it refers to the unconverted. His new understanding has made a significant change in his self-image; he sees the struggles in the Christian life carried out in an atmosphere of victory and not of constant defeat. Passages like 1 John 3:9 teach that a believer does not

---

3. Kruger, "Saint or Sinner?"

4. Hoekema speaks here of words from these rites in the Christian Reformed Church.

5. Hoekema, "The Christian's Self-Image" (Sept 1971), 23–24.

live a life of habitual sin, and if it does occur we ought to be a bit surprised rather than disheartened.[6] This more positive self-image is encouraged by rightly interpreting Paul's other references to the old and new self. They are not both parts of a believer so that we are partly old and partly new, but each is a different way of living. For the believer, the old self has been crucified and the new self is our current identity. The NT use of words signifying struggle, battle, a race, and soldiering reminds us we must fight the good fight. The foundation we stand on is newness in Christ; if we sin, we momentarily step off our foundation. There must be balance here—to think more highly of ourselves is pride and to see ourselves as less than the Scriptures teach is false modesty. The goal is to make an honest appraisal of ourselves, realizing our life is one of progressive transformation and renewal (Rom 12:2). When we see ourselves that way our self-image is dynamic—we are complete at this moment but will never be ultimately complete until we meet Jesus in his resurrection (1 John 3:2).[7] Hoekema has some excellent insights into how Christians should view themselves, a view that comports well with the biblical portrayal in the NT and the conclusions of Model 3.

Personal Reflections

This book's discussion has personal ramifications for me, the author. I have experienced first-hand the effects of a dysfunctional family and of parental divorce; the sins of those around me have had profound effects. I have dealt with my own mid-life struggle, with anxiety and clinical depression, and the attempt to discern physical causes from personality, family, and personal sins. I have struggled with my own fleshly desires in the area of impure thoughts, anger, and a people-pleasing and perfectionistic personality. Looking outward, I have taught private and public school junior-highers and have observed the effects of the flesh and the world on their behavior. This age group lacks some of the judgment that comes with physical and emotional maturity and is capable of both moral highs and lows. I have also worked in a professional setting where the effects of gossip and innuendo created hard feelings among colleagues and upward in the chain of command.

These negatives are either direct or indirect results of sin and they have affected and formed my current self. However, they are not my identity. They may hinder, but do not prevent me from pleasing God with my motives, thoughts, words, and deeds.

---

6. Ibid., 27–28.
7. Hoekema, "The Christian's Self-Image" (Oct 1971), 18, 20.

Working within Existing Church Beliefs

A further implication for those adopting Models 1 and 3 is that they may have difficulty fitting in with some Christian groups or denominations. These Models do not fit some denominational statements of faith and this could hamper one's ability to serve with them. On the other side of that coin, there are opportunities to positively affect Christian doctrine and practice if one is persistent and irenic.

MODELS 1 AND 3'S IMPLICATIONS FOR THE CHURCH

If the church at whatever level would adopt the conclusions of this book, certain changes would be necessary. First, since tradition and experience are very powerful interpretive factors in many sectors of the church, it would have to ask itself if it is willing to go wherever the Scriptures go, even if it is against tradition or present experience. What is God's truth worth?

Next, there would be a change in teaching and preaching. The doctrines on original sin, sin, the flesh, and sometimes holiness would be redefined. Human responsibility for sin would increase; we are not at the mercy of our fleshly desires. What counts as sin would decrease for some denominations, since sin would not be defined in relation to God's performance with his unlimited attributes and perfect character. For some groups what counts as sin might increase, since it refers to the heart motive and not just outward conduct. In concordance with sin's definition, holiness expectations would adjust discipleship expectations and instruction based on these changes. Regardless which direction the sin definition moved, the church would know it could actually please their Lord on a regular basis. This positive outlook would lift the countenance of the church as a whole, make it look more like the body of its head, Christ, and be a more winsome draw to the world around it.

Other teaching changes would affect evangelism since a common strategy in evangelism is to teach that all are sinners and justly deserve to be separated from God forever. If the recipients are thinking sinners, they will ask why all people sin and will likely be given the reason that it is because of Adam's sin—we are all sinners because of him or because we possess fleshly desires that we all must give into. Getting sinners' minds beyond the injustice of that logic and also trying to get them to feel guilty for a sin they didn't commit are sure ways to get people to walk away in disgust. The heart cannot accept what the mind rejects. Teaching the conclusions of Models 1 and 3 would help apologetic and evangelistic efforts by presenting a God who understands the finiteness of his creatures, wishes them to be like him, and will empower them to do so if they change their allegiance.

Formal church rites would be affected. In some instances the liturgy would change from confession and forgiveness only to one that included repentance from mediocrity and prayers and entreaties for power to live Christlike. Times for testimony of how God has worked in believers' hearts would be appropriate. The meaning of baptism would be reconsidered for some (especially infant baptism), since the need for original sin's forgiveness or removal is unnecessary. Statements of faith would certainly change to accommodate changed beliefs. Whether Christian sectarian bodies are willing to make these changes is unknown, but there is always hope!

Epilogue

IF THERE WAS A short message summarizing the gist of this book's message and the heart of its author, what would it be? Three points will suffice. The first point is to not be afraid to think, question, challenge, and seek when pursuing biblical truth. Don't take a poll of your friends or look at your own wants, but dig deep into God's word and use the mind God gave you. The promise of the Holy Spirit leading us into all truth in John 16:13 is not a guarantee that when we read the Bible the Holy Spirit will pump in answers to every one of our nagging questions. The most spiritual and intelligent people of history have wrestled with various theological questions over the centuries and there is still disagreement on certain issues. What the verse seems to imply is that the Holy Spirit will reveal the main truths of the gospel; these are plain. It is unclear whether he sees fit to nudge us toward truth on secondary issues. If he does, the church and its scholars haven't been paying attention, because there is still much debate. Consequently, it seems God wants us to use the skills he has blessed us with to dig up other nuggets with a miner's dedication. That has been my interpretation of Scripture and my experience. A look at Christian tradition yields the same answer.

Tradition is another realm where Christian theologians must eschew fear. Tradition must be balanced between taking it as an unquestioning source of truth and not paying any attention to it. On the one hand there is formal and informal pressure within Christian segments or denominations to conform to existing dogma. Unlike the declarations of the Scriptures, these positions were arrived at by fallible human beings using various hermeneutical priorities and existing doctrinal commitments. Therefore, well-established dogmas are not a guarantee of truth. In spite of this, rocking a theological boat can have significant relationship altering and career jeopardizing consequences. To stand up for what one believes is true until sufficient evidence is presented otherwise involves counting the cost; I encourage you to pay it, just as Martin Luther did at the Diet of Worms.[1] On the other hand a theologian must not be afraid to give significant deference to the wisdom of the centuries. Most doctrines have been studied deeply by numerous Christian thinkers and it is negligent to not seriously consider their conclusions.

A second point is that God is not the author of sin. God forbid—he wants the whole world to give it up and come to their senses! He also wants all people to know what pleases and displeases him so we won't stumble into sins we can avoid. He has defined sin and given us examples of what to do and not to do. He outlines the character traits that fit with following him and the ones that fit with following the devil and inordinate fleshly desires. He has given his followers the Holy Spirit to abide within and to empower them to love like him.

It seems there are two extreme errors that we should avoid regarding sin. On one hand, the world chooses to be oblivious to the details of sin—they have dulled the moral conscience they once had by neglect. Even some Christians rationalize what they know is against God's will and do it anyway to satisfy their own desires. Their spiritual aim is low to medium; they lack courage; they lack vision; they make excuses for lack of spiritual progress; they pray seldom; they risk little for the kingdom of God. What work they do for God is burned up and they themselves barely escape, singed with fire (1 Cor 3:15).

The other extreme is for believers to think that everything they do is tainted with sin. They believe none of their motives are pure; they surely can't go a day without sinning. Even if they can't put a finger on an intentional sin, they figure they've sinned in some way—they must have. This is purported to be an expression of humility; to say any more would be prideful. However, pride may still be there—in the form of a spiritual worm. Where does this thinking come from? What does it say about the power of

---

1. Historical reports affirm that Luther defended his convictions about errors in the Roman Catholic Church with these words: "Unless I am convinced by the testimony of the Scriptures or by clear reason (for I do not trust either in the pope or in councils alone, since it is well known that they have often erred and contradicted themselves), I am bound by the Scriptures I have quoted and my conscience is captive to the Word of God. I cannot and will not recant anything, since it is neither safe nor right to go against conscience. May God help me. Amen." Brecht, *Martin*, vol. 1, 460. Although the author agrees wholeheartedly with Luther's sentiments, he disagrees with Luther's conclusions on original sin, the freedom of the will, and the level of holiness achievable in this life. This situation reminds us that each new generation of Christian theologians must reevaluate the methods and conclusions of those who have come before, all the while being ready to defend one's conclusions with the Bible, a defendable hermeneutic, a humble dependence on the Holy Spirit, and a willingness to follow the evidence wherever it leads.

God's Spirit to overcome the flesh? Who are we giving more credit to for our spiritual condition?

The backside of this second point is about how we were created. We concluded in chapters 3 and 4 that God doesn't lay a burden of an irresistible sin nature on our heart so that we can do nothing but sin. That sounds like something the devil might do if he had the power! Adam is also not the cause of our sin. God didn't cause or allow him to condemn the rest of humanity for one broken commandment. On the contrary, sin is something we do (ch. 2) and not a part of what we are (our being or essence). Even though sin is not part of our being, none of us, even Adam and Eve, started out neutral. Their surroundings were wonderful but they still had desires that they could allow to dominate God's will. Satan was around to tempt them and he's still here today, working as hard as ever. God tests us just as he tested them, but only up to what we can bear (1 Cor 10:13). Unlike them, we grow up in a world plagued by sin—the culture and people around us draw us toward it. Furthermore, if we practice sin enough we get really good—it becomes second nature and a bondage; it can define our overall character. Sometimes the Bible writers use language that suggests we are naturally sinners and this habitual indulgence certainly can become our ultimate choice. But it need not be—if we forsake our old ways, God will abundantly pardon (Isa 55:7) and transform us by his grace (2 Cor 3:18).

A third point is to focus on what God says about us as Christians. There is truth in the expression that "our attitude determines our altitude." Peter tells us that God has given us all the divine power we need to live godly. As we make every effort to add godly virtues, God will empower us to be like him. To not aim at God's best is nearsighted and blind (2 Pet 1:3–11). In fact, this Godward attitude should reflect positively on our self-image as Christians. God continually used his servants to call us what we are— saints, adopted, new creatures, crucified with Christ, Christ's body, and many more. This doesn't mean we can't or won't sin, but sin does not define or characterize our lives. He calls us to act like who we are. We are continually reflecting more clearly Christ's likeness. Read Anthony Hoekema's articles to get a good idea of how God wants us to see ourselves. Relatedly, we shouldn't be afraid to see ourselves as holy (remember the Barna article!) if we are obeying all the spiritual light we have. Holy does not mean we've never sinned or that we don't do it on occasion, it means our hearts chase after God's heart like King David's did. As we know, King David sinned, in some ways much greater than most of us. Considering ourselves holy is not prideful; we have not generated character by pulling up our own bootstraps. We are in a dynamic relationship with God and he is working in us by his grace to make us like a brilliant gem. I pray you will join me in that journey, the same journey that Christian and Christiana were on in *The Pilgrim's Progress*. Though they faced repeated temptations from those who would discourage them and several hills and valleys, they persevered along the King's Highway. Unfortunately, they occasionally diverted themselves away from the good path by following the likes of Mr. Worldly Wiseman and those folk from the Valley of Destruction. However, with the help of many good aides, such as Faithful and Mr. Greatheart, and the graces of Interpreter (the Holy Spirit), Goodwill (Jesus Christ, who we can surmise is also the Prince of the Celestial City!), and the Lord of the Hill himself (God the Father), they were both permitted entrance into the City. May that be the story of each of us as we pursue the Lord of the Hill!

Appendix
Informal Fallacies of Logic

A LOGICAL FALLACY IS a defect in an argument other than having false premises. Fallacies are frequently divided into two groups—formal and informal. A formal fallacy involves a false argument form, seen mainly in deductive arguments. Informal or material fallacies involve false argument content or language and are seen mainly in inductive arguments. Most of the fallacies that occur in theology seem to be from the informal side. Logic textbooks frequently list and describe informal fallacies and group them into categories. There is no agreed-upon final number of informal fallacies, so lists and categories differ somewhat. However, the following list is representative of the major informal fallacies. Most have an accompanying Latin description and these names are included.

Fallacies of Relevance: Fallacies in which the premises of an argument are *logically* irrelevant to the conclusion arrived at. Many times these premises are *psychologically* relevant because they try to divert us with non-logical, but emotionally appealing or repelling factors.

- *Ad hominem* (against the person, therefore distracting one away from the argument)
    - *Ad hominem* abusive (poisoning the well): A personal attack on an arguer's character, trustworthiness, or motives instead of the argument.
    - *Ad hominem* circumstantial (genetic fallacy): An attempt to discredit an arguer by claiming personal circumstances predispose the arguer toward his or her views. The attack is on the source of the argument (the person, i.e., their "genetics"). For example: "You are only against abortion because you are a priest."

- *Ad hominem, tu quoque* (you too): Presenting the arguer as a hypocrite in an attempt to discredit the argument.
- *Ad Populum* (appeal to the people)
  - Direct version: Exciting the emotion of a large group in order to gain acceptance of your argument. Frequently used in propaganda and advertising. Example: Many in-person political speeches.
  - Indirect version: Targeting one or two members of a group, using their relationship to the crowd to sway them.
    - The bandwagon. If you, as an individual, do so-and-so like everyone else, you'll be part of the group. If not, you'll be the odd person out. "Eighty percent of your colleagues believe in naturalism. You'd be a fool to believe in creationism."
    - Appeal to vanity. Associate your argument with an admired person. If you accept the appeal, you'll be admired too. "Buy this cereal because Peyton Manning is on the box."
    - Appeal to snobbery or membership in an elite group. For example, implying that only the smartest people believe this-and-such theory. Negatively, "Are there any honest lawyers or politicians?" Positively, "If you drink Gatorade like most elite athletes do, you'll become a superstar."
- *Ad Verecundiam* (appeal to illegitimate or unqualified authority): The appeal to valid authority is legitimate, but when the authority is false in some way, this is fallacious. Kreeft qualifies an authority as illegitimate when the proposed authority is irrelevant to the subject matter at hand, unreliable, unnecessary to support the argument, or when the appeal is dogmatic and closed as opposed to open or is uncritical when assessing the authority's trustworthiness.[1]
  - Related to this is the *appeal to tradition*. In itself tradition is a neutral source, since what is older or has lasted longer is not necessarily better or worse. Whether a Christian tradition is valid or good is based on other criteria, such as God, his Word, and solid hermeneutical principles.
- *Ad baculum* (appeal to the "stick"/force): Using the threat of harm (psychological, physical, monetary, withdrawal of approval or privileges, etc.) to win an argument. "If you don't convert to our religious faith, we'll kill you." The opposite, the *appeal to desire*, has not been

---

1. Kreeft, *Socratic Logic*, 82.

INFORMAL FALLACIES OF LOGIC   271

named, but is similar in action to *ad baculum*. This means what we want to be true we count as true.[2]

- *Ad Misercordiam* (appeal to pity): Eliciting pity or sympathy from an audience in order to gain approval of an argument. "If you don't help support missionaries in this remote area, these heathens will surely end up in hell."

- Straw man: A straw man argument attacks a weaker or distorted form of an opponent's argument (the "straw" as opposed to the "real" man), then claims that the opponent's stronger or more reasonable form is defeated. This is irrelevant to the real argument and is fallacious. For example, employees in "Dept. A" of Depts. A-K request cooling fans be used in their high-heat area. Management responds that they cannot afford to air-condition the whole plant, therefore the request is denied.

- *Ignoratio Elenchi* (Ignorance of the Refutation): This fallacy, frequently called *missing the point* or *irrelevant conclusion*, puts forth premises that support a certain conclusion, but the arguer then makes a different or only vaguely related conclusion. The arguer ignores the logical direction her premises take and veers off to another conclusion, "missing the point" of the premises. For example, "The rapid increase of worldwide terrorism threatens the safety of all democratic nations. Therefore NATO must bomb all suspected terrorist hide-outs and freeze all assets of nations who support them."

- Red herring: Similar to *ignoratio elenchi*, a red herring is an argument that diverts opponents by drawing attention away from the real argument onto side issues, just like the scent of the potent red herring drew hunting dogs away from the scent of their true prey. The side issue may be related in some way to the true issue, but then answering this side issue is substituted for dealing with the one at hand. Red herrings are frequently used by children who want glasses of water or repeated tellings of stories to distract parents from putting them to bed.

Fallacies of Presumption: Presumption means the arguer presumes or assumes ahead of time what the argument was designed to prove once it is completed.

- *Petitio Principii* (Requesting the Source): This is frequently translated as *begging the question* and is sometimes called *arguing in a circle*.

2 . Ibid., 83.

The "requester of the source" is the astute hearer of the argument. In response the arguer "begs" or provides an inadequate answer to the question, "How do you know your shaky premise is true?" Thus, the arguer "creates the illusion that inadequate premises provide adequate support for the conclusion by leaving out a possibly false (shaky) key premise, by restating a possibly false premise as the conclusion, or by reasoning in a circle."[3] In arguing in a circle, the conclusion is smuggled back into the argument as a premise, thereby supporting itself falsely. In all these three there is an inadequate source (premise).

- Example of first type: Worshipping idols is wrong. That being the case, eating meat sacrificed to idols is wrong. The begging question is, "Is eating meat sacrificed to idols idol worship?"

- Example of second type: "Tithing one percent of one's gross income is appropriate in this poor economy because one percent is a reasonable amount for those with partial incomes and high taxes." The conclusion merely restates the premise and is thus unproven.

- Example of third type: "King David was the most effective Israelite king. He was the most effective because he eliminated more Canaanites from the Promised Land than any other king. He was able to eliminate them because God's power was with him. God's power was with him because David oversaw the "golden age" of Israelite history. Only the most effective king in Israel's history could oversee Israel's golden age." There is no source to this reasoning. It goes in a circle with unsupported premises.

• False dichotomy: This "either-or" fallacy posits only two options to a question when it is likely there are more and better options present. The illusion is that the arguer has been exhaustive in presenting alternatives. "Either you believe the un-evangelized are going to hell or you really don't believe what the Bible says about sinners."

• *Argumentum ad temperantiam* (argument to moderation or the golden mean): asserts that truth is found in the middle ground between two extremes. Compromise is elevated since it is frequently a necessity in modern democratic society. A middle ground position may indeed be best, but it is best because of other reasons, not because it is in the middle.

3 . Hurley, *Concise Introduction to Logic*, 149.

Fallacies of Induction: In these fallacies, the connection between the premises and the conclusion is so weak that the conclusion cannot be reasonably supported.

- *Ad ignorantium* (appeal to ignorance): This is sometimes phrased *the argument from silence*. Affirms that an argument is true because there is no evidence against it. There can be an exception to this rule if qualified and expert researchers investigate the existence of some phenomenon over an extended time and if they find no evidence for it that counts as positive evidence against its existence.[4]

- Hasty generalization: A generalization in which insufficient data fail to adequately support a generalization. The data are faulty because they are too few, too homogeneous, too atypical, or not randomly selected.

- Selective or suppressed evidence: Instead of failing to amass sufficient evidence as in a hasty generalization, the selective evidence ploy intentionally neglects evidence that would prove damaging to one's argument. This expresses itself frequently when a researcher negates the effects of variables that do not fit into her favorite theory.

- False cause: Occurs when the causal link between premises and conclusion is either very weak or nonexistent.
    - *Post hoc ergo propter hoc* ("after this, therefore caused by this"): This fallacy, a variety of false cause, assumes that since one factor precedes another that the former causes the latter. However, events occurring in close proximity need not have this relationship. For example, because a young person always sees milk arrive at home after mom comes home from the grocery store does not mean the store produces the milk. Imagine the surprise when the youngster first visits a dairy farm.
    - Oversimplified cause: Many effects have multi-factorial causes. If this is the case and an arguer selects only one or a few and declares these are solely responsible for the effect, then he has committed the fallacy of oversimplified cause.
    - Slippery slope: This fallacy asserts that an initial action will precipitate a chain of other events which culminates in some dire outcome. If the chain of events is unlikely to occur or there is no known causal link between these events, this is a fallacious move. Also, the greater the number of intervening events,

---

4 . Ibid., 134.

the more likely the argument is fallacious. Good judgment and having a lot data is required to determine how likely the chain of events is to occur, therefore it is sometimes difficult to assess such arguments.

- The speculative or "what-if" hypothesis: In this case hypothetical connections are used to support a theory. These hypotheticals (X) are "contrary to fact"—they don't exist, but if they did, the arguer ventures that Y would have happened. "If only the Seattle Seahawks would have run the ball with Marshawn Lynch instead of throwing a slant pass, they would have beaten the New England Patriots in the last seconds of Super Bowl XLIX."

- False or weak analogy: In this case an analogy is used in an inappropriate way to support an argument. Analogies are good when they illustrate connections between things that are similar. However, when the analogy does not highlight true similarities or when the arguer assumes that when two things are alike in one respect that they are alike in another respect, then the analogy is false or weak. Peter Kreeft notes that Jesus used a false analogy to test the faith of the Canaanite woman who asked him to heal her demon-possessed daughter. Though Jesus compared Canaanites to dogs who were trying to get food from the children's (Israel's) table, the woman responded that even dogs eat the crumbs that fall from the master's table. He sensed her faith, and even though she was a Gentile, he healed her daughter (Matt 15:21–28).[5]

Fallacies of Language: When the words used in an argument are unclear or used improperly, fallacies of language result. Sometimes this category is called *ambiguous language.*

- Equivocation: This involves using one word or phrase with two different meanings in the same argument. Think of the dialog by Abbott and Costello—"Who's on first?"

- Amphiboly: In this case the ambiguity is not with the words but with the syntax of a sentence—its grammar or word order. For example, "John told Mark that he had made a mistake." It is unclear from the sentence structure which of the two made the mistake.

Fallacies of Grouping: Wrongly assuming the attributes of parts applies to wholes and vice versa.

---

5 . Kreeft, *Socratic Logic*, 103.

- Composition: The attribute of a part of something is wrongly applied to the whole. "Sandy swears when she is angry therefore Sandy is an evil person." "Iron atoms are invisible therefore an iron fence is invisible."
- Division: This wrongly affirms what is true of the whole is necessarily true of its parts. "This vase is square so each of its molecules must be square." "Harry comes from a Christian family. He must be a Christian."

Bibliography

Akin, Daniel L. *1, 2, 3 John*. The New American Commentary, 38. Nashville: Broadman and Holman, 2001.
Althaus, Paul. *The Theology of Martin Luther*. Philadelphia: Fortress, 1966.
Arnold, Bill T. *1 & 2 Samuel*. The NIV Application Commentary. Grand Rapids: Zondervan, 2003.
———. *Genesis*. New Cambridge Bible Commentary. New York: Cambridge University Press, 2009.
Arnold, Clinton E. *Ephesians*. Zondervan Exegetical Commentary on the New Testament. Grand Rapids: Zondervan, 2000.
Barna Group. "The Concept of Holiness Baffles Most Americans." *Barna.org* (February 2006). https://www.barna.org/barna-update/article/5-barna-update/162-the-concept-of-holiness-baffles-most-americans#.VFKETWdowdU.
Barnett, Paul. *The Second Epistle to the Corinthians*. The New International Commentary on the New Testament. Grand Rapids: Eerdmans, 1997.
Bartholomew, Craig G. *Ecclesiastes*. Baker Commentary on the Old Testament Wisdom and Psalms. Grand Rapids: Baker Academic, 2009.
Batson, C. Daniel. "Empathy-Induced Altruistic Motivation." Lecture for the Inaugural Herzliya Symposium on Pro-social Motives, Emotions, and Behavior. (March 24–27, 2008) 1–32. http://portal.idc.ac.il/en/symposium/herzliyasymposium/documents/dcbatson.pdf.
Bauckham, Richard J. *Jude, 2 Peter*. Word Biblical Commentary, 50. Nashville: Thomas Nelson, 1983.
Bergen, Robert D. *1, 2 Samuel*. The New American Commentary, 7. Nashville: Broadman and Holman, 1996.
Block, Daniel I. *The Book of Ezekiel: Chapters 1–24*. New International Commentary on the Old Testament. Grand Rapids: Eerdmans, 1997.
Blomberg, Craig L. *Jesus and the Gospels*, 2nd ed. Nashville: B & H Academic, 2009.
Blomberg, Craig L., and Mariam J. Kamell. *James*. Zondervan Exegetical Commentary on the New Testament. Grand Rapids: Zondervan, 2008.
Bock, Darrell L. *Luke 1:1—9:50*. Baker Exegetical Commentary on the New Testament, 1. Grand Rapids: Baker Academic, 1994.
Brecht, Martin. *Martin Luther*. Vol. 1. Translated by James L. Schaaf. Philadelphia: Fortress, 1985.
Brown, Colin, ed. *The New International Dictionary of New Testament Theology*. 3 vols. Grand Rapids: Zondervan, 1986.

Brown, William P. *Ecclesiastes*. Interpretation. Louisville: John Knox, 2001.
Byrne, Brendan. *Romans*. Sacra Pagina, 6. Collegeville, MN: Liturgical, 1996.
Calvin, John. *Institutes of the Christian Religion, XX*. Edited by John T. McNeill and translated by Ford Lewis Battles. Philadelphia: Westminster, 1960.
Canons of the Council of Orange. http://www.reformed.org/documents/canons_of_orange.html.
Cassian, John. *The Conferences*. Translated by Boniface Ramsey. New York: Paulist, 1997.
Catechism of the Catholic Church. http://www.vatican.va/archive/ENG0015/_INDEX.HTM.
Catholic Encyclopedia, "Sin." *New Advent*. http://www.newadvent.org/cathen/14004b.htm.
Christensen, Duane L. *Deuteronomy*. Word Biblical Commentary, 6a. Nashville: Thomas Nelson, 2001.
Christensen, Michael M. "A Description and Analysis of Pelagius' Views on Original Sin." http://www.academia.edu.
———. "A Description, Comparison, and Critique of Compatibilism and Incompatibilism." http://www.academia.edu.
———. "Original Sin from Justin Martyr to Augustine." http://www.academia.edu.
Church of the Nazarene Statement of Faith. http://www.nazarene.org.
Ciampa, Roy E., and Brian S. Rosner. *The First Letter to the Corinthians*. Pillar New Testament Commentary. Grand Rapids: Eerdmans, 2010.
Clark, David C. *To Know and Love God: Method for Theology*. Wheaton: Crossway, 2003.
Clines, David J. A. *Job 1–20*. Word Biblical Commentary, 17. Dallas: Word, 1989.
———. *Job 31–37*. Word Biblical Commentary, 18a. Dallas: Word, 1989.
Cockerill, Gareth Lee. *The Epistle to the Hebrews*. New International Commentary on the New Testament. Grand Rapids: Eerdmans, 2012.
Confession of Faith in a Mennonite Perspective (July 1995). Published by the Mennonite Church and the General Conference Mennonite Church. http://mennoniteusa.org/confession-of-faith/.
Cooper, Lamar Eugene, Sr. *Ezekiel*. The New American Commentary, 17. Nashville: Broadman and Holman, 1994.
The Council of Trent, Fifth Session. https://history.hanover.edu/texts/trent/ct05.html.
Craigie, Peter C. *Psalms 1–50*. Word Biblical Commentary, 19. Waco: Word, 1983.
Cranfield, C. E. B. *The Epistle to the Romans*. The International Critical Commentary, 1. New York: T & T Clark, 2004.
Davies, W. D. *Paul and Rabbinic Judaism: Some Rabbinic Elements in Pauline Theology*. Philadelphia: Fortress, 1980.
DeYoung, Kevin. "Temptation is Not the Same as Sin." *The Gospel Coalition*. http://www.thegospelcoalition.org/blogs/kevindeyoung/2013/09/26/temptation-is-not-the-same-as-sin.
Diehl, Bill, Jr., ed. "The Meaning of Righteousness in Scripture." *Present Truth Magazine* 33 (n.d.) chapter 3. http://www.presenttruthmag.com/archive/XXXIII/33-2.htm.
Dunbar, Robin, et al. *Evolutionary Psychology*. Oxford: Oneworld, 2007.
Dunn, James D. G. *Romans 1–8*. Word Biblical Commentary, 38a. Nashville: Thomas Nelson, 1988.
———. *The Theology of the Apostle Paul*. Grand Rapids: Eerdmans, 1998.

Duvall, J. Scott, and J. Daniel Hays. *Grasping God's Word*. 2nd ed. Grand Rapids: Zondervan, 2005.
Erickson, Millard J. *Christian Theology*. 2nd ed. Grand Rapids: Baker Academic, 1998.
Evangelical Lutheran Church in America. "Faith: ELCA Teaching: Scriptures Creeds and Confessions." *ELCA.org*. http://www.elca.org/Faith/ELCA-Teaching/Scripture-Creeds-Confessions.
Evans, C. S. *Pocket Dictionary of Apologetics & Philosophy of Religion*. CD-ROM. Downers Grove: InterVarsity, 2002.
Fairbairn, Donald. *Eastern Orthodoxy through Western Eyes*. Louisville: Westminster John Knox, 2002.
Falk, Gerhard. "Bar Mitzvah—Bat Mitzvah." http://jbuff.com/c032901.htm.
Fee, Gordon D. *Galatians*. Pentecostal Commentary. Dorset, UK: Deo, 2007.
———. *Paul's Letter to the Philippians*. New International Commentary on the New Testament. Grand Rapids: Eerdmans, 1995.
Feinberg, John S. *No One Like Him: The Doctrine of God*. Wheaton: Crossway, 2001.
Foster, Douglas A., et al., eds. *The Encyclopedia of the Stone-Campbell Movement*. Grand Rapids: Eerdmans, 2004.
Friedmann, Robert. "The Doctrine of Original Sin as held by the Anabaptists of the Sixteenth Century." *Mennonite Quarterly Review* 33 (1959) 206–14.
Gammie, John G. *Holiness in Israel*. Minneapolis: Fortress, 1989.
Gantt, Edwin E., and Jeffrey S. Reber. "Sociobiological and Social Constructionist Accounts of Altruism: A Phenomenological Critique." *Journal of Phenomenological Psychology* 30 (Fall 1999) 1–21. http://web.a.ebscohost.com/ehost/detail/detail?sid=a2309c07-0e6b-4239-a639-763982773fd6%40sessionmgr4003&vid=15&hid=4201&bdata=JnNpdGU9ZWhvc3QtbGl2ZQ%3d%3d#db=aph&AN=2930785.
Garland, David E. *1 Corinthians*. Baker Exegetical Commentary on the New Testament. Grand Rapids: Baker Academic, 2003.
Goldingay, John. *Old Testament Theology*. Vol. 2. Downers Grove: IVP Academic, 2003.
———. *Psalms 1–41*. Baker Commentary on the Old Testament Wisdom and Psalms, 1. Grand Rapids: Baker Academic, 2006.
———. *Psalms 42–89*. Baker Commentary on the Old Testament Wisdom and Psalms, 2. Grand Rapids: Baker Academic, 2007.
Goodrick, Edward W., and John R. Kohlenberger III. *The Strongest NIV Exhaustive Concordance*. Grand Rapids: Zondervan, 1999.
Green, Gene L. *Jude and 2 Peter*. Baker Exegetical Commentary on the New Testament. Grand Rapids: Baker Academic, 2008.
———. *The Letters to the Thessalonians*. Pillar Commentary on the New Testament. Grand Rapids: Eerdmans, 2002.
Grenz, Stanley, et al. *Pocket Dictionary of Theological Terms*. CD-ROM. Downers Grove: InterVarsity, 1999.
Hagner, Donald A. *Matthew*. Word Biblical Commentary, 33a. Dallas: Word, 1993.
Haight, Roger. "Sin and Grace." In *Systematic Theology, Roman Catholic Perspectives*, 2, edited by Francis Schüssler Fiorenza and John P. Galvin. Minneapolis: Fortress, 1991.
Hamilton, Victor P. *The Book of Genesis: Chapters 1–17*. New International Commentary on the Old Testament, 1. Grand Rapids: Eerdmans, 1990.

Harris, Murray J. *The Second Epistle to the Corinthians*. New International Greek Testament Commentary. Grand Rapids: Eerdmans, 2005.

Hawthorne, G. G., et al. "Flesh." In *Dictionary of Paul and his Letters*. CD-ROM. Downers Grove: InterVarsity, 1993.

Hoekema, Anthony A. "The Christian's Self-Image." *Reformed Journal* 21:7 (Sept 1971) 23–28.

———. "The Christian's Self-Image." *Reformed Journal* 21:8 (Oct 1971) 17–20.

Hurley, Patrick J. *A Concise Introduction to Logic*. 10th ed. Belmont, CA: Thomson Wadsworth, 2008.

Jobes, Karen H. *1, 2, 3 John*. Zondervan Evangelical Commentary on the New Testament. Grand Rapids: Zondervan, 2014.

———. *1 Peter*. Baker Exegetical Commentary on the New Testament. Grand Rapids: Baker Academic, 2005.

Johnson, Gregg. "Inadequacies of Sociobiological Explanations of Altruism." In *Investigating the Biological Foundations of Human Morality*, edited by James P. Hurd, 93–106. Lewiston, NY: Edwin Mellen, 1996.

Kane, Robert, ed. *Free Will*. Malden, MA: Blackwell, 2002.

———. *The Significance of Free Will*. New York: Oxford University Press, 1996.

Kantzer, Kenneth S. "A Systematic Biblical Dogmatics: What is it and How is it to be Done?" In *Doing Theology in Today's World*, edited by John D. Woodbridge and Thomas Edward McComiskey, 463–93. Grand Rapids: Zondervan, 1991.

Keener, Craig S. *The Gospel of John*. Vol. 2. Peabody, MA: Hendrickson, 2003.

———. *The IVP Background Commentary: New Testament*. CD-ROM. Downers Grove: InterVarsity, 1993.

Kelly, J. N. D. *Early Christian Doctrines*. Rev. ed. New York: HarperOne, 1978.

Kittel, Gerhard, and Gerhard Friedrich, eds. *Theological Dictionary of the New Testament*. Vol. 9. Grand Rapids: Eerdmans, 1976.

Klein, William W., et al. *Introduction to Biblical Interpretation*. 2nd ed. Nashville: Thomas Nelson, 2004.

Koszarek, Sister Clare. *The Catechesis of Original Sin*. Collegeville, MN: St. John's University Press, 1969.

Kraus, Hans-Joachim. *Psalms 1–59: A Commentary*. Vol. 1. Translated by Hilton C. Oswald. Minneapolis: Augsburg, 1988.

———. *Theology of the Psalms*. Translated by Keith Crim. Minneapolis: Augsburg, 1986.

Kreeft, Peter. *Socratic Logic*. 3.1 ed. South Bend, IN: St. Augustine's, 2010.

Kruger, Michael J. "Saint or Sinner? Rethinking the Language of Our Christian Identity." *Canon Fodder*. http://michaeljkruger.com/?s=saint+or+sinner&x=0&y=0.

Kruse, Colin G. *The Letters of John*. Pillar New Testament Commentary. Grand Rapids: Eerdmans, 2000.

———. *Paul's Letter to the Romans*. Pillar New Testament Commentary. Grand Rapids: Eerdmans, 2012.

Lane, William L. *Hebrews 1–8*. Word Biblical Commentary, 47. Dallas: Word, 1991.

Lewis, C. S. *Mere Christianity*. New York: Touchstone, 1996.

Lewis, Gordon R., and Bruce A. Demarest. *Integrative Theology: Three Volumes in One*. Grand Rapids: Zondervan, 1996.

Lincoln, Andrew T. *Ephesians*. Word Biblical Commentary, 42. Dallas: Word, 1990.

Longenecker, Richard N. *Galatians*. Word Biblical Commentary, 41. Dallas: Word, 1990.
Longman, Tremper III. *The Book of Ecclesiastes*. New International Commentary on the Old Testament. Grand Rapids: Eerdmans, 1998.
———. *Job*. Baker Commentary on the Old Testament Wisdom and Psalms. Grand Rapids: Baker Academic, 2012.
Lundbom, Jack L. *Jeremiah 21–36*. The Anchor Bible. New York: Doubleday, 1999.
Luther, Martin. *A Compend of Luther's Theology*. Edited by Hugh Thomson Kerr. Philadelphia: Westminster, 1943.
———. *Luther: Lectures on Romans*. Translated and edited by Wilhelm Pauck. Philadelphia: Westminster, 1961.
MacLean, P. D. *The Triune Brain in Evolution*. New York: Plenum, 1990.
Maddox, Randy L. "The Enriching Role of Experience." In *Wesley and the Quadrilateral*, edited by W. Stephen Gunter et al., 107–28. Nashville: Abingdon, 1997.
———. *Responsible Grace: John Wesley's Practical Theology*. Nashville: Kingwood, 1994.
Marmion, Declan, and Mary E. Hines, eds. *The Cambridge Companion to Karl Rahner*. New York: Cambridge University Press, 2005.
Martin, Ralph. *The Fulfillment of All Desire*. Steubenville, OH: Emmaus Road, 2006.
Matera, Frank. *Romans*. Paedeia Commentaries on the New Testament. Grand Rapids: Baker Academic, 2010.
Matusiak, John. "What is Sin?" *Orthodox Church in America*. http://oca.org/questions/sacramentconfession/what-is-sin.
McCartney, Dan G. *James*. Baker Exegetical Commentary on the New Testament. Grand Rapids: Baker Academic, 2009.
McDermott, Brian O. "The Theology of Original Sin: Recent Developments." *Theological Studies* 38 (1977) 505–12.
McGrath, Alistair E. "Engaging the Great Tradition." In *Evangelical Futures: A Conversation on Theological Method*, edited by John G. Stackhouse, 139–58. Vancouver: Regent College Publishing, 2000.
———. "The 'Wretched Man' Revisited: Another Look at Romans 7:14–25." In *Romans and the People of God*, edited by Sven K. Soderlund and N. T. Wright, 70–81. Grand Rapids: Eerdmans, 1999.
McGuckin, John Anthony. *The Orthodox Church: An Introduction to its History, Doctrine, and Spiritual Culture*. Malden, MA: Wiley-Blackwell, 2011.
McKnight, Scot. *The Letter of James*. New International Commentary on the New Testament. Grand Rapids: Eerdmans, 2011.
Meyer, Heinrich. "Ephesians 2:3." *Bible Hub: Meyer's New Testament Commentary*. http://biblehub.com/commentaries/meyer/ephesians/2.htm.
Michaels, J. Ramsey. *The Gospel of John*. New International Commentary on the New Testament. Grand Rapids: Eerdmans, 2010.
Moo, Douglas J. *The Epistle to the Romans*. New International Commentary on the New Testament. Grand Rapids: Eerdmans, 1996.
———. *Galatians*. Baker Exegetical Commentary on the New Testament. Grand Rapids: Baker Academic, 2013.
———. *The Letter of James*. Pillar New Testament Commentary. Grand Rapids: Eerdmans, 2000.
Moore, G. F. *Judaism in the First Centuries of the Christian Era*. Vol. 1. Cambridge, MA: Harvard University Press, 1946.

Moreland, J. P., and William Lane Craig. *Philosophical Foundations for a Christian Worldview*. Downers Grove: InterVarsity, 2003.
Motzkin, Julian C., et al. "Reduced Prefrontal Connectivity in Psychopathy." *The Journal of Neuroscience* 31 (Nov 2011) 17348–57.
Netland, Harold. *Encountering Religious Pluralism*. Downers Grove: InterVarsity, 2001.
Noble, Thomas A. "Prolegomena for a Conference on Original Sin." *European Nazarene Theology Conference* (April 2000). http://didache.nazarene.org/index.php?option=com_docman&task=cat_view&gid=44&Itemid=51.
———. "Scripture and Experience." In *A Pathway into the Holy Scripture*, edited by Philip E. Satterthwaite and David F. Wright, 277–96. Grand Rapids: Eerdmans, 1994.
O'Brien, Peter T. *The Epistle to the Philippians*. New International Greek New Testament Commentary. Grand Rapids: Eerdmans, 1991.
———. *The Letter to the Ephesians*. The Pillar New Testament Commentary. Grand Rapids: Eerdmans, 1999.
———. *The Letter to the Hebrews*. The Pillar New Testament Commentary. Grand Rapids: Eerdmans, 2010.
Olson, Gordon C. *The Moral Government of God*. Minneapolis: Men for Missions, 1974.
Osborne, Grant R. *The Hermeneutical Spiral*. 2nd ed. Downers Grove: IVP Academic, 2006.
———. *Matthew*. Zondervan Exegetical Commentary on the New Testament. Grand Rapids: Zondervan, 2010.
Oswalt, John N. *The Book of Isaiah: Chapters 40–66*. New International Commentary on the Old Testament. Grand Rapids: Eerdmans, 1998.
———. *Called to be Holy*. Anderson, IN: Francis Asbury, 1999.
Packer, J. I. "Is Systematic Theology a Mirage? An Introductory Discussion." In *Doing Theology in Today's World*, edited by John D. Woodbridge and Thomas Edward McComiskey, 17–38. Grand Rapids: Zondervan, 1991.
Pearcey, Nancy. *Finding Truth*. Colorado Springs: David C. Cook, 2015.
Peters, Ted. *Playing God? Genetic Determinism and Human Freedom*. New York: Routledge, 1997.
Peterson, David. *Possessed by God: A New Testament Theology of Sanctification and Holiness*. Grand Rapids: Eerdmans, 1995.
Peterson, Michael, et al. *Reason and Religious Belief*. 4th ed. New York: Oxford University Press, 2009.
Pomazansky, Michael. *Orthodox Dogmatic Theology*. 3rd ed. Translated and edited by Hieromonk Seraphim Rose. Platina, CA: St. Herman of Alaska Brotherhood, 2009.
Rad, Gerhard von. *Old Testament Theology*. New York: Harper, 1962.
Rapinchuk, Mark. "Universal Sin and Salvation in Romans 5:12–21." *Journal of the Evangelical Theological Society* 42 (Sept 1999) 427–41.
Rea, Robert. "'Holiness' in the Writings of Early Stone-Campbell Movement Leaders." *Stone-Campbell Journal* 8 (Fall 2005) 163–79.
Rich, Tracey R. "Bar Mitzvah, Bat Mitzvah, and Confirmation." *Judaism 101* (2011). http://jewfaq.org/barmitz.htm.
Ridgway, Andy. "The Human Brain: Hardwired to Sin." *Focus Magazine* (Feb 2010). http://www.sciencefocus.com/feature/psychology/human-brain-hardwired-sin.

Ritenbaugh, John W. "What Sin Is & What Sin Does." *Church of the Great God* (Feb 1996). http://www.cgg.org/index.cfm/fuseaction/Library.sr/CT/PERSONAL/k/489/What-Sin-Is-Does.htm.

Romanides, John S. *The Ancestral Sin*. Translated by George S. Gabriel. Ridgewood, NJ: Zephyr, 2008.

———. "Original Sin According to St. Paul." *St. Vladimir's Seminary Quarterly* 4:1–2 (1955–56). http://www.romanity.org/htm/rom.10.en.original_sin_according_to_st._paul.01.htm.

Samples, Kenneth Richard. *A World of Difference*. Grand Rapids: Baker, 2007.

Sanday, William, and Arthur C. Headlam. *The Epistle to the Romans*. The International Critical Commentary. 5th ed. Edinburgh: T & T Clark, 1902.

Schauss, Hayyim. "History of Bar Mitzvah." *MyJewishLearning*. http://www.myjewishlearning.com/article/history-of-bar-mitzvah/.

Schechter, Solomon. *Some Aspects of Rabbinic Theology*. London: Adam and Charles Black, 1909.

Schloss, Jeffrey P. "Sociobiological Explanations of Altruistic Ethics: Necessary, Sufficient, or Irrelevant?" In *Investigating the Biological Foundations of Human Morality*, edited by James P. Hurd, 107–45. Lewiston, NY: Edwin Mellen, 1996.

Schoonenberg, Piet. *Man and Sin*. Translated by Joseph Donceel. Notre Dame: University of Notre Dame Press, 1965.

Schreiner, Thomas R. *Galatians*. Zondervan Exegetical Commentary on the New Testament. Grand Rapids: Zondervan, 2010.

———. *Romans*. Baker Exegetical Commentary on the New Testament. Grand Rapids: Baker, 1998.

Shaw, Timothy J. "The Human Brain, Religion, and the Biology of Sin." In *Investigating the Biological Foundations of Human Morality*, edited by James P. Hurd, 147–63. Lewiston, NY: Edwin Mellen, 1996.

Smith, David L. *With Willful Intent: A Theology of Sin*. Wheaton: BridgePoint, 1994.

Smith, Gary V. *Isaiah 1–39*. The New American Commentary, 15a. Nashville: Broadman and Holman, 2007.

———. *Isaiah 40–66*. The New American Commentary, 15b. Nashville: Broadman and Holman, 2009.

Stuart, Douglas K. *Exodus*. The New American Commentary, 2. Nashville: Broadman and Holman, 2006.

Swanson, Dwight D. "'Original' Sin in the Primeval Narratives." *European Nazarene Theological Conference* (April 2000). http://didache.nazarene.org/index.php?option=com_docman&task=cat_view&gid=44&Itemid=51.

Sweeten, Harold W. *Must We Sin?* Kansas City, MO: Nazarene, 1919.

Swinburne, Richard. *Responsibility and Atonement*. Oxford: Clarendon, 1989.

Tate, Marvin E. *Psalms 51–100*. Word Biblical Commentary, 20. Dallas: Word, 1990.

Tennant, F. R. *The Sources of the Doctrines of the Fall and Original Sin*. New York: Schocken, 1968.

Teo, Adrian. "Human Altruism in Evolutionary Psychological Perspective: A Critique." *Journal of Psychology and Christianity* 21 (2002) 169–80.

Thils, Gustave. *Christian Holiness*. Tielt, Belgium: Lannoo, 1961.

Thomas, Gordon J. "Old Testament Proof-Texts for Original Sin." *European Nazarene Theological Conference* (April 2000). http://didache.nazarene.org/index.php?option=com_docman&task=cat_view&gid=44&Itemid=51.

Toews, John E. *The Story of Original Sin*. Eugene, OR: Pickwick, 2013.

VanGemeren, Willem A., ed. *New International Dictionary of Old Testament Theology and Exegesis*. Vols. 1–4. Grand Rapids: Zondervan, 1997.

Vanhoozer, Kevin. "Christ and Concept: Doing Theology and the 'Ministry' of Philosophy." In *Doing Theology in Today's World*, edited by John D. Woodbridge and Thomas Edward McComiskey, 99–145. Grand Rapids: Zondervan, 1991.

Wainwright, William J. "Doctrinal Schemes, Metaphysics and Propositional Truth." In *Religious Pluralism and Truth*, edited by Thomas Dean, 73–86. Albany, NY: State University of New York Press, 1995.

Walton, John H., et al. *Psalm 51:5*. The IVP Bible Background Commentary: Old Testament. CD-ROM. Downers Grove: InterVarsity, 2000.

Ware, Kallistos. *The Orthodox Way*. Crestwood, NY: St. Vladimir's Seminary, 1996.

Weaver, Rebecca Harden. *Divine Grace and Human Agency: A Study of the Semi-Pelagian Controversy*. Macon, GA: Mercer University Press, 1996.

Weingart, Richard. "The Meaning of Sin in the Theology of Menno Simons." *Mennonite Quarterly Review* 41 (1967) 25–39.

Wells, Jo Bailey. *God's Holy People*. Sheffield, UK: Sheffield Academic, 2000.

Wenham, Gordon J. *Genesis 1–15*. Word Biblical Commentary, 1. Nashville: Thomas Nelson, 1987.

Wesley, John. *A Compend of Wesley's Theology*. Edited by Robert W. Burtner and Robert E. Chiles. Nashville: Abingdon, 1954.

———. *A Plain Account of Christian Perfection*. Kansas City: Beacon Hill, 1966.

———. "Sermon 44, Original Sin." In *The Works of John Wesley*, vol. 2, edited by Albert C. Outler. Nashville: Abingdon, 1985.

———. *The Works of John Wesley*. Vol. IX. 3rd ed. Grand Rapids: Baker, 1978.

Westerholm, Stephen. "The Righteousness of the Law and the Righteousness of Faith in Romans." *Interpretation* 58 (July 2004) 254–64.

Westminster Larger Catechism. Calvin College: Christian Classics Ethereal Library. http://www.ccel.org/ccel/anonymous/westminster2.i.html.

Wigoder, Geoffrey, ed. *The New Encyclopedia of Judaism*. New York: New York University Press, 2002.

Wiley, H. Orton. *Christian Theology*. Vol. 2. Kansas City, MO: Beacon Hill, 1945.

Williams, N. P. *The Ideas of the Fall and of Original Sin*. New York: Longmans, Green, and Co., 1927.

Williams, Patricia A. *Doing without Adam and Eve: Sociobiology and Original Sin*. Minneapolis: Fortress, 2001.

Wilson, E. O. *Sociobiology*. Cambridge, MA: Belknap, 1975.

Wright, Christopher J. H. *Deuteronomy*. New International Biblical Commentary. Peabody, MA: Hendrickson, 1996.

Wright, N. T. *Justification*. Downers Grove: IVP Academic, 2009.

———. *What Saint Paul Really Said*. Grand Rapids: Eerdmans, 1997.

Yarbrough, Robert W. *1–3 John*. Baker Commentary on the New Testament. Grand Rapids: Baker Academic, 2008.

Ziesler, J. A. *The Meaning of Righteousness in Paul*. New York: Cambridge University Press, 1972.

www.ingramcontent.com/pod-product-compliance
Lightning Source LLC
Chambersburg PA
CBHW070236230426
43664CB00014B/2328

AFTER SATURDAY COMES SUNDAY

Understanding the Christian Crisis
in the Middle East

Elizabeth Kendal

RESOURCE *Publications* • Eugene, Oregon

AFTER SATURDAY COMES SUNDAY
Understanding the Christian Crisis in the Middle East

Copyright © 2016 Elizabeth N. Kendal. All rights reserved. Except for brief quotations in critical publications or reviews, no part of this book may be reproduced in any manner without prior written permission from the publisher. Write: Permissions, Wipf and Stock Publishers, 199 W. 8th Ave., Suite 3, Eugene, OR 97401.

Resource Publications
An Imprint of Wipf and Stock Publishers
199 W. 8th Ave., Suite 3
Eugene, OR 97401

www.wipfandstock.com

PAPERBACK ISBN: 978-1-4982-3986-8
HARDCOVER ISBN: 978-1-4982-3988-2
EBOOK ISBN: 978-1-4982-3987-5

Manufactured in the U.S.A.

Unless otherwise indicated, all Scripture quotations are from the ESV® Bible (The Holy Bible, English Standard Version®), copyright © 2001 by Crossway, a publishing ministry of Good News Publishers. Used by permission. All rights reserved.

Scripture quotations marked NIV are taken from the Holy Bible, New International Version®. NIV®. Copyright © 1973, 1978, 1984 by International Bible Society. Used by permission of Zondervan. All rights reserved worldwide.